Editing for Today's Newsroo

Carl Sessions Stepp's second edition of *Editing for Today's Newsroom* arrives at just the right time. In today's "anyone can be a journalist" environment, Stepp reminds us that editors and editing stand between journalistic mediocrity and excellence. Readers will find crisp technique, context and encouragement in this coherent, accessible text. Certain to emerge as the standard.

John F. Greenman, University of Georgia

Carl Stepp thoroughly understands every phase of editing. He knows editing's past and present, and, most importantly, he leads us toward its future. *Editing for Today's Newsroom* provides insightful point-by-point guidance on everything from applying basic grammar rules to making decisions about coverage.

This book will inspire the college student working toward his first job. It will restore confidence to the veteran desk person struggling to keep pace with a growing demand for speed (don't miss Carl's discussion of the RECESS method). It will encourage a veteran reporter just promoted to a seat on the city desk, and it will motivate a longtime editor who's striving to provide leadership in the changing newsroom environment. Anyone who edits, studies editing or teaches aspiring editors should read *Editing for Today's Newsroom*.

Bill Cloud, Julian W. Scheer Term Associate Professor and director of the Summer Institute for Midcareer Copy Editors, University of North Carolina at Chapel Hill.

A young editor once asked Carl Sessions Stepp whether editing was a job or a lifestyle. Stepp's answer is this book, which covers the "breathtaking breadth" of editing as a way of life. Updated to reflect journalism's transformation by the Internet, *Editing for Today's Newsroom* is a guide to the job of editing in all its roles: leader, coach, quality controller, umpire—even, thanks to the linking nature of online journalism, brand manager. Stepp pulls powerful examples of the best and worst editors from his own career, as well as from the experiences of other professionals, to leave readers chuckling—and sometimes flinching, occasionally quaking. In the end, students of editing, novice and pro alike, are deeply impressed by the imperative to focus on the heart of editing—making news decisions that are grounded in fact and fairness and helping writers to express their ideas in the most effective way possible. If future editors heed the wisdom in this book, journalism's future will be in surer hands.

Deborah Gump, Committee of Concerned Journalists

LEA's COMMUNICATION SERIES
Jennings Bryant / Dolf Zillmann, General Editors

Editing for Today's Newsroom

A guide for success in a changing profession

Second Edition

Carl Sessions Stepp

Routledge
Taylor & Francis Group

NEW YORK AND LONDON

First published 1989 by Lawrence Erlbaum Associates
This edition published 2008
by Routledge
270 Madison Ave, New York, NY 10016

Simultaneously published in the UK
by Routledge
2 Park Square, Milton Park, Abingdon, Oxon OX14 4RN

*Routledge is an imprint of the Taylor & Francis Group,
an informa business*

© 1989 LEA; 2008 Taylor & Francis

Typeset in Sabon by
Swales & Willis Ltd, Exeter, Devon
Printed and bound in the United States of America on acid-free paper by
Edwards Brothers, Inc.

Library of Congress Cataloging in Publication Data
Stepp, Carl Sessions.
Editing for today' newsroom / by Carl Sessions Stepp.
    p.cm.
Includes index.
ISBN 978-0-8058-6217-1 – ISBN 978-0-8058-6218-8
ISBN 978-1-4106-1602-9
1. Journalism–Editing.   I. Title.
PN4778.S73 2008
070.4′1–dc22   2007044233

ISBN10: 0–8058–6217–X (hbk)
ISBN10: 0–8058–6218–8 (pbk)
ISBN10: 1–4106–1602–9 (ebk)

ISBN13: 978–0–8058–6217–1 (hbk)
ISBN13: 978–0–8058–6218–8 (pbk)
ISBN13: 978–1–4106–1602–9 (ebk)

Contents

Preface to the Second Edition

I encountered my first editor shortly after I turned 14 and my latest one about half an hour ago. Though the experiences took place more than four decades apart, in one key way they were the same.

My first editor was the redoubtable Annie Laurie Kinney of the *Marlboro Herald-Advocate* in Bennettsville, S.C., my home town. I tell her story in more detail later, but the short version is that I paraded into her newsroom one day, announced I was there to be a reporter, and was overjoyed when she took me seriously, lectured me about community journalism, and sent me away with an assignment.

My most recent encounter was with Rem Rieder, the editor of *American Journalism Review*, where I have served as senior contributing editor. Rem Rieder is much different from Annie Laurie Kinney in style and personality, but he too has the gift of taking writers seriously. We discussed a potential assignment—his idea—and he listened carefully to my thoughts, added his own, and signed off on a mutually formulated plan for proceeding.

Our discussion underlined, for the umpteenth time in my career, a paramount lesson about editing, which I first learned all those years ago in my home town: Good editors treat all writers with respect and seriousness, be they greenhorns or graybeards. That is the backbone of the relationship. That insight remains, to this day, one of the foundations of my career.

What I didn't know at first, but soon came to appreciate, was how rare good editing and good editors can be and how sadly and inexplicably our profession neglects them. In journalism schools and professional seminars, in the literature and the mythology of our practice, we dwell on writing and reporting, with token bows to editing. We glamorize reporting but too often marginalize editing.

In this book, I seek to help rectify this condition by sharing some of what I have collected and learned about our craft. I hope to encourage us all to think of editing in new and wider ways.

The book is intended primarily for advanced students of editing, as well as professional journalists who are considering editing or who have, as countless newspeople do, gone into editing with little formal preparation. I try to cover a range of skills that editors may need over the course of a career, from the fundamentals of line editing to the subtleties of supervising.

In this new edition, as in the first, I view editors broadly as newsroom decision makers and quality controllers, whose duties may begin with editing copy but often range further and further from that starting point. Accordingly, the book features strategies and techniques for coping with a broad spectrum of editing duties.

Recognizing that the ability to edit copy is a touchstone, it covers basic and advanced copyediting skills. But beyond the basics it seeks to give intellectual context to the editor's role, critically examining the history of editing and the changing job of the contemporary editor.

Then it devotes specific attention to a spectrum of skills and duties: developing ideas, evaluating copy, working with writers, making news judgments, understanding presentation and design, directing news coverage, managing people, making decisions under pressure, and coping with a variety of legal, ethical, and professional considerations, all while operating in today's multimedia, multiplatform news arena.

Changes in the second edition include:

- Updated examples, references, and terminology
- Incorporation of new thinking about editing and its best practices, drawing on current research, editor-training initiatives, and several projects I have participated in or observed
- Up-to-date material to help editors deal with the demands and opportunities presented by the rise of the Internet, web publishing, interactivity, and other changes transforming the news media
- New insights based on my own decades of work as a teacher, writer, and consultant specializing in editing and newsroom change and innovation.

The goal of this edition remains to help prepare editors not just for their first, techniques-oriented job but for careers as journalistic leaders. In those careers, editors will meet many challenges.

Good editors must know how to be tough on the copy, but gentle on the ego. They recognize the wild spark that fires the writer-beast, and they thrill in the incendiary challenge of inciting it to the creative brink.

As part-time language police and full-time ego massagers, they live in a dual world, shuttling through what may seem a professional mind warp: at one moment, operating in lone-eagle style as sharp-eyed copy surgeons; at the next, presiding grandly over expansive projects, marshaling some elusive blend of wisdom, patience, temper, and octane to best stimulate the ferocity and fragility of each newshound.

Unhappily, too few editors span these points successfully. In the

45 years or so since meeting Annie Laurie Kinney, I have worked with editors of many flavors. I have become an editor myself. I have studied journalism and taught in a journalism school. From this all, I have come away fascinated and enthralled by the intricacies of editing, and disappointed and let down by the haphazard, ineffective way too many journalists approach it.

I have had good editors and bad, and I have done good editing and bad. From this experience, nothing thunders more loudly to me than this point: Editing is the essential difference between excellence and mediocrity in journalism. Like movie directors, editors are behind-the-scenes catalysts and coordinators whose efforts fundamentally define the ultimate product.

Some readers may find material here that seems elementary and repetitive; others may find the same passages fresh and eye-opening. That is precisely because we have no standard system for producing editors and no set body of knowledge that all editors share. Appointees arrive on the job with vastly differing backgrounds and abilities and, likewise, with differing knowledge gaps and blind spots.

No one text can serve them all, of course, but I have tried to view the subject and the audience broadly enough to bring many strands of editing together into something coherent. I hope it helps.

Acknowledgments

In writing this material, I think of Annie Laurie Kinney and Rem Rieder and so many other editors from whom I have gained: her husband Bill, who brought a dignity to every story and person; her son, Bill Jr., who shot enthusiasm into both his journalism and mine; Professor Ed Trayes of Temple University, who introduced me to the best practices of editing; Buzz Merritt, who exemplified the meaning of editor–reporter teamwork; Joe Distelheim, the best editor I ever worked for; my teachers at the University of South Carolina; and Laura Sessions Stepp, my wife and also the best editor I ever saw at moving a team of reporters toward the goal line.

And many others: James Batten, Bob Boyd, Ginny Carroll, Pat Carter, John Curley, Stu Dim, Mark Ethridge, Bill Fuller, Clark Hoyt, David Lawrence, Luisita Lopez, Walker Lundy, Pete McKnight, Ron Martin, Bill Monroe, Rich Oppel, John Quinn, Rachel Smolkin, Larry Tarleton, Gil Thelen, John Walter, Nancy Woodhull, and so many more.

Because of them all, I believe that editing is vital, it is fun, and we all have much to learn about it.

In addition, thanks go to many current and former colleagues for assistance and encouragement with this book.

Reese Cleghorn, my former dean at the University of Maryland Philip Merrill College of Journalism, gave special support, especially for the original version of this book, and my current dean, Thomas Kunkel, has been a similar bulwark for this edition.

So many of these ideas were first explored or presented in the pages of *American Journalism Review*, and I again thank its editors for their encouragement.

Appreciated contributions have come from many campus colleagues including Steve Barkin, Maurine Beasley, Alice Bonner, Chris Callahan, Jon Franklin, Penny Fuchs, Alex Greenfeld, Bob Grover, James Grunig, Chris Harvey, Ben Holman, Kathy McAdams, Gene Roberts, Jan Schaffer, and Eric Zanot. Also helping in innumerable ways were Shirley Biagi, Jennings Bryant, Jerry Ceppos, Roy Peter Clark, Marty Claus, Don Fry, Jane Harrigan, Maxwell McCombs, Duncan McDonald, Michele McLellan, Raleigh Mann, Steve Weinberg, and Robin Marks Weisberg.

Readers for the second edition offered excellent ideas and included Jacqui Banaszynski of the University of Missouri, Bill Cloud of the University of North Carolina, John Greenman of the University of Georgia, Deb Gump of Ohio University, and Lil Swanson of APME NewsTrain. At Lawrence Erlbaum Associates, my editor Linda Bathgate offered steadfast support and guidance, as did Karin Wittig Bates, Kerry Breen, Amy Lee, and others in the editing and production process.

Many other friends and colleagues played roles, and my students contributed in more ways than they know. My family showed particular patience and love.

I appreciate it all.

One final word should be said about the genesis of many ideas here. Although I have tried to attribute material as scrupulously as possible, it seems impossible to trace many of my views back to original sources. I readily take responsibility for all the material I present, but I cannot honestly take credit for it.

If I have slighted any sources or seemed to usurp any ideas that others uttered long before me, then I apologize. An editor becomes a different person every day, absorbing lessons and insights from everywhere. I owe especial debts to those who have written about editing before me.

In my evolution as reporter, editor, and teacher, I have been profoundly influenced by innumerable co-workers and colleagues; by practically every editor and writer I ever observed; by my teachers and my students; by books, magazines, newspapers, websites, and lectures; and by presentations at seminars, conventions, and gatherings of all sorts.

Their ideas filled my head and made me want to pass them on. It is in that spirit, and with thanks to all, that I present this book.

Carl Sessions Stepp
Summer 2007

1 The dynamic world of editing

In the life of city editor Joe Carmean, no single day is typical, certainly not this one.

On the morning I visit his newsroom, Carmean is coping with an unusual challenge at his news organization, the 30,000-circulation *Daily Times* in Salisbury, Maryland. The paper's press has broken down the night before, so today's edition is being printed out of town, very late. The phone is ringing constantly from bereft subscribers, some of whom are even coming to the *Times* office scouting for copies. By noon, Carmean has reporters out on numerous stories, is readying an update for the paper's website, and is fending off various crises because his boss, the executive editor, has been drafted to help deliver the late-arriving issues.

Still, Carmean is willing to take a few minutes to discuss the multimedia, multidimensional role of today's editor. It is busy, complex, and multi-faceted. It is ferociously challenging, and it is enormously satisfying.

The biggest recent change? The need to adapt to the nearly 24-hour news cycle created by the Internet.

What motivates him? Working with his reporters to keep his news organization competitive and vital, both on paper and online.

What it takes? Long days and nights of hard work.

The satisfaction? "Joy in the achievements of my reporters," he answers. "Watching a reporter I've groomed succeed and develop instills the kind of pride I think only a parent can feel."

* * *

Of all jobs in journalism, the editor's is probably the most misunderstood. In fact, even though *editing* is a central, everyday term in journalism, it is, like *news*, a concept that frustrates easy definition.

Typically, we think of editing as copy reading. We imagine owlish grammarians and wordsmiths poring over articles, sweating out headlines, and designing pages and websites. But the term *editor* also applies in many other ways: to city editors, feature editors, photo editors, managing editors, editorial page editors, news editors, and home page editors, all with distinct duties. To designers, web producers, and art directors, who may never touch a reporter's copy. To broadcast editors, who process tape and digital content. To magazines editors, to whom the term means everything from manager to contributor to reporter. To online editors, with multimedia duties of every kind.

Editors certainly edit copy. At least many of them do. They also are teachers, counselors, negotiators, schedulers, taskmasters, disciplinarians, ethicists, motivators, ombudsmen, and referees. They are managers and judges, facing the daily idiosyncrasies of human relations and news gathering . . . and the inflammatory tasks of deciding where new furniture goes in the newsroom and who has to work on New Year's Eve.

What all these editors have in common is their role as decision makers. More than anything else, editing is *newsroom decision making under pressure*.

A good newsroom decision maker needs the following three qualities:

- First, *technical skills*, or substantive knowledge of the issues being decided, such as what makes news or a strong lead or an inviting web page. A good editor should be a solid journalist.
- Second, *conceptual skills*. A good editor should have exceptional ideas and vision.
- Third, *people skills*. A good editor should be a capable coach, manager, and leader.

Although most journalists can be assumed knowledgeable about the substance of the news business, rarer are those people with the last two qualities: the conceptual aptitude for envisioning excellence and the humane finesse for working with others to achieve it.

Few people grow up intending to be editors. Writers often feel the urge to write in elementary or middle school, and many are committed by high school. But in interviewing hundreds of editors over the years, I have encountered only a handful who decided to become editors while in grade school. So editors tend to emerge through one of two relatively haphazard ways: (1) They discover the satisfactions of editing while working on their college papers, begin their careers as copyeditors or designers, and eventually ascend to supervisory jobs, or (2) more commonly, they start as reporters or artists or web producers, and come to assigning editing jobs after several years, frequently drafted for a vacancy when an editor has quit, retired, or died.

In both these cases, the fledgling mid-level editor will have adequate if not superior technical skills, but will not be systematically prepared for the conceptual and administrative challenges of leading a staff.

This book is intended to help in all three areas. It will offer the copyediting techniques required of almost every editor. But it also will construe editing in the broader sense of leadership. It will encourage a modernized view of editing. Instead of pigeonholing editors based on particular duties some may have, it seems wiser to foster the idea that editors form a professional class of journalists whose responsibilities at any one time may be as narrow as writing cutlines or as broad as running a converged newsroom. In the material that follows, we will consider editors as *newsroom professionals prepared for decision-making authority over content, presentation, assignments, journalistic issues, and, perhaps above all, personnel.*

In short, our guiding principle will be that editors are *quality controllers*. Whatever the particulars of any individual editing job, the common element is the responsibility to envision and achieve the highest possible quality.

The goal is to help journalists better understand the fuller dimensions of editing, with particular attention to assignment editors, those who deal regularly with reporters, photographers, and others directly producing the content.

The bumpy path to editing

Quality control is not the role for which editors historically have been readied.

A friend of mine, the late reporter and editor Gary Blonston, once observed that the most common "training" a new editor receives is being told, "Sit over there." John Greenman, a former publisher involved in training for editors, found that just 21 percent of those in one of his programs had received any training at all before their first editing job.[1]

Few more important long-range problems confront journalism than the challenge of finding, preparing, and nurturing good editors. In too many cases the selection and training of editors takes place through an outdated and inadequate system that no longer produces the quality and quantity of talent needed to handle the complexities of contemporary newsrooms. Too few people want to be career editors, and even fewer people win recognition as good editors. Insufficient attention goes into finding and grooming editors, and inadequate effort is spent on encouraging those editors who do persevere.

To make a decision as an editor means acting under pressure, weighing competing priorities, considering others' opinions, understanding a newsroom's policies, respecting the role of precedent, predicting the consequences, and gauging risks and benefits. Not every good journalist is a good decision maker under those conditions. Many reporters, for instance, excel at making spot decisions that govern their own work but don't feel comfortable operating in the group setting that editors face. Others react well instinctively but cannot articulate their reasoning or formulate it in ways that colleagues can follow.

Typically, an editor must work indirectly, building consensus where possible, motivating others to carry out policies, and following up tactfully but firmly. Again, many otherwise good journalists don't possess such dexterity. They can become frustrated and ineffective when called on to work with and through others rather than simply forging ahead themselves. As team leaders, editors succeed only to the extent that they can recognize what motivates each member of the group and then tailor their methods to get the most out of everyone involved.

Instead of being trained broadly for this range and variety of duties, however, students and novice editors too often are simply instructed in basic copyediting and design, and then, later, slotted into a supervisory editing job and left alone to navigate the newsroom's white waters.

As anyone who has both reported and edited can testify, the requirements for the two roles are not the same. Editors also need specialized conceptual and people skills that reporting doesn't necessarily require. Good reporters tend to be fast-moving, aggressive extroverts whose ego gratification comes from the thrill of the chase and the rush of seeing the next byline. Good editors, their aggression tempered with patience, are more often introverts, accepting their anonymity and drawing contentment from their roles in coordinating an overall team effort.

As a result of a tradition of simply shifting good reporters into editing slots, however, too many editors are forced to learn on the job, relying on hunch and guesswork, rather than proper preparation, to make the split-second judgments required hour after hour.

This system seems roughly like selecting brain surgeons by scanning an operating room to see who is the best nurse or orderly or technician, and then assuming that competence in one aspect of medicine carries over to others. Editing may not be brain surgery, but it is a complex, challenging specialty that deserves more careful attention to recruiting, training, and development.

Given this irregular pipeline for editors, is it any wonder that so much tension separates editors and reporters, or that journalists have the reputation of being hopeless managers? Or that news organizations report that good editors are getting harder and harder to find, and harder and harder to keep? Good editing comes hard, and too much of today's editing is so hurried, careless, and cloddish that, even when it succeeds, everyone ends up too frazzled to notice.

In many respects, editors resemble sports referees and umpires. We notice them only when they blow a big call. In most newsrooms, it is a daily routine to hear reporters growling that "some editor" has fouled up their copy or that the managing editor has sold out to the business side's demand for earlier deadlines. But how often do reporters offer testimonials to the editor who noticed a careless libel, or inserted a magical phrase that brought sizzle to a lead, or suggested one last interview that yielded the perfect closer quote? Or the web editor who brilliantly assembled text, audio, and video? Or the city editor who deftly motivated an under-achieving reporter to a new level of excellence?

"Most of my time is spent editing stories, and a lot of time is spent in meetings," Tim Cotter, an editor for the *Day* in New London, Conn., once wrote. "But the most important role I play is communicating with reporters, through weekly beat notes, brief conversations during the coaching process, longer meetings about . . . ideas, and feedback during critique sessions. . . . I just would like more time to do it."[2]

My own memories as an editor do not dwell on great leads I helped sharpen or days when my news judgment seemed especially keen or times when I wrote a one-column headline that fit the first time.

Instead, I remember things like:

- Facing a mother who approached me pleading that we leave out an investigative story that would, she was convinced, cause her son to kill himself
- Confronting an agitated reporter who, after working feverishly overnight on a story, had produced only a computer screen full of gibberish
- Negotiating by telephone with a man who claimed to be an underworld figure and wanted $5,000 to provide me with pictures of a prominent local official taking payoffs—if I would join in a cloak-and-dagger scheme involving notes taped to park benches and pay phones at the local library.

I remember, perhaps most vividly, the everyday stresses and strains of supervising people, competing for tight space and resources, defending stories in news meetings, trying to motivate recalcitrant reporters and rein in overzealous ones, and attacking the scores of daily dilemmas in producing good journalism.

And I remember the thrill of the job, tough as it was; the excitement and gratification of being a central participant in moving news to the public. For all its strains, editing is a powerful and rewarding way of life.

Viewing editing this broadly is not intended in any way to disparage language and grammar skills or to belittle the role of good copyeditors. They are vital, and all too scarce. The point is this: Most editors, including copyeditors, have jobs dominated by the need for intelligent decision making and human relations, but those qualities are not what come to mind in teaching, training, and choosing editors.

At the University of Maryland, journalism students can enroll in a class especially designed for those who hold editing jobs, with either student or off-campus news organizations. Each week, they bring to class a short report on editing problems encountered on the job. The students report on all sorts of issues: editing technique ("When does an editor decide to change the tone of a story?"), logistics ("The entire printing-typesetting system failed at 12:30 a.m."), and design ("The problem this week involved not having enough good quality photographs"). But, year in and year out, the dominant category involves problem solving in human relations—how to deal with sources, readers, reporters, publishers, advertisers, and an assortment of other cranks, creeps, and cry babies.

Consider problems such as:

- What you tell a reporter who has gotten a death threat for writing that a local boxer was "a career loser"
- How you edit the weekly column from a local preacher
- How you advise a reporter who feels she is being sexually harassed by a local official's dinner invitations and suggestive remarks
- What you tell an advertiser who pushes to "sponsor" a section of community news
- How you react when a reporter refuses a dicey assignment.

These are real-life issues the students have grappled with outside class, sometimes to the point of despair. "We spend so much time settling little squabbles between ourselves and among others," one student editor wrote ruefully.

Issues such as these have long vexed journalists. But they have taken on new and ominous dimensions as the newsroom environment has changed in recent years. Editing today is hard and becoming harder, as journalism, society, and individuals evolve.

Editors, would-be editors, and managers can identify several conditions that underlie the dearth of good editing candidates and the difficulties they face. We will examine some of them before turning to more positive issues of what can and should be done.

Lifestyles of the nonrich and the nonfamous

In the lore of the news business, reporters stand as the glamour figures, energy burners with strong egos lubricated by the sight of their names regularly on the page or screen. Editors, by contrast, tend toward offstage duties outside the spotlight and without the glory that accompanies public credit.

Once I asked an editing seminar who could name the two *Washington Post* reporters who won fame by exposing the Watergate scandal. Every hand in the room went up. Bob Woodward and Carl Bernstein were well-known names. Then I asked: "Who was their immediate editor?" Pause. A hand went up tentatively; the guess was wrong. Then silence. No one remembered Barry Sussman, Watergate editor.

Yet his role was central. Here's how Woodward and Bernstein themselves describe it in *All the President's Men*:

Sussman had the ability to seize facts and lock them in his memory, where they remained poised for instant recall. More than any other editor at the *Post*, or Bernstein and Woodward, Sussman became a walking compendium of Watergate knowledge, a reference source to be summoned when even the library failed. On deadline, he would pump these facts into a story in a constant infusion . . . Watergate was a puzzle and he was a collector of the pieces.[3]

It is no wonder, perhaps, that the editor's life is hardly the dream of tender journalists-to-be. While the reporter is at the stadium interviewing the star shortstop, the editor is bent over the terminal piecing together the agate box score. While the writer is hobnobbing with presidents and rock stars, the editor is rounding up mug shots for the obit page and website.

Few would doubt that reporting rather than editing is, to most tastes, the more exciting introduction to the news business.

For that reason, among others, news organizations face a chronic shortage of editors. Ask any journalism school placement officer: Editors, especially those with multimedia skills, are hot property. Dozens of applications from prospective writers flood newsrooms for every one that trickles in from an editor hopeful.

The shortage starts at the copydesk, which is the entry point for many editors, and it spreads throughout the newsroom. "How many times have you heard this," began one article in a professional magazine. "We can't find enough qualified copyeditors. And if we find them, we can't keep them."[4] A survey by the American Copy Editors Society (ACES) found that fewer than a third of newsrooms had a fully staffed copydesk. Almost all had hired copyeditors within the past year and were looking for more, and 55 of 64 editors queried criticized college journalism programs for not encouraging more students to enter editing.[5]

The problem is not limited to copydesks. "It is very hard to find good line editors—assigning editors who are the first-read editors for reporters," a key editor for the *San Jose Mercury News* once told me. "It's hard to find someone who has had reporting experience, is a good writer, can see the big picture, and is a good teacher. I have had a devil of a time finding assistant city editor candidates who have that combination of everything."[6]

Keeping good editors can be as hard as finding them. "Newsroom retention . . . is an increasingly challenging issue as labor pools and average tenures shrink," editor Leslie Ansley reported to a group of newsroom training officers.[7]

In fact, the lifestyle of the editor is difficult, and getting more so year by year. This is a fact of life that aspiring editors cannot ignore. Editors are potent figures with decisive influence over every aspect of journalism. But their lives can involve high stress, low recognition, long hours, and tough working conditions, especially in break-in jobs like the copydesk, round-the-clock web desks, or weekend assigning desks.

Editors regularly work nights, weekends, and holidays. At one morning newspaper where I was an editor, the building escalators were turned off around 7 p.m., even though the night staff, including a full shift of editors, worked till well past midnight. It was as if normal needs and courtesies did not apply to such a strange breed of owls.

Today's workers, perhaps more than those of earlier generations, prize leisure time and want to reduce work-related interference with personal life. For single workers, working the weekend and wee hours common in editing offers little hope of a stimulating social life. For young parents, the odd and inflexible hours make raising a family, finding child care, and reading bedtime stories next to impossible. For journalistic graybeards, Saturday night and holiday duties seem an indignity when their peers in, say, the law or medicine are routinely lolling on sailboats and enjoying the material fruits of success.

Beyond status questions, it has become common, in today's health-conscious environment, to hear journalists lament the risk of burnout and stress—two all-too-real dangers of the business.

Sharon Peters, in one of the most systematic studies of mid-level editors called *Caught in the Middle*, cited "long hours, intense pressure, little respect from below, little support from above." These perennial pitfalls have become "inarguably more challenging," Peters continued, because of "ever-changing technology, shrinking news hole, reduced staffing, shifting public perceptions, ever-evolving competition and a regularly metamorphosing workforce."[8] A Poynter Institute survey found that 44 percent of newsroom managers were very or somewhat dissatisfied with work–life balance and that two-thirds of all responding journalists felt their work had a very or somewhat negative impact on their health.[9]

It should go without saying here that editors stand on both sides of this equation. As employees, they confront the stress and must work in difficult newsroom environments. But, as *managers*, they bear much responsibility for what the newsroom climate has become. They can become, all too often, stress carriers, inflicting damage on others as well as themselves.

Whereas in some occupations high salaries may help offset high stress, that hardly applies in editing, at least in the beginning. A 2006 survey by the Inland Press Association found the average salary for city editors was $54,000.[10] Broadcast executive producers, who have roughly equivalent jobs to assigning editors in print and online, had a similar median salary of about $50,000.[11] That's about half of what a first-year lawyer makes. Data from the Bureau of Labor Statistics showed editors making less than lawyers, doctors, and nurses; more than clergy and claims adjusters; and about the same as teachers, police, and mail carriers.[12]

Certainly, the preceding catalogue of issues is sobering, but it should not throw the overall picture out of whack. Editing is a tough business with its share of tribulations, but it also can be enormously enriching. In the next section, we examine the enduring satisfactions awaiting good editors.

On top of the newsroom

Perhaps the most famous editor of all time, Max Perkins, masterminded the work of F. Scott Fitzgerald, Ernest Hemingway, Thomas Wolfe, and Marjorie Kinnan Rawlings, among many others. "Why don't you write yourself?" a friend once asked, observing that Perkins seemed more talented than many of his big-name protégés. "Max just stared at me for a long time," the friend recalled, "and said, 'Because I'm an editor.' "[13]

Some people, like Perkins, seem born to edit. Others find roundabout ways to the job. But almost all editors live stimulating, creative, exciting, and intellectually challenging lives. Few ever complain of boredom or monotony. Editors occupy the centers of power in every news and literary enterprise. A reporter may touch one or two stories at a time; an editor may touch dozens. Editors are almost certainly the most powerful figures in journalism.

Asked what makes the job satisfying, assigning editor Dick Rogers of the *San Francisco Examiner* replied, "The chance to learn something new and convey it to others creatively. It's a far cry from warehouse work." Karanja Ajanaku of the *Commercial Appeal* in Memphis put the appeal in sports terms: "I'm an ex-football player and the daily demands are like getting the ball from the 2-yard line to the goal line every day. I like to see the entire field and know what everybody else is doing."[14]

"Being an editor is not easy," the veteran newspaper editor Gregory L. Moore, who headed the *Denver Post* among other papers, has said. "Many of us who do it, however, really love it. We love shaping the news report; we love dispatching the troops; we love solving problems and being in the thick of things. And we love having a powerful role in directing coverage."[15]

Sharon Peters, whose study *Caught in the Middle* identified several stress factors of editing, also found a long list of appeals of the job. She found that nearly 60 percent of mid-level editors were happy enough to want to stay in newsroom leadership for the remainder of their careers. Appeals of the job included:

- Opportunity to direct, improve, and shape content
- Decision-making authority
- Control
- The chance to effect change
- The teaching aspects of editing
- The chance to work with people and watch them grow.[16]

Editors stand in the vortex of the news flow, influencing both the content of journalism and the character of journalists. And their gratification comes quickly. Hard work is promptly rewarded, with a website that can be viewed instantly, a newspaper page that will greet thousands of readers within 24 hours, a magazine cover that will grace the news racks for days.

"You're really doing something worthwhile and rewarding, and it makes a difference, and it's fun," said Julia Wallace, top editor of the *Atlanta Journal-Constitution* and other papers as well. "There is not much else like that in the world."[17]

The changing nature of journalism

One Wednesday in September 2005, about 140 people watched anxiously as television news showed live shots of an airliner approaching Los Angeles with faulty landing gear.

Remarkably, the 140 people were the troubled aircraft's own passengers, viewing their fateful drama as it happened, over the plane's satellite TV news channels. Seeing emergency vehicles lining the runway, some passengers dialed out on their cell phones. Others punched in emotional text messages. Others just watched, spellbound. After landing safely, relieved travelers called their real-time news experience "weird" and "surreal."[18]

Surreal it may have seemed, but this one early example illustrated an increasing trend that has altered how editors and other journalists work: the intersection of news makers, news producers, and news consumers. The interactivity and interconnections of the Internet turn those with camera phones, web cams, and other high-tech devices into simultaneous transmitters, receivers, and commentators in a live-all-the-time 24/7 news cycle.

The revolution spawned by technology is just one of many profound changes confronting today and tomorrow's journalists. Other forces include the changing habits of readers and viewers; shifting definitions of news; and the three Cs of modern media business, concentration, consolidation, and commercialization. All are affecting the duties and roles of editors, and the skills and strategies required for success.

Breakthrough, breakneck technology. If you study the history of journalism and mass media, you quickly detect that major changes in content and direction are associated with technological innovations. The invention of the telegraph, for instance, underlay the very concept of "news," allowing people for the first time to develop the expectation of learning about events in a timely way. The rise of television and its insistent visual imagery changed not only our living rooms but our brains, moving us from linear, print-dominant learners to a visual, right-brain-dominant culture fed by fast-paced images and sounds.

The computerized, digital ascendancy is having a similar far-reaching influence. It offers audiences nearly instant access to vast, almost infinite volumes of information, in text, audio, and video formats. Satellite and electronic signal distribution enables immediate, two-way, real-time global connections. Mobile hand-held instruments keep consumers in touch at all times and places. The result is a far more democratic information environment, diminishing the hegemony of media professionals. Audience members create and consume news on their schedules and whims, not the commercialized mass media's. The explosion of weblogs (more than 50 million created in their first decade of existence) provided just one indicator of how popular and powerful interactivity would become in this multidimensional, multimedia age.

Changing consumption patterns. Various social forces, from technology to lifestyle considerations, are leading consumers to change how, when, and where they seek information. For several decades, a fairly stable pattern held. People tended to read their daily newspaper at the breakfast table, tune into an occasional radio newscast during the day, and watch the evening news for a roundup of the day's doings. Today, fewer people read daily papers, especially among the young, and fewer wait until the dinner hour to tune in the news. Headlines, updates, and depth discussion and analysis are available through the day and night, via cable news channels, mainstream Internet sites, and thousands of specialized websites, blogs, podcasts, forums, and feeds, most of them downloadable to portable devices whose settings can be personalized for easy consumption anytime and anywhere.

Shifting definitions of news. The falloff of attention to newspapers and other mainstream media coincided with a perceived decline in participation and interest in public affairs, again notably among young people, and with ever-changing eclectic tastes of the aging baby boomer consumer bloc as well. News has always been a transaction between seller and buyer, and so these social and cultural shifts prompted journalists to adjust their news offerings.

In the revisionist news formula, for example, the dutiful monitoring of routine government and civic affairs yields typically to increased "softer" tales of relationships, lifestyles, and leisure. You may see fewer stories about Congress or international affairs, more about lifestyle topics such as parenting, commuting, exercising, and shopping. Targeting of information for localized and specialized constituencies (such as a well-to-do suburb or a minority group) has increased, at the expense of material aimed vaguely at the audience at large or of material (such as routine government coverage) whose constituency was believed to be in decline.

These generalizations did not hold in every medium on every day, but overall they have had the result of modernizing the mix of information and entertainment that editors are expected to deliver.

Concentration, consolidation, and commercialization. Many full books have been written on this phenomenon, because it represents possibly the defining development within the mass media over the past 50 years. Mainstream news media are held in fewer and fewer hands, with more corporate, shareholder control and less independent, mom-and-pop ownership. Organizations that once focused exclusively on news have been swallowed by diversified conglomerates for whom the news is just one branch. The steady demand for increased profits to satisfy investors competes with journalistic considerations in decisions about staffing, resources, and coverage. News organizations, once viewed as society's ragtag troubadours and watchdogs, increasingly find themselves inseparable from the insider zone of big business.

Like most major changes, all this shifting has both positive and negative aspects, but our concern here is relatively narrow. How does it affect editors?

The impact of change seems deep indeed:

- It speeds up nearly everything about the editing job. Information is now being produced and posted nearly nonstop from early morning to late at night.
- It requires multimedia proficiency. The typical news organization now has print, audio, video, and online components, with many editors expected to be capable in them all.
- It brings consumers into the action much earlier, as "citizen journalists" producing or contributing to news from the outset, as lobbyists for various stories or segments, and as instant critics and responders to what is being disseminated.
- It empowers the audience. With more choice and access than ever, consumers can tip the balance among competing media, create irresistible demand for various products and services, and virtually dictate which timetables and formats flourish in the marketplace.
- It makes journalism, and therefore much of what editors do, more visible to the public. Few topics earn more newsroom discussion these days than ethics, credibility, and journalists' relationship to their audiences.
- It makes editing more fun. Almost every innovation gives editors new tools for bringing more and better information to audiences in a speedier, more effective, more dramatic manner. Technology has banished many limitations of time and space that once frustrated and hamstrung journalists. Never before have there been so many options for enhancing clarity and drama in news reporting and storytelling.
- It makes editing more important than ever.

In this era of momentous change, the vital role of editing should be obvious. The trust and credibility of media, as competition rages and change explodes, rest heavily on the foundation of quality control provided by editors. Editors specialize not in information collection, not in information processing, not in information distribution, but in information assessment. It is editors who, exercising their professional judgment, help test information for all-important reliability and relevance; select, sort, arrange, and present information in the most useful, accessible, and effective ways; provide backup and oversight to other journalists struggling toward accuracy and clarity in the nonstop news cycle; and serve both individual consumers and the larger interests of society by policing the integrity of the information stream.

For editors, the aggregate impact of all this is clear. This is noble, difficult, essential work, with profound rewards and satisfactions. A pattern of changing personal, professional, and social conditions has made the editor's life—never easy—more complex than ever, and given editors more tools and opportunities than ever. These changes also underline the weaknesses of our old-fashioned system of training editors and demand renewed attention to producing the well-rounded talent needed for these challenging professional times.

Conclusion: Today's editor at work

It's only 9 a.m., and this morning's paper copy of the *Houston Chronicle* has barely hit people's doorsteps, but Sylvia Wood, the *Chronicle*'s local online news editor, already is working on a breaking, and heartbreaking, story.

A 15-year-old boy has been killed playing with a pistol with three friends. As seems so common, the boys thought the gun was unloaded. They pulled the trigger once. A harmless click. The second time, the ninth-grader was shot in the chest.

Wood has posted a brief at chron.com, her news organization's website. She has a reporter on the way and is scrambling to locate a yearbook photo of the victim. She's also juggling two more spot stories while around her, in a newsroom as quiet as a library, print colleagues shuffle in sipping from their coffee cups and grunting their good mornings.

By noon, Wood has found and posted a yearbook photo of the ninth-grader and a staff-written story on the shooting. Now she is racing after other stories, all before colleagues involved with the next day's print edition have moved into second gear.

Wood's speeded-up pace is one encountered more and more often as mainstream newsrooms adjust to becoming two-worlds-in-one. The rollercoaster rhythm of print—the steady early climb followed by the precipitous plunge to deadline—is being overtaken by the web's all-out, all-day news cycle. Like the arrival of a gigantic planet next door, multimedia online newsrooms have exerted a culture-changing gravitational pull on the lives and work of traditional journalists.

If there is one thing all these sites and their editors have in common, it is moving faster, as the almost-24-hour web cycle becomes increasingly important in the newsroom tempo, work flow, and culture.

One consequence is that today's editors tend to be more identified by their function than their medium. As newsrooms turn into diversified information retailers, they need skilled editors who can assemble, prepare, and distribute content of all kinds via print, broadcast, the Internet, and other channels.

"The endgame," said Sylvia Wood's boss, Houston editor Jeff Cohen, "is to have all our excellent journalists producing content, and 'air traffic controllers' putting in on the various platforms."

Or, as Wood herself put it: "Whether it is the web or print or handhelds, the future is giving people news when they want it and how they want it."[19]

It is that future for which editors must prepare.

Sidebar 1: Advice from the pros

Journalists, I have found, enjoy helping one another. With that in mind, I asked several editors to share thoughts on how their jobs are changing and on strategies that would be most helpful for incoming editors. Here are some of their comments.

Learn to listen

If you're going to become an assigning editor, learn to listen.

That's the short version.

The longer version: Talk enough with your [staff] to find out what they like and hate about their jobs, what inspires or dispirits them. Then try to feed them more of the former and less of the latter. Find out how they prefer to be edited—face-to-face conversations, notes in the copy, whatever—and try to do it that way as much as possible. Find out what their intermediate- and long-range goals are, then work with them to find ways toward those goals. Whenever you're tempted to give direction, ask questions instead and see whether the reporter comes to the same conclusion you do.

No one told me any of this when I got promoted, and I wasn't smart enough to figure it out quickly on my own. I suffered for that.

Lex Alexander, citizen-journalism coordinator *News & Record*, Greensboro, N.C.

Publish now!

1   This isn't necessarily new, but it has intensified: You are expected to turn up more and more with fewer resources.
2   The news cycle is gone. It's publish now! We have to get reporters to submit whatever they can as soon as they can with breaking stories, so that the news can be placed online.

3   We have more outlets for our news. We have to think, with reporters, about how to use blogs, online publications, and online video and audio to publish our material. This makes our jobs more complex.
4   The Internet has made it much easier to research stories and trends as we think about coverage. It also has made it vastly easier to turn up background information for stories and check facts (although information found online must be used with diligent caution).

> Dan Duke, Entertainment Editor *Virginian-Pilot*, Norfolk, Va.

Broaden your skills

The job has changed dramatically with the advent of the web and with the need for more powerful and visual forms of storytelling.

Today's editors are expected to be proficient in a wide range of skills—coaching writers, working with them to settle on the appropriate story form, getting the breaking news online, thinking in terms of display and multimedia.

The job is no longer just about assigning and editing the story; it's about assigning the story and then working with the reporter and the online folks and the visual folks to come up with a whole package. Sometimes the editors write the early versions for online, in order to leave the reporter with more time to get the print story done.

With the push (not a bad push, but a push nevertheless) for more entry points to a page, the assigning editor is often the one who is left to launch the graphics, create the text boxes, work with photographers and copyeditors to come up with richer cutlines and display type. There's just so much more juggling.

And then when all that is done, they still have to edit the story on deadline.

Some of the most important things that people should learn to become assigning editors haven't changed. They need to be organized. They need to stay calm in a crisis. They need to be fast. They need to have excellent people skills, changing their methods to fit with each writer. They need to be able to juggle. But these things have always been true.

Beyond that, more than ever before, they need to learn and understand story structure. They need to learn to coach writers through stories, not just assign on one end and edit on the other. They need to learn to be web-proficient. They need to learn to keep the reader in mind.

> Laurie Hertzel, Projects Editor *Star Tribune*, Minneapolis

Think!

Back in the day (before the Apple Macintosh and *USA Today*) in the 1980s, we thought we had hard jobs. We had to talk to reporters, edit stories and go to meetings. We were beleaguered.

We focused on reporting and writing skills. Then the coaching movement taught us how to actually help reporters improve. And we editors got better. We had to go to meetings, talk with reporters, edit side-by-side. Then some editor . . .

- wanted a Want to Go? box to go with the story. We started to actually think about readers as consumers.
- wanted a photo to go with the story.
- wanted a go box, photo, and a graphic to go with the story.
- wanted us to actually meet with our colleagues in design, photo and copydesk to discuss the best way to illustrate the story.
- wanted us to post the story online before the reporter got back to the office.
- wanted us to update the online story and get the reporter on the 5 p.m. TV news with our news partner before the reporting and writing is finished.

We've evolved from a job that was limited to working with reporters for the next day's print newspaper to a 24/7 job where we're responsible for collaborating with other divisions (advertising, circulation, online, TV) and colleagues in the newsroom.

As a result, we're producing much more sophisticated news reports for a more sophisticated readership. It's a lot more work, but a lot more fun, too.

Important things for modern editors to know:

- Most important: Learn how to think.
- Be a teacher. The best leaders are the best teachers.
- Acquire skills in reporting, writing, storytelling. Learn how those skills apply to the different platforms. Acquire knowledge in photography and design.
- Be a great collaborator.

Michael Weinstein, Features Editor *Charlotte Observer*

Gain lots of experience

As a deputy business editor at the *Plain Dealer*, I've gone through two noticeable changes in the last few years:

- An increased emphasis on alternative story forms (Q&As, grids, etc.). I've long encouraged these on my own, but in recent years the paper as a whole has embraced the concept, which means that I have to lead reporters toward a different way of thinking about writing. It's a gradual process. First efforts usually require a lot of hand-holding, and it's an editor-driven process to even conceive of stories in different ways, but in time it becomes part of the mindset.

* A new emphasis on online. I've become the online coordinator for our department, which means not only transferring stories from the print-edition computer system to online but also posting items on my own—rewritten news releases, for example—to get things up as quickly as possible. I'm also hosting a weekly podcast, which involves editing tapes of reporters' interviews, doing some original interviews, recording narration. And I'm blogging on topics related to special reports we do.

I've long felt that the best preparation for being an assigning editor is to hold as many different kinds of newsroom jobs first: not just reporting, but copyediting, design, photo editing, wire editing.

Editors whose only experience is in reporting seem to have a much harder time coordinating all the aspects of the job, have less sympathy for other parts of the process (tending to ignore deadlines, for example, to the copy desk's pain) and come to the job with less understanding of the types of problems they may run into. A reporter who's been diligent and self-motivated, for example, may be shocked as an assigning editor to discover that his former colleagues include some who are lazy, sloppy, or resistant to change.

John Kroll, Deputy Business Editor *Plain Dealer*, Cleveland

Learn to collaborate

How have mid-level editing jobs changed most in the past few years?

* Greater demands to acknowledge and take advantage of web opportunities, including staffing for print and online and developing new skills, such as audio, video, and Flash.
* Greater financial pressure on the newsroom which translates into harder budget decisions related to overtime, travel, and equipment.
* Greater personnel management demands as a result of Generation Y & X staffers being part of the newsroom mix. Their motivation, career expectations may be quite different than the Baby Boomer generation that lived and breathed the newsroom. The Gen Ys and Xs may have a much different

(and healthier) view about their job in the bigger context of their overall lifestyle.

What are the most important things people should do or learn to prepare to become assigning editors?

- Alternative storytelling. Routinely (and boringly) churning out the 12–15 inch stories with or without photos will not cut it any longer. Mid-level editors have to be more creative in presenting information to their audiences, print and online. They need to know the different devices they can employ to provide information in print, as well as the multimedia possibilities for delivering compelling content online.
- Audio and video. They must know the basics of how to record, shoot, and edit in these formats. They will be filling the role of multimedia coach for online stories, just as we expect them today to be a reporting/writing coach for the print edition.
- Efficiency. We know that efficiency is a critical skill for any journalist but the need is magnified for multi-tasking mid-level editors. Yet where do we as an industry acknowledge, train, and reward this quality? It can take many forms (clutter, procrastination, organization, email, phone calls, meetings), but show me where significant value is attached to efficiency in the newsroom environment. If anything, the well-organized editor is viewed (and often derided) as an anal/obsessive curiosity. Is it coincidence that one of the most frequent writing deficiencies cited by mid-level editors is the lack of organization in stories? We've overlooked this critical part of a journalist's makeup for too long. We've focused instead almost solely on the writing/reporting skills and failed to acknowledge how efficiency and organization dramatically impact both.
- People skills. The most frequent undoing of any mid-level editor is the inability to get along with others, collaborate with others, listen to others, motivate others, coach others. Again, we haven't had the greatest newsroom models to learn from, so these skills must be valued, nurtured, developed, and rewarded.

Michael Schwartz, Manager of Editorial Training COXnet
and Cox Newspapers

Vignettes

Surprises often await newcomers to editing, who may expect work days consumed by arcane debate over great writing but instead spend their days absorbed by a variety of duties, at least as many involving *people* as *copy*.

Here are some situations encountered by student editors I have taught:

- "What do you do when you edit a story, can't get in touch with the reporter, do what you consider your best, and then, after the story is printed, the reporter comes back to you and is not at all pleased? I think I finally got him to understand that if he had been available, he would have been able to come in and make the changes himself."

- "When editing a letter to the editor, and the argument within that letter sounds unfocused and the rambling of a mad man, how far should an editor go to make the letter tight and a cohesive argument?"

- "A recent article included interviews with people who had been unemployed. The story had been written earlier and was held. We got a phone call from a man who was upset because by the time the article came out he already had gotten a new job. His boss had seen the article and suspected that the man may be pretending to be unemployed to obtain more money from unemployment benefits."

- "What do you do when you think you are falling in love with [a colleague]? Or at least like? You work closely with your colleagues. This is sometimes bound to happen."

- "This editing problem involved helping a reporter who was hesitant to interview friends and family of a campus student who was murdered last weekend. The reporter is one who is very capable and very adept at dealing with people. In fact, he is just the person I would choose to deal with people in such a touchy situation. Because he always seems so confident and well-mannered, I was surprised when he told me he was uneasy about going to the victim's dormitory. As it turned out, I ended up going along with the reporter to talk to the victim's hall mates. Although some did refuse to talk to us, two girls that lived next door did give us some information. The experience was not as unpleasant as I imagined. As an editor, I think it made me feel good to be able to help out a reporter with something that was so emotionally draining."

2 What makes a good editor?

> One should fight like the devil the temptation to think well of editors.
> They are all, without exception—at least some of the time—incompetent
> or crazy.
>
> John Gardner[1]

Considering how much power they have, editors have never had a very
good press. Anyone who has spent time in newsrooms can recall besotted,
post-deadline rounds of editor bashing, listening to the disgruntled
rabble spin horror tales exposing editors as the literary equivalent of ax
murderers.

Much of the imagery verges on the violent. Writer Jon Franklin has
said that to edit is "to kill babies."[2] Mark Twain once said: "How often
we recall, with regret, that Napoleon once shot at a magazine editor and
missed him and killed a publisher. But we remember with clarity that his
intentions were good."[3] This level of passion testifies to the profound,
intimate attachment people have to what they write. Writers pour body
and soul into their work, and few occasions provoke more naked terror
than delivering one's handiwork to an aloof, all-powerful editor who
stands like St. Peter, passing ultimate judgment on creative achievement
and controlling admission to that journalistic heaven: publication, with a
byline.

Yet almost every journalist has also had at least one ideal editor, that
gifted literary companion whose stalwart partnership inspires our souls
and improves our copy. As the newspaper writer Barry Bearak once
told me, "There's nothing a reporter wants more—with the exception of
a good spouse—than a good editor." In fact, I once interviewed a writer–
editor team who had actually fallen in love and married. "I loved him first
as a writer," editor Jan Winburn explained.

So far, we have concentrated on what editors *do*. Another path is to
consider what editors *are*, or at least what they *should be*, as they attempt
to achieve their many and complex goals in ways that nurture rather than
fracture professional relationships.

In describing what editors should be, journalists reach for a range of adjectives: creative, energetic, skeptical, curious, challenging, experienced. They apply descriptors that sometimes seem polar: able to write, able to coach; able to teach, able to learn; able to juggle, able to focus; able to stand firm, able to stay flexible; able to lead, able to follow. No wonder such big game is hard to bag. The gamut of desired editorial qualities runs wide. Just as wide are the ranges of people who make editing their careers and of their styles for relating to writers.

Writers and editors

It should not be surprising that writers often come predisposed to view editors as adversaries, or at least formidable rivals for control over what gets published.

In his classic book, *On Writing Well*, William Zinsser crisply set out the basic dichotomy for judging editors: "Are they friends or enemies—gods who save us from our sins or bums who trample on our poetic souls?"[4]

They are, of course, both. Indeed, when one listens to reporters and writers discussing their editors, the conversations tend to lurch from one pole to the other, portraying a love–hate relationship of mutual dependence and battlefield-like tension and exhilaration.

Once, the editor, especially the city editor, was the unquestionable colossus of journalism. Newsrooms were fiefdoms, and many editors seemed to take glee in autocratic, arbitrary actions. Little challenge was tolerated. Orders required obedience.

Yet, looking back, many older-generation journalists tend to remember these editors affectionately and to recall them as teachers and mentors passionately devoted to getting the story and getting it right.

That era has largely passed, of course, and with good reason. Today's assigning editors tend to be more responsible but less colorful. The top-down management style has yielded to more collegial approaches. They do more planning, work across more kinds of media, and spend more time managing than muscling. They work with writers in what is far closer to a collegial relationship of equals than a boss–subordinate hierarchy.

The Pulitzer-winning writer and teacher Donald Murray echoed those who see the writer–editor pairing as akin to wedlock. "Every writer needs at least one editor, most of us need two," Murray has written. "Although I've been married twice, I find the marriage relationship easier than the one between the writer and editor. Writers and editors depend on each other; without the writer there is no copy and without the editor there is no publication."[5]

What resounds from many such comments is one of the overpowering truisms of editing. Editors work with people as much as copy. That is, editors must deal first with human beings and then with their copy. It often is the intangibles, such as respect and trust, or their absence, that cement or fragment a writer–editor relationship, and that govern the ultimate quality of copy. This is what writing teacher Roy Peter Clark calls "the human side of editing."[6]

For some editors, this feel for people is innate and natural. For others, it must be rigorously acquired and honed. But it is the starting point, and perhaps the most important single ingredient, that charts the direction of writer–editor collaborations.

Writer Madeleine Blais once captured the essence of the writer's longing, for an editor who is "an eminently trustworthy reader of what you do."[7] Few things are quite so depressing as those occasions when writers recognize that they and the editor have irreconcilable visions of the direction and purpose of a cherished project. And there is nothing quite so thrilling as the synergistic chain reaction that comes from the teamwork of a writer and editor in synchronization.

In striving for such camaraderie, it is vital to appreciate the different starting points of writer and editors. For the editor, burdened with a range of responsibilities and commonly expected to oversee a thundering herd of writers, working with one reporter's copy may be one single aspect of a complex day's work. For the writer, that one piece of copy is *everything*. No matter that the editor has 15 other articles to move and a website to update; no matter that the publisher has just called to shrink the news hole by 10 columns; no matter that the payroll report is overdue, the news desk is breathing fire over busted deadlines, the police radio is blaring something about an airliner in trouble, and the company lawyer is on hold to discuss the libel trial. It is the urgent, inescapable duty of the editor to close out the distractions, train full attention on the writer, and approach the copy as if it were a precious, fragile, and unique contribution to literary history. Which, of course, it is.

And it is important that the actual moment of copyediting not be the editor's first raw exposure to the reporter's effort. The good editor is prepared for the copy's arrival. She or he will have worked with the writer planning and conceiving the idea, monitored the reporting, and collaborated on possible approaches to the writing.

Occasionally, editors protest that there is not time for such consultations. But in the long run there is not time *not* to have them. To neglect them makes no more sense than for a banker to invest money without regard for the interest rate or for a lawyer to go into court without first reading the depositions. Such preliminary decisions are an irreversible investment in the outcome, and whatever is locked in at the moment of investment determines, to a large extent, the ultimate payoff.

Too often, however, writers and editors regard each other not as teammates but as adversaries, and they may even avoid each other at times during a story's infancy and as it progresses toward production. I know writers who, when they see the editor heading their way, will seize the phone and pretend to be involved in an important call, just to avoid dealing with the editor.

In a marvelous essay called "A View from the Trenches: The Editor as Enemy?" writer Jim Schutze provided an insightful look at how "editors and reporters actually may live in different worlds." Schutze described his shock as a reporter when an editor appeared angry upon learning Schutze's weather story included information on a record number of snow-related deaths. Schutze, who had been proud of his reporting, relayed his confusion to an older reporter, who explained:

> "The thing is, [the editor] promised a funny story at the morning meeting. Now that your story is depressing, he'll have to explain to the afternoon meeting why he doesn't have a story for the funny hole."
>
> "So what? Who cares about the meetings? We're talking about real life here."
>
> He stared at me and then looked off toward the bar as if he hated talking to me worse than anything else on earth. "Look," he said, "what went on out there in the blizzard is your idea of real life. For editors, real life is the meeting."[8]

Such a view of editors, as remote figures drifting into and out of various fog-shrouded meetings, isn't altogether far from reality. As we have seen, editors do far more than process copy: They manage newsrooms, administer budgets, hire and fire and supervise, help run the business, and participate in an assortment of activities that remove them from what writers consider their true responsibilities. These distractions crop up inevitably, but the editor must not let them crowd out discussions with reporters.

Writers use many words and images, some of them pejorative, to characterize editors. At worst, they see editors as nagging parents, peremptory drill sergeants, or tin-eared tyrants. At best, they see editors as collaborators, teammates, and coaches, always tough but also helpful and benevolent.

Concentrating on the good examples seems wise. Editor Jack Hart once asked numerous writers at several newsrooms to talk about their best editors:

> Their best editors, the respondents say, were great teachers. They took a personal interest in young journalists and showed an obvious concern for them and their futures. They took time. They listened intently. They set high standards and established challenging goals. They laughed a lot. And some of them were even—dare we say it?—gentle.[9]

Editor and website operator Bob Baker listed the key qualities reporters want from their editors. They included:

- I want you to listen to me.
- I want to be able to brainstorm with you.
- I want to sound like me, not you.
- Help me bring more context, wisdom, and perspective to my work.
- Don't rewrite me unless you have to.
- Tell me the truth.
- Don't be a bureaucrat. Be a leader.[10]

Or, as one writer told longtime editor and teacher Gene Foreman: "Be like my mom—someone who is really enthusiastic, who genuinely cares about me."[11]

In summary, what may be most vital is a quality described not so much by journalists as by singing legend Aretha Franklin: R-E-S-P-E-C-T. Writers crave respect. They want to be challenged, prodded, and led, but not by a dictator. They want to be treated as equal professional colleagues in a grand creative enterprise. Achieving such a relationship starts with mutual respect.

Characteristics of a great editor

First, as we have already discussed, come the technical skills. Outstanding editors must master the art of producing excellent content under deadline. Whether they specialize in print, broadcast, online journalism, or a combination, whether they deal in words, sounds, images, or a combination, the best editors have top copyediting, design, or other journalistic know-how. The test is simple: Good editors make the content better, not worse.

For example, the typical assigning editor should know how to:

- Help reporters select the best possible ideas
- Provide assistance and guidance, as needed, during the reporting
- Coach writers through the organizing, writing, and revising phases
- Coordinate copy, illustrations, online and multimedia packaging, and other presentation requirements
- Edit the copy for accuracy, clarity, drama, and maximum impact.

The final step in the above list—editing copy to make it better—is crucial. William Zinsser described the process this way:

> What a good editor brings to a piece of writing is an objective eye that the writer has long since lost. . . . A good editor likes nothing better than a piece of copy that he hardly has to touch. A bad editor

has a compulsion to tinker, proving with busywork that he hasn't forgotten the minutiae of grammar and usage. He is a literal fellow, catching cracks in the road but not enjoying the scenery.[12]

The flair for "enjoying the scenery," while not losing sight of the need to patch the cracks, is a quality that seems to mark strong editors. Perhaps no one has better summarized the daunting requirements of such a super editor than writer Lillian Ross, in the introduction of her book *Reporting*:

> What most writers need is not another writer but an editor—someone to talk to about their work, someone capable of giving guidance and help without getting in the writers' way.
>
> A helpful editor should have the following qualities: understanding of and sympathy for writers; the editorial talent to recognize and appreciate journalistic and literary talent; an openness to all kinds of such talent; confidence and strength in his own judgment; resistance to fads and fakery in publishing; resistance to corruption and opportunism, to exhortations from people, including writers and other editors, who are concerned with "popularity" and "the market"; moral and mental strength, and the physical strength to sustain these; energy and resourcefulness in helping writers discover what they should write about; literally unlimited patience with selfishness and egotism; the generosity and character required to give away his own creativity and pour it into a group of greedy and usually ungrateful writers. This kind of editor is a rarity. If you're lucky, you may find one.
>
> Avoid the following kind of editor: one who does not like writers.[13]

Most editors begin as writers. How soon some forget! Wherever the careers propel them, editors should never forget several fundamental lessons that help illustrate and separate the roles of editors and writers:

- Reporting is very hard. Editors should have been reporters. They should have been lectured by uppity scientists, threatened by angry police sergeants, yelled at by mayors, and forced to confront a dead cell phone in the pouring rain after their car battery has died while pursuing, on deadline, a vital source who lives in a part of town they have never been to.
- Writing is very hard. Editors should firmly remember the terror of staring at the blank screen and the insecurity of having to prove, time after time, that they still can produce marvelous copy. Writer after writer tells of fearing that, no matter what their prior successes, each new article will expose their weaknesses and unveil them as pretenders. As they move away from daily reporting and writing, editors must hold onto those feelings.
- Editors are not writers. Editors are editors. They help others write.

They supervise writers. They often rewrite. And they edit (which involves writing, but doing so unnaturally, that is, in the style of the original writer or of the publication). Editors must do their jobs but leave room for writers to exercise themselves. They must let go.

- Editors are advisers. They are expected to give advice without dominating a project. If a reporter needs to locate a source or document, editors should help. Editors don't have to *know* everything, but they should know how to *find out* almost everything. A good sign of a strong reporter–editor relationship is when the reporter's first thought, on encountering a problem with a story, is to consult with the editor. A bad sign is when reporters avoid their editors.

No list of desirable traits for editors can be exhaustive, but it can be fruitful to single out several important virtues that seem associated with successful editing.

Attitude. Good editors care. They respect writers and their copy. Harold Ross, the editing giant who founded the *New Yorker*, exemplified this quality as well as any editor in history. His biographer, Thomas Kunkel, credited "Ross's intrinsic understanding that writers and artists are different from other people and must be treated . . . as such." Kunkel goes on to say:

> And talent, the editor understood, was the key. He never stopped searching for it, or, once he had found it, nurturing it. . . . Ross had a respect for creative people that bordered on veneration; everyone else, himself included, was meant to be in their service. Needless to say, this was an attitude that writers and artists didn't come across every day. Once they understood Ross's mystical, unwavering faith in them, they were free to validate it. He championed them.[14]

Intelligence. Editors need to be quick-witted, street-smart, and well informed. They must, through a lifetime of reading and the instinct of paying attention, display a general familiarity with how things work—from international politics and genetic engineering to local zoning and celebrity hairstyles.

I once worked alongside a man who had been copyediting for 30 years. He seemed to remember every story he had ever edited. His memory was encyclopedic, and the newsroom depended on him. Another editor I worked for had a near-photographic memory. She could recall specific dates and details of news, page numbers where stories appeared months earlier, and the capital of any obscure country whose name cropped up in a wire service article.

Curiosity. Editors are annoying buttinskies because they are so curious. Like fidgety children, they want to get their hands on everything. They are always tossing off story ideas, meddling in the reporting, tinkering with the layouts, peeping at the website to see what is happening. This can, of course, be irritating but for the most part it is an important quality. Because of it, editors are always stumbling into new and exciting places. "Our best editors," David Halberstam once wrote in reference to magazine visionary Henry Luce, "have always been at least partly hick—everything is new and fresh and possible for them, they take nothing for granted."[15]

Resourcefulness. Editors get things done. They understand that life consists of a procession of problems to which it is their job to find solutions. Perhaps nothing better defines successful editors than saying they operate as problem solvers rather than problem creators: looking for the most effective solution to the nonstop crises of the news business, without unduly whining about the oppressive deadlines, incompetent staffing, uncooperative computers, hostile sources, and unreasonable management that bedevil them all.

I recall once slumping into my managing editor's office complaining that we were missing a tremendous story because no reporter with the proper blend of reporting skill and writing sensitivity was available. "Why don't you send the columnist?" the managing editor replied. Indeed, sitting right before my eyes was perhaps the best writer on the staff, our daily columnist, but I had so pigeonholed him as a column writer that it never occurred to me to send him on assignment. I did, and the story worked brilliantly, all because the managing editor was resourceful enough to imagine something innovative.

Analytical skill. Before they can solve problems, editors first must have enough analytical ability to recognize and understand the problems.

Mona McCormick has identified steps that can help a person critically evaluate information and situations:

- Identifying main issues
- Recognizing underlying assumptions
- Evaluating evidence (by testing claims or checking conclusions against facts)
- Evaluating authority (by checking the credibility of sources)
- Recognizing bias
- Understanding problems of language (such as generalities and clichés that produce misunderstanding)
- Relating information to ideas (to make sure facts contribute to proper conclusions).[16]

Good editors save time and increase their efficiency by going through these, or similar, steps regularly.

Flexibility. The editor is a kind of newsroom handyperson, whose dealings over time may skip from managing people to designing pages to conceiving story ideas to editing obits to fending off lawsuits. For most editors, a linear approach—one thing at a time—is fruitless. Editors juggle. They switch from right hemisphere to left hemisphere in the same way web browsers jump from one screen to another. This is a ragged and disconcerting way of operating, and it requires good humor and good gears.

One executive editor told me that staff vacancies had forced him to work a double shift for several weeks. During the day, he ran the newsroom, planned coverage, worked on his paper's budget proposals for the coming years, and handled other broadscale administrative duties. At night, he worked on the copydesk, fine-tuning stories and writing headlines. His flexibility kept him from drowning in the flood of work.

Good-hearted toughness. Editors must be skeptics and taskmasters. They cannot be faint-hearted in the ongoing swordplay of newsroom politics. They strive to project a near-the-brink blend of charity and fury that instills just the right touch of fear and affection. But all this must be carried off in a good spirit and without triggering newsroom warfare. I recommend practicing (perhaps in front of a mirror) the ability to smile pleasantly and speak evenly while delivering the most intellectually scathing message.

One editor I know told of waking up in the middle of the night, rehearsing the exact words he would use to tell a reporter who was failing. On another occasion, I worked for an editor who exuded poise and self-confidence in even the roughest situations. One day, just before he was to give a difficult speech, I caught him sneaking off to the bathroom to be sick. On the outside, both these editors were solid anchors for their staffs. Inside, they were just as nervous as the rest of us. Both took special care in handling the tough chores, even to the point of practicing their lines.

Fairness and diplomacy. Nobody likes a bully. Editors do not have to win every battle, inside the newsroom or outside, and few things prove more important than knowing when to retreat. Good editors listen to everyone and then try to react judiciously. Of course, staff members will vie for an editor's attention and good will in much the same way children contend for their parents' blessings. Editors need to consciously delegate time to each individual, each duty, each part of the operation.

I remember once being accused of treating some reporters better than others because, on my route to my desk each morning, I routinely stopped to chat with several reporters along the way. It was habit and geography, not favoritism, that underlay my conduct. But after the complaint I took different routes to my desk each day.

Tenacity. On the other hand, sometimes editors must display the persistence of the pit bull. This quality sometimes emerges early. As a youth, editor Max Perkins wrote a friend, "I kissed the dickens out of a pretty girl this afternoon. It took about three hours of steady arguing to get it out of her, but finally she gave me permission." After that, editing tough writers like Hemingway must have seemed like a vacation.[17]

Energy. Editors work hard, physically and emotionally. In general, the bitterest newsroom arguments that I have witnessed (and participated in) occurred when people were pushed beyond their capacity to endure. Most editors, like most people, tend to be reasonable and understanding most of the time, but become increasingly churlish, stubborn, and itchy-fingered as pressure mounts and weariness sets in. A bit of advice: Watch the eyes. When hard steel replaces the usual twinkle, an editor is over-drafted at the energy bank. Back off. Wait until the next morning to make your pitch for covering the elections in Bermuda.

Sense of humor. Special indeed is the editor who, amidst the tensest newsroom crisis, can make everyone chuckle. Few weapons are so dis-arming as wit, in particular the wisdom to laugh at yourself. Humor and tomfoolery provide important escape valves in many newsrooms. Staff members at the *Philadelphia Inquirer* still talk about the reporter return-ing from an exotic foreign assignment who walked into the editor's office with a camel and a goat.

Thoughtfulness. This means basic politeness and respect for others. It also means something else: Editors should think about everything they do. Given the rugged demands of the job, it is tempting to rush through mundane tasks and to plunge through the people and duties of the job as if they were items on a checklist. This is almost always a mistake.

Once when I was a copyeditor, I struggled for hours to polish a major investigative story and to write a punchy headline for it. I went home thinking I had significantly helped the article but realizing that no one would notice. When I arrived for work the next day, there was a note of appreciation from the executive editor. The copydesk chief had recognized my effort and notified the executive editor, who took the time to relay his thanks. That kind of thoughtfulness is doubly repaid in loyalty.

Ability. Here is where we started this section. Should skills and ability come first on the list, or last? Editors must have a range of capabilities and accomplishments: knowledge of news, language, style, usage, grammar, graphics, headlines, photos, cutlines, design, websites, audio and video feeds; plus speed, efficiency, decisiveness, and carefulness. They must be strong writers, able rewriters, and clinical copy surgeons. They must be, in the usual sense of the word, excellent journalists. These qualities are sine qua non.

But remember: They are the starting point of good editing, not the end-ing point. Editors who never build beyond these basic abilities will, more often than not, find themselves thwarted and frustrated before very long.

Personalities of successful editors

For several years, I participated in a training program for a major news-paper chain's assigning editors. We always began by asking these new and aspiring newsroom leaders to describe the best editors they ever had. Listening to hundreds of such testimonials, I was struck by the huge differences in personality and style among the editors singled out as memorable.

Some were loud, others soft-spoken. Some were tough, others gentle. Some were gruff, others congenial. Some were brash, others mannerly. Some were distant, others pushy. Some preferred the big picture, others the details. All the differences raised the obvious question of whether successful editors have anything at all in common.

The more I listened and thought, the more it seemed that these special editors shared at least two attributes:

- An exceptional vision of great journalism and a passion for achieving it
- Almost uncanny insight into motivating each person as an individual to reach unexpected levels of accomplishment.

Short of a saint, what kind of person can have, or acquire, these qualities and the many others demanded of good editors? Are editors born, or can they be taught? It seems to me that some editing talents do seem to come naturally, giving certain editing candidates an edge. But it also seems clear that almost anyone can learn to edit *better*. Surely it helps to have the inborn gift. Some people are natural editors in the same way that others are born ballet dancers or math geniuses or baseball pitchers. But there is much to learn through careful study of editing.

Many different types of people become good editors, and almost everyone can become a better one.

Conclusion

Based on all the testimonials, research, and analysis, it seems fair to conclude that success in editing tends to correspond with journalistic proficiency plus leadership ability. Editors and writers have different roles. The editor is the orchestra conductor; the writer is the virtuoso first violinist. The editor is the team coach; the writer is the star goalkeeper. These differing roles inevitably produce some conflict and tension, but they also dramatically reward teamwork and smooth relationships.

As team builders and leaders, editors spend their days making and enforcing decisions. In the following chapters, we will explore how the role of editing has evolved through history, how editors make decisions, and how they can better prepare for the challenges they face.

Sidebar 2: Skills of frontline editors

In the quest to itemize the virtues of good editors, one direct contribution has come from the Frontline Editors Project, sponsored by the

Knight Foundation and administered by Michele McLellan and others at Northwestern University. As part of the project, several editors, writers, and teachers (including myself) tried to identify some personality traits that correspond with success in editing. The idea wasn't to build a rigid formulaic model, but to help individuals and newsrooms select, train, and nurture editing candidates.

From this research, McLellan, a former editor herself, and Jacqui Banaszynski, the Knight Chair in Editing at the University of Missouri School of Journalism, developed a list they called "23 skills of effective frontline editors."

Editors, they concluded, need to be *sellers, thinkers, leaders, partners, coaches*, and *administrators*. Their research identified 23 applicable skills, including 10 that were labeled as "essential" and 13 others considered "important" or "relevant." They also discussed possible problems of relying either too much or too little on each attribute.

Essential skills

1 *Persuasive*
   Likes debate and negotiation
   Can sell self and ideas to others and enjoys that
   Enjoys winning people over.

   Too much? May not be a good listener.
   Too little? May not like to pitch ideas.

2 *Appreciative of what makes people tick*
   Interested in why people do things
   Thinks through likely motives and reactions of others and
      takes human nature into account.

   Too much? Not likely.
   Too little? May fail to motivate staff, peers, and bosses.

3 *Confident*
   Comfortable meeting people for the first time
   Comfortable in a variety of settings.

   Too much? May be a poor listener.
   Too little? May be uncomfortable, make others feel that way.

4 *Evaluative*
   Evaluates information carefully
   Looks for potential limitations or errors.

   Too much? Not likely but be gentle.
   Too little? Holes in stories.

5   *Fact-based*
Comfortable with data and numbers; likes to have them
Also comfortable when stories don't have quantifiable infor-
mation.

Too much? Struggles without data.
Too little? False premises, holes, and errors.

6   *Innovative*
Generates new ideas, original solutions
Enjoys brainstorming and coming up with new ways of look-
ing at things.

Too much? Not likely.
Too little? Doesn't help make journalism fresh, engaging.

7   *Optimistic*
Expects things will turn out well in the long run even when
there are problems along the way
Has a positive and realistic attitude.

Too much? May miss potential pitfalls.
Too little? Always negative focus.

8   *Collaborative*
Consults with others
Lets team influence decisions rather than dictating.

Too much? Decisions don't get made.
Too little? Others feel left out.

9   *Trusting*
Prepared to believe others are reliable and honest
Skeptical enough not to be easily fooled.

Too much? Too ready to believe, perhaps easily taken in.
Too little? Thinks the worst of people (and they know it).

10 *Caring*
Sympathetic and considerate towards others
Supportive when problems arise
Will consider making allowances without being overly drawn
into people's problems.

Too much? May make unfair allowances for individuals.
Too little? May be insensitive to significant problems.

Important and relevant skills

1   *Achieving* (sets high goals and works hard)

2 *Willing to take charge*
3 *Affiliative* (enjoys being with others but can work alone)
4 *Able to plan*
5 *Detail conscious*
6 *Rule conscious* (supports rules but uses nonstandard approach when warranted)
7 *Adaptable*
8 *Independent-minded*
9 *Tough-minded*
10 *Candid*
11 *Modest*
12 *Emotionally controlled*
13 *Self-aware.*

Michele McLellan, Frontline Editors Project Medill School of Journalism, Northwestern University[18]

Vignettes

What do managers look for in assigning editors? Here are excerpts from ads posted on the same day at the online site JournalismJobs.com:

- *For a city editor:* "The desirable candidate will have at least five years of experience in news reporting, editing, and management; a solid grounding in journalism ethics and values; computer skills that include word processing, use of the Internet for research, and databases; and some knowledge of online publishing as it applies to newspapers. This is a job for a dedicated, flexible, and creative journalist, committed to high standards of journalism, and eager to play a major role in shaping the future of [this news organization]."
- *For a sports editor:* "The future sports editor will be a versatile leader who can motivate and coach a talented staff. He/she will be able to think visually and is innovative in print as well as the online product, including multimedia presentation. . . . The chosen candidate will excel in working with other departments in the paper as collaboration and playing as a team member are crucial to success on the newsroom management team."
- *For a deputy lifestyles editor:* "The ideal candidate will have: Two or more years of management experience handling writers and stories for a major news organization; the ability to see the big picture and sweat the details; proven experience handling several tasks simultaneously; experience with both hard news and features; familiarity with online publishing; technical understanding a plus; an inquisitive mind eager to continually embrace change."

- *For an assistant features editor:* "The perfect candidate will have a few years of hands-on news or features reporting or editing experience and exceptional organizational and planning skills. We work in a collaborative environment that prizes these traits in managers: flexibility, creativity, planning, and coaching."

3 The rise of the new editor

During the Civil War, a nearsighted Hungarian teenager was recruited to join the Union Army. He was put aboard ship from Europe to Boston, where the agent who signed him would earn a $300 bounty. As the ship neared the United States, however, the enterprising teenager jumped into Boston Harbor, swam to shore through chilling waters, and took a train to the recruiting station, where he collected the bounty for himself.

The teenager was Joseph Pulitzer, and he soon proved a lousy cavalryman. He turned instead to journalism and became one of America's legendary editors.[1]

As for his swimming-to-America beginning, it holds at least one unforgettable lesson: The most outstanding editors often show the most remarkable energy, drive, and resourcefulness. They swim the extra lap to succeed.

From long before Pulitzer's time, of course, American newspaper editors had been hard workers with a true ink-stained heritage. They began as printers and writers. Colonial newspapers typically were run by maverick pamphleteers blessed with the typographical know-how to set the type and run the presses. Writing for them was a bit of a sideline. Over time, their one-person shops gradually yielded to layered news operations, and the editor's role as partisan editorialist gave way to that of professional news disseminator.

Steadily, over the past 200 years, editors drifted away from day-to-day absorption in writing and processing copy. New responsibilities emerged. Although some editors remained at the typewriter and later the terminal, others removed themselves one or more steps, into news gathering and coordination. Eventually, editors came to preside over ever-expanding, complex, multimedia organizations whose administrative demands left less and less time for any one individual to attend to writing, assigning, and editing the copy. The editor's world broadened to encompass a full range of editorial, executive, and leadership duties.

Today's editor, to be fully prepared, requires the skills of all these predecessors and more. Writing, editing, coordinating, producing, and managing all belong in the repertoire of the individual we call the *new editor*:

a professional journalist armed for decision-making responsibility in the modern news organization.

The new editor does not reside only in the prestigious positions atop the masthead. She or he may be a copyeditor, assignment editor, or designer; in features, news, or on the web; a longtime writer enticed into a desk stint, or a career desk person dedicated to the editing track. The new editor may specialize in one medium or work across what have come to be called "platforms." What distinguishes new editors is not the particular job they hold at the moment. Instead, it is their preparation and capacity for understanding and performing a spectrum of contemporary editorial duties.

As we have already discussed, editors belong to a neglected species. That neglect has given editing something of a bad name and produced misunderstanding about the role, duties, and qualifications of the job. The result is a kind of spiral. Young journalists do not prime themselves for editing careers or receive sufficient guidance in that direction from management. So those who are selected for editing often move into the job poorly prepared and lacking confidence. They reinforce the stereotypes. The spiral continues. Coupled with the vast changes taking place in journalism, this syndrome has created problems in producing the quality of editing that modern times demand.

To address these issues, we first briefly examine some stages editors have gone through historically. The evolution of editors from "writers" to "executives" should appear clearly. In the final part of this chapter, we further define and flesh out the duties and roles of editors.

In reviewing the origins and development of editing, it is worth noting how each successive phase builds on the past, adding duties, broadening the editor's role, and imposing new requirements. Ironically, as editors increasingly come to specialize, the range of knowledge and ability needed for an editing career (assuming that one will hold several different editing positions over time) increases noticeably.

The editor in history

It may seem a stretch, but let's think of Johann Gutenberg as the first editor. In the 1450s, Gutenberg combined moveable, or re-usable, type along with a press adapted from the wine industry into a practical printing system. The priceless Gutenberg Bibles came from his presses. Similar technology may have been used in Korea, China, and elsewhere, but history has celebrated Gutenberg for this world-changing invention.

Less well known is the fact that Gutenberg had a partner, Johann Fust, who provided loans for this work. These two men almost immediately got into a ferocious argument. The details remain murky, but Fust accused Gutenberg of diverting money intended for printing bibles into more lucrative publishing ventures. Fust sued and won, and Gutenberg had to forfeit his printing operation.[2]

The precedent was rudely established. Put two journalists together, and friction results, often a clash between sacred public service duties and more worldly profit motives. The tension between the competing priorities of service and profit marked journalism early and carries forward to this day.

Like Gutenberg, the earliest American editors were, above all, skilled printers. Their job required mastery of typography, access to presses, and, at least at first, licenses from authorities. Thus equipped, they could spread their messages. Ben Franklin, for instance, signed on as a printer's apprentice at age 12, composed type for his brother James's *New England Courant*, and eventually rose to editing and publishing on his own.

Franklin had a flair for editing: He substituted the word "self-evident" in Thomas Jefferson's draft of the Declaration of Independence that originally read, "We hold these truths to be sacred and undeniable."[3]

Franklin also showed an editor's sensibilities. In his *Autobiography*, he boasted of having "excluded all libelling and personal abuse" from his publications, and he cautioned "young printers ... not to pollute their presses and disgrace their profession by such infamous practices."[4] Despite his wide-ranging accomplishments, Franklin never forgot his origins. In proposing his own epitaph, he called himself "Benjamin Franklin, printer."

These early editors were essayists and editorialists, not news gatherers, and their work grew overtly partisan as they associated themselves with specific parties and philosophies. Isaiah Thomas, an apprentice printer at age 6, became one of the young nation's leading publishers by championing the patriot cause against Britain. Noah Webster, best known today for his dictionaries, won fame in his own time by editing one of the country's leading Federalist journals.

The great turning point for American media came in the 1830s, when a combination of events, including industrialization, urbanization, and the movement toward widespread literacy, produced a new kind of newspaper, the mass daily. It was supported not by government contracts, moneyed patrons, or factional underwriting but by the pennies of ordinary readers and the advertising support that followed them. Launched in 1833 by 23-year-old Benjamin Day and his *New York Sun*, the Penny Press era introduced the financial and professional model that would sustain U.S. journalism from then on: advertiser-supported media aimed at the needs and interests of the huge middle-class audience.

With the mass press came a new breed of editors, people like James Gordon Bennett who recognized the commercial value of relatively straightforward news and who moved aggressively to capitalize. Bennett's penny-a-copy *New York Herald* opened in 1835, offering unparalleled local, national, and foreign news coverage. Among its innovations was aggressive reporting on sports, finance, crime, and society, everyday topics that quickly won the interest of the burgeoning New York mass audience.

Unlike many of his predecessors, Bennett chose the role of news gatherer and disseminator over that of opinion writer. Perhaps more than anyone else, Bennett developed the modern notion of "news."

Later, editors such as Joseph Pulitzer and William Randolph Hearst responded to political and economic upheaval and led the way into the 20th century by synthesizing Bennett's hard-news model with their updated version of the old political evangelizing. The resulting extraordinary aggressiveness in both news gathering and editorial crusading begot the era of muckraking and yellow journalism. As the century turned, newspapers, although increasingly big businesses, had top editors who still could personally oversee news coverage and editorial policy making. But the growing complexity of news operations brought departmentalization and specialization and gave rise to a new kind of professional editor.

Such a person was Carr V. Van Anda, a brilliant mathematician hired in the early 1900s to be managing editor of the *New York Times*. Van Anda was not the paper's top editor or business strategist (Adolph Ochs was). But he ran the news operation, and stories of his stewardship are legend. It was Van Anda who, based on his own mathematical calculations, decided that the supposedly unsinkable *Titanic* had indeed sunk and led his paper with the scoop. On another occasion, he noticed an error in a complicated equation that Albert Einstein had used during a lecture. During World War I, he monitored the movement of armies, dispatching his correspondents to cover expected battles with what David Halberstam called "a surprisingly prophetic instinct."[5]

As the 20th century advanced, editors and subeditors grew increasingly specialized. Newsrooms became small empires. Line editors oversaw routine chores of producing the daily news report. Top editors managed. The higher on the ladder editors rose, the more likely they were to be rewarded for production and executive abilities, not simply journalistic flair. Yet most had begun as writers and subordinate editors, and many felt unsteady and insecure as they climbed from rung to rung, progressively distancing themselves from the kind of work that had initially drawn them.

As discussed earlier, the modern period has accelerated and intensified these trends, as the newsroom empire found itself surrounded by increasingly elaborate corporate and marketing structures and by expansion into multimedia avenues of presentation. Today, the new editor must build on all this ancestry, and overcome the insecurity. An understanding of writing, reporting, presentation, coordination, and production remains vital. But added to it is the need to maneuver in the modern news environment, a place where journalists increasingly share space and power with publishers and various other associates from the once-segregated "business side"; with other colleagues associated with multiple forms of media; and with an increasingly active audience that includes "citizen journalists," bloggers, and others.

In this integrated environment, today's editor is a multimedia manager. The new editor remains a decision maker about news, copy, and design, but in formats ranging far beyond the traditional print standard. Beyond that, she or he is likely to have expanded duties in making decisions about numerous other issues that may lie outside the traditional journalistic and editorial purview. These issues typically touch such areas as law, ethics, management philosophy, marketing strategy, and business direction. They call for editors of breadth and depth, at all levels of the newsroom.

David Stoeffler, a top editor at Lee Newspapers, put it this way:

> The difference between the average newspapers and the best newspapers is all about the leadership. It certainly starts at the top, and by that I mean both the editor and the publisher, but it's really critical to have strong leadership at the mid-level management of the newspaper.[6]

As Stoeffler suggests, these changing times affect all editors, not just those at the top. Today, it is not unusual for a city editor to have a year-end financial bonus tied in part to the newspaper's overall circulation gains or the website's traffic growth, or for a copyeditor to sit on an inter-departmental committee helping map the news organization's five-year multimedia plan.

The demand for better- and broader-trained editors extends throughout the newsroom and is felt in every editing job. An individual launching an editing career can encounter a path of jobs with diverse responsibilities and requirements. Not every editor will follow this path in a hierarchical fashion. Some, such as a talented reporter chosen to be city editor, begin in the middle. Others, such as a high-powered outsider brought in as editor in chief, may start at the top. More typically, however, editors move through several of the following jobs in a rough progression:

Line editing. Copyeditors, headline writers, page designers, photo editors, web producers, and others work directly with copy, usually on deadline. They need language proficiency, precision, speed, multimedia know-how, and cool heads.

News editing. News editors, wire editors, and section producers are gatekeepers who decide what content will appear and how it will be played. They must have vision, news judgment, and understanding of their audiences along with the efficiency and copyediting skills to process copy.

Assignment editing. So-called department heads, such as city editors, sports editors, features editors and their assistants, spend less time with copy and more time with ideas, reporters, artists, and other editors. They, too, must be accomplished technicians able to edit rapidly and accurately. They also need imagination and the nose for news, the ability to make clear assignments and direct reporters' work, a flair for juggling all the hectic elements of a news day, and sophisticated planning and administrative abilities to effectively deploy their limited resources under severe time pressures. In addition, they must understand their special areas (for example, sports, foreign news, or graphics) and serve as advocates for the material their staffs produce.

Specialized editing. At about this point, some editors find themselves attracted to various specialties, such as editorial writing, photo editing, or online production coordination, where particular talents or knowledge may be required.

Managing editing. Depending on the size of a news organization, several editing jobs may be primarily administrative. The managing editor and various deputies, as well as executive editors and others in similar posts, stand one step further from constant involvement with copy or daily assignments. Typically, they handle major stories, oversee page-1 and section-front copy and design, and try to allot time for some hands-on editing. But they also must hire, fire, and supervise; handle matters like scheduling; administer budgets; plan long-term coverage; and frequently serve as liaisons with other parts of the news organization such as the website, the cable station, or the production staffs. On top of their skills as editors of copy, they must be executives and diplomats, counselors and critics, planners and prodders.

Executive editing. These are editors, editors in chief, senior editors, associate editors, and so on. By whatever title, editors at the peak of all but the smallest newsrooms have vast corporate and administrative duties that may, on some days, keep them completely out of the news flow. They are likely to oversee various kinds of media, including print, broadcast, cable, and online operations. Whatever their journalistic talents, they must be effective planners, organizers, and overseers on a strategic level.

To cope with the jobs just listed, the new editor needs preparation for a variety of roles, many of them fairly far removed from basic writing and copyediting. In the following sections, we examine one by one the roles of the new editor. Although not all roles apply to each job, most new editors can expect to fulfill most or all of the following roles at some time during a career.

The editor as businessperson

"One part writer, one part editor, one part businessperson." That is how one expert's post on the career site monster.com described the editor's evolving role.[7]

While the business role is growing, however, it isn't new at all. Editing has long been connected to entrepreneurship. Early editors, as we have seen, were printers running their own small enterprises. The very phrase "family-owned newspaper," which applied to most papers for decades and still applies to many, suggests an ongoing business venture. Editors in the United States have almost always worked within for-profit environments. But, as we discussed earlier, concentration and competition have steadily raised the stakes of the business aspects of editing.

Geneva Overholser, a longtime editor herself, documented the trend in an extensive report for a series called "The State of the American Newspaper." Here is what she found:

> Over the years, with the decline in newspaper readership, the emergence of the publicly owned newspaper company, and the concomitant ascent of the business side, the editor's role has evolved. Dramatically. . . . Declining readership compels editors to be marketers. Corporatization compels them to be entrepreneurs.[8]

Editors today hide from reality if they regard the newsroom as a barricaded bunker protected from the ricocheting flak of market competition. However, do not misunderstand the editor's role here: It is *not* to serve as a businessperson first, newsperson second. Nor is it to maximize profit at the expense of quality, nor to abandon news duties in a rush to the boardroom. News organizations have important social responsibilities that underlie their First Amendment protection. The editor's role is to grow in understanding the corporate culture as well as the news side, in order to have an informed, powerful voice in representing the newsroom, asserting its interests, and sustaining the commitment to social responsibility and to reasonable corporate success. With more and more news firms in the hands of conglomerate managers not backgrounded in journalism, editors become more important than ever to ensuring that bottom-line mentalities do not crowd out public service and long-term quality.

What has changed is not the editor's values and standards, but the breadth of knowledge and preparation necessary to maintain them effectively and the environment (including financial concerns and potentially less-sympathetic ownership) where decisions get made. Long ago, then *Washington Post* publisher Donald Graham addressed the point eloquently in a speech:

> One of the ultimate questions in any organization is, what yardstick do you measure yourself by? We ought to be familiar with the yardsticks of the manager, of the marketer, and of the public corporation, but the ultimate test comes when the reader opens the door in the morning, looks at the paper and says: "Is there a good story here?"[9]

The editor as planner

I once spoke with a young journalist from Brazil who had spent several months as a visiting writer here. Asked what surprised her about United

States newsrooms, she replied without hesitation, "These Americans, they debate *everything*!"

Perhaps it stems from the nonstop growth of journalistic corporations, or from modern journalists' much-proclaimed yearning for involvement, or simply from society's increasing demands for fuller communication. But editors no longer can get away with barking out unilateral orders and expecting underlings to leap to carry them out.

Publishing today requires as many committee meetings as a busy day on Capitol Hill. It demands carefully plotting everything from long-range marketing strategy to multimedia coverage plans for next week's first day of school. It includes meetings inviting subscribers to "talk back" and counseling sessions with staff members in trouble. Increasingly, as we discuss later in the book, it involves marshaling teams of writers, artists, designers, assignment editors, news editors, copyeditors, TV producers, and webmasters that cross over traditional turf lines. Building consensus and reducing friction rank high on the editor's duty list. Good planning has priority.

A routine work day may compel editors to look ahead in numerous ways: to decide which of next week's papers will feature special sections, who will cover night cops while the beat reporter attends a stress-management seminar, what comics might be eliminated if budget cutbacks materialize, or whose applications will be approved for new blogs on the website. One of my earliest tasks as the first national editor of *USA Today* was to create from scratch a futures calendar of events covering the entire country.

Various studies suggest that editors spend from one-third to two-thirds of their time on administrative and planning activities outside of actually writing, editing copy, or designing pages or sites. In addition, these activities increasingly take place outside of the newsroom entirely. Editors may spend several hours a week or a month in meetings with other divisions of their news organization. They may spend time meeting with individuals in their communities or making speeches to civic organizations.

All this requires anticipation, oversight, coordination, and strong time management, along with the flexibility to shift from one setting to another and maintain efficiency.

As an example, consider a hypothetical suburban editor for a good-sized regional newspaper. The job combines fundamental journalism (assigning stories, editing copy, designing pages, feeding the web) with awesome planning challenges. Suburban editors grapple with such issues as:

- How to set priorities to cover council meetings, school boards, and police and fire departments in dozens of outlying communities, without sufficient staff to cover a fraction of the potential beats
- How to deploy bureaus and reporters efficiently (and economically) in a vast geographic area

- How to direct these forces on deadline each day
- How to balance the need for constant web updates with the reporting and writing time required for depth print reports
- How to assemble copy and illustrations in time to meet inelastic production deadlines that begin with the web and end with multiple daily editions, each zoned to a different area
- How to keep peace among staffers being asked to record suburban school lunch menus when their true goals are to lay siege to larger, more glamorous front-page stories.

For some editors, these demands can be maddening. Journalists tend to have driven, can-do personalities, more geared to quick action than to planning, coordination, and direction. In this, as in other aspects of editing, the training and attributes that led a journalist to early success in the trenches can create problems when the individual moves into editing. There, subtlety, discretion, efficiency, and soft stepping may count more than individual heroics.

To help address the need for planning and priority setting, one university program began experimenting with a new newsroom title: executive editor for innovation. The idea, according to Prof. Jacqui Banaszynski of the Knight Center in Editing Excellence at the Missouri School of Journalism, is to develop "a leader of change" inside newsrooms. The experiment recognizes that newsrooms need to be "live laboratories for change," to "identify the urgent challenges facing the industry" and "to plan for the newsroom of the next 10 years."[10]

While it seems sensible to consider deputizing one editor with those special duties, it also seems clear that almost all editors will have a role in the kind of intense planning that today's and tomorrow's journalism demands.

The editor as manager

You edit people, not just copy. How many journalists have heard that hoary slogan? Of course, it is hoary because it is true. Nothing is more important to editors than appreciating that people lie at the heart of the job.

"My job," a *New Orleans Times-Picayune* editor once told me, "is to be calm, reasonable and fair when faced with people who are unreasonable, unfair and not calm."[11]

We commonly think of management as the direction of people. However, editors also manage in other ways: They manage resources (more and more news organizations are making mid-level editors responsible for administering five- and six-figure budgets). They manage time, including their own and the time of others. They manage reputations, of their staffs and their news operations.

To many derring-do journalists, few things seem more alien than management. After all, journalists take pride in their iconoclasm. They prize independence and shout at presidents. What preparation is there in such a life for the moment that often serves as its capstone: appointment to management?

Not much, of course, and therein lies trouble. Given all the changes in journalism discussed so far, it should be clear that managing has surged higher and higher on most editors' charts. But training and preparation for that role have not nearly kept pace.

The new editor must manage proficiently. As always, good journalism comes first. Without an understanding of journalistic values, a manager—no matter how well trained in personnel policies—cannot master the complex forces of the newsroom universe. So, a key goal for journalism schools and media training programs is to help journalists become competent managers. Otherwise, editors risk finding themselves outmaneuvered and their newsrooms outflanked by deft outsiders better able to manipulate corporate power levers.

Robert Giles, in his book *Newsroom Management*, lists several qualities required of editor-managers. They include the following:

- The need to be effective in running a staff that is ambitious, well-educated, and sophisticated in its expectation of sensitive management.
- The need to be supportive of women and minorities.
- The need to help staffers motivate themselves.
- The need to build a climate of trust.
- The need to let staffers know where they stand.
- The need to help staffers chart career paths.
- The need to understand . . . high technology.
- The need to develop and execute changes in news content and news focus based on marketing and readership research.[12]

In so many ways, editors serve as stewards. Copyeditors are stewards of writers' copy; assignment editors, of the trust and talents of their staffs; managing editors, of the news organization's ideals and content; web editors, of the collaborative work of staff members and citizen contributors.

Exercising such stewardship can seldom be accomplished alone. Through thoughtful, sensitive management, the new editor tries to harness the gifts and energies of others. Unified, a news staff is an awesome force. Dispirited, it chugs toward mediocrity.

Geneva Overholser, the former editor quoted earlier in this chapter, has advised editors to reshape how they think of themselves and their roles, with stronger focus on management. "You can't care enough about keeping your staff engaged," she believes. "Not happy necessarily, but engaged. A well-attended machine is going to work better than one that is neglected."

Overholser, former editor of the *Des Moines Register*, says editors should pay special attention to staff development: teaching staff members the history of their community and news organization, pairing old-timers with newcomers to help transfer the "lore of the newsroom," and spending more personal time "just cruising the newsroom."[13]

Gregory Favre, onetime executive editor of the *Sacramento Bee*, puts it this way: "To me, people need to be the center of the editor's universe." Favre suggests working harder on attracting "the best and the brightest," treating them as individuals, and offering a range of incentives to help them avoid burnout and lead balanced lives.

"The single most important thing we do," according to Favre, "is surround ourselves with good people and try to create the kind of workplace where they can express themselves and do their best work."[14]

The difference between smoothly functioning newsrooms and the dysfunctional newsroom rests with the management, and the management rests with the editors.

The editor as journalist

In describing the roles of the new editor, we began with the furthest from the daily news operation ("the editor as businessperson") and moved inward toward the center. Squarely at the bull's-eye is the editor as journalist. Nothing ranks higher. The first editors knew that, and the new editor knows it too.

No matter what else she or he can do, the new editor should be a more-than-competent journalist. Credibility and authority rise from there. Just like Ben Franklin and the earliest American editors, the new editor must come prepared to make productive command decisions day in and day out. What does this role entail?

Essentially it subdivides into four key categories, decisions about coverage, content, structure, and presentation.

Making decisions about coverage. In the large sense, editors represent their publications and have responsibility for generating suitable overall content. They decide what gets through the gates and into the paper, onto the air, and onto the web. From the view of the audience, few jobs could be more vital. Every day brings hundreds of potential topics, forcing editors into rapid-fire decisions that govern what kind of content will emerge. Editors, then, must understand their news organizations' values and expectations, and apply them. That involves understanding what makes news (or features or good websites or whatever the expected product is for a given editor) and demonstrating the ability to supply it.

Making decisions about content. Editors need the basic critical-thinking skills to analyze each piece of work and help make it of the highest quality possible. The best editors think conceptually, helping evaluate whether articles and artwork are accurate, balanced, complete, fair, well conceived, well documented, well organized, and appropriate in tone, taste, and style. From the very conception of a story idea, the good editor serves as a partner in proceeding toward making it reality. As a "copy doctor," the editor needs the talent of an intellectual surgeon *and* the wisdom to know what to leave alone.

Making decisions about structure. Editing requires many gears. At the content editing level, an editor may rev up the engines to top throttle and fly around the ethers of deep thoughts and high ideas. But a crucial next step is to gear down, so to inspect copy word by word and mark by mark. This is fine-tuning. It is nitpicking. And it is quality control at its most precise. Style, spelling, grammar, punctuation, and word usage must be meticulously inspected. All editors, somewhere in their careers, must prove their ability to furnish the final product: clear, clean, correct, publishable copy, on deadline.

Making decisions about presentation. Ben Franklin did not have to worry about photographs, and certainly not about pie charts, fever lines, infographics, podcasts, and web chats. The new editor does. Gone is the world divided into "word people" and "the artsy types." Broad-casting, computerization, pagination, the Internet, and other techno-logical marvels have blurred the old forms. The new editor must know not only what is news, how to get it, how to write it, and how to cor-rect it, but also how to design and display it for maximum effect for a busy distracted audience. Although some editors seem uncomfortable with the new visual or multimedia world, they should see it as an asset. It presents editors with extremely powerful tools for conveying their messages with greater force than ever. The new editor welcomes that opportunity.

The technological revolution stands as one highly visible symbol of change, but it is not the only way that the editor's journalistic role has matured. In making decisions about coverage, the new editor faces unprecedented questions involving privacy, access, credibility, sources, and balance. Competition from other media, ever-changing audience tastes, and today's emphasis on trends and depth reporting require a re-evaluation of traditional notions of news.

In content editing, editors no longer wield unbridled, capricious power over copy. Writers demand more sensitive, consultative editing manners. With space and resources at a premium, every story and illustration faces scrutiny. New writing styles, experiments, and risks must be considered. Format differences among print, broadcast, and online publication must be balanced.

In structural editing, the editor remains the reader-of-last-resort, as copydesks or web production units get the final chance to scrutinize copy before it goes public. Structural editing includes putting the final touches on copy and formatting it for various production processes. Editors use time-honored fact-checking methods, including their own hunches and knowledge as well as standard reference materials. Increasingly, web-based research tools and electronic diagnostic programs can help evaluate everything from addresses to potential plagiarism.

In each of these roles, change confronts the new editor. Subsequent chapters attempt to help editors prepare for their changing duties.

Conclusion

Someone once said that journalists tend to be bomb-throwers, at least metaphorically. That seems to suggest a pretty strong image for the role of the new editor: a newsroom executive paid for tending to the bombs.

Of course, the job does not necessarily require stamping out the controversial ideas of a reporter, artist, or web master. One editor I know thinks today's journalists are too docile and says he fights constantly to goad his staff into stirring things up.

To lob the bomb or to spit on the fuse: That is the editor's question. The new editor contends with swirling changes within journalism and society. No longer a one-person shop, no more a whimsical individualist, the new editor makes decisions against a backdrop of swift change.

Yet to dwell on the pressures, frustrations, and complications of editing misses a far larger point: The new editor has powers and opportunities like never before. Potential audiences have never been larger, nor the stakes of journalism more serious. As executive, manager, planner, and teacher, the new editor derives daily, even hourly, satisfaction from producing vibrant products with a central role in our information-based society. Editors work daily with enthusiastic, devoted staffs who see journalism as a mission and a calling, not just a job.

One editor's influence extends far further, typically, than any one writer's. Editors touch dozens of stories in a given day. Their vision can embrace every part of journalism: the ideas, the reporting, the writing, the presentation.

Although new editors must make more decisions than ever before, in a more difficult environment than ever before, they also have more help than ever before. Reporters have never been better educated. News has never been more interesting. Technology has enabled editors to aspire to creative artwork and display unimagined just a few years ago. And for all the financial strains felt in the business, news organizations generally remain healthy, solid enterprises.

Without a doubt, editing is a complex, frustrating, not always appreciated job. But the best new editors hold true to the spirit of their inky-fingered ancestors. As editors always have, they grow toward a future that is once again changing, broadening, and complicating their lives.

In the next chapters, we examine in more detail the techniques and skills required for the job, beginning with the single most common act in editing: making decisions.

Sidebar 3: Defining the typical editor—"How come so many of them tend to be geeks?"

Dave Barry

First of all, we ought to define "editor." I say this because, as you have probably noticed, American journalism has become title happy, so that in most newspapers everybody covered by the dental plan is editor of something. You meet people with impressive-sounding titles like Associate Lifestyles Editor, and it turns out their primary responsibility is deciding how many stars to give the Late Movie.

For our purposes, I'm going to rule out these lower level personnel. I'm also going to rule out editors listed on the masthead with titles such as Extreme Exalted Editor, because as a rule these are aged, out-to-pasture coots who wear green eyeshades and refuse to learn how the computer system works, so they use their 1927 Royal typewriters to pound out philosophical op-ed pieces about the change of seasons, only they keep getting the actual seasons out of sequence

No, what I'm going to talk about are the *real* editors, the skilled and highly paid upper-level professionals who bear the heavy responsibility of performing the essential tasks of modern-day newspaper journalism, which are:

1   Making up budgets
2   Telling job applicants that their credentials are very impressive, especially the two Pulitzer Prizes, but due to budget considerations no new people can be hired until at least three current employees retire and then die
3   Going to budget-related meetings
4   Deciding that, due to budget considerations, you are going to rely on the wire services to cover the mass slaying in your lobby
5   Fretting about the Decline in Readership.

So that's what real editors *do*, but who *are* they? What makes them tick? What do they feel, deep inside? How come so many of them tend to be geeks? To answer these questions, we must first understand how these people came to be editors.

Most of them developed their interest in journalism very early. In high school, while the other kids were out playing sports, buying condoms, etc., our young editor-to-be was hard at work on the school paper, cranking out lengthy, dated articles that could be used to sedate hyperactive children. During college, our future editor typically got a summer job as a reporter for a small newspaper with a name like the Buford County Register-Calibrator, where he learned the three basic rules of reporting:

1   Never quote anybody accurately unless you want to make him sound like a jerk.
2   Always describe relatives of plane-crash victims as "grief-stricken." Women who have just seen their husbands reduced to objects the size of cigar boxes in freak trash-compactor accidents are "shocked."
3   If you go to a meeting of the Regional Area Water, Zoning and Sewage Appeal Board Authority Commission, and it lasts three-and-a-half hours and absolutely nothing newsworthy happens, you should engage in cynical, hard-bitten-newsman-style banter with the other reporters about what a waste of time it was, then write a 37-inch story with at least two sidebars.

After college, our editor-to-be gets a full-time job as a reporter with a bigger newspaper, and he quickly realizes that if he moves up to the copydesk, he won't have to talk to the public any more. So he learns the three basic rules of copyediting:

1   Whatever way the reporter has spelled "Caribbean," you should change it to another way.
2   Headlines . . . ideally should be completely unintelligible (*House Unit Airs Solons' Parley Plea*).
3   If you are editing a story in which the reporter has risked his life to get an exclusive interview with a machete-wielding, hostage-holding, homicidal maniac, and it is a brilliant piece of deadline writing, a crackling, gripping, tension-filled, firsthand account, you should wait until the newsroom is fairly quiet, then yell to the reporter: "Dammit, Johnson, our style is to use a colon to introduce a complete, one-sentence quotation within a paragraph!"

So our boy gets a job on the copydesk. The problem there, of course, is that according to government figures, working on the copydesk kills your brain cells at the rate of over 4 million a day. So as soon as he can, our savvy editor-to-be makes the move up the ladder to full-fledged editor, with direct responsibility for not hiring people, not spending money, and writing lengthy and vaguely threatening memos to the staff about using the [office telephone] line for personal calls.

If he handles these tasks well, our editor is promoted to an upper level post where, along with his peers, he is responsible for fretting about the Decline in Readership, which is caused by the fact that the average reader buys the paper mainly for sports and the Kmart insert, and pays no attention to the lengthy front page stories about Lebanon, the deficit, and important meetings of the Regional Area Water, Zoning and Sewage Appeal Board Authority Commission.

Most of this fretting is done in-house, but from time to time our editor will attend week-long Fretting Conferences in warm locales with high-level editors of other papers that are also suffering from Declining Readership. They sit around, day after day, trying to figure out what the hell the public wants, which is not easy because the last time any of them dealt with the actual public in person was back when they were just out of college, and all they can remember is that it seemed to be grief-stricken. Eventually, they decide that what they need to do is humanize the paper, which means use more interviews with Dolly Parton in the Lifestyles section.

What we have in our typical editor, then, is a person who leads a sheltered existence: After about age 30, he hardly ever deals professionally with anybody except other editors. This tends to make him insecure. At home, in his suburban development, he's surrounded by neighbors with real jobs at large corporations that own railroad cars and huge vats of chemicals and entire Third World nations, neighbors who routinely deal with high-level financial concepts such as debentures. These concepts are far beyond the comprehension of our editor, whose only major investment move in his entire life was to join a Christmas Club, in which he lost money.

Oh, our editor tries hard to be one of the guys, to appear as though he has an important job with important problems, just like his neighbors. He starts wearing three-piece suits. He carries a briefcase. He goes out of his way to talk business at cocktail parties. "Bob," he'll say to a neighbor, "how's business?" And Bob will say, "Well, Ed, I had to lay off 67,000 people today, and the division I'm in charge of lost $3.28 billion in the last fiscal quarter because of unexpected fluctuations in the composite annualized national bond accrual, but, hey, it's nothing we can't handle. How about you?" And Ed says, "Well, we're thinking seriously about dropping 'Dick Tracy.'" And he knows, deep in his soul, that Bob does not view him as a heavy hitter. He knows that if Bob faced a wimpy little problem such as Declining Readership, he would punch some figures into his giant corporate mainframe computer and have it solved before lunchtime.

No, our boy realizes, in the end, that he's an editor, not a businessman. So he trudges back to his cubicle and he looks out across the newsroom at the young, enthusiastic reporters violently pounding out stories, and he thinks: "Maybe it's time I let a new generation take over the tasks of fretting and not hiring. Maybe it's time I slowed down a little, thought a little more about the meaning of life, maybe even did a little piece about the changing of the seasons." Of course, he realizes he must wait until the current Extreme Executive Editor suffers a fatal heart attack. . . . Budget considerations, you know.[15]

Vignettes

I once asked several retired newspaper editors what they would do differently if they could return to the newsroom. Here are some of their answers:

- From Ben Bradlee, former executive editor, *Washington Post*: Don't let daily chores divert you from concentrating on content. "When you come to work in the morning, there is an awful lot preventing you from sitting down with other editors and reporters and saying, 'What are we going to put in the paper?' Get it in the paper, get it in the paper, make a call, get it in. The sense of excitement that comes from all that, that is what I would try to re-create."
- From Pam Luecke, former editor, *Lexington Herald-Leader* in Kentucky: Stop fouling up the basics. "My husband and I edit heavily at the breakfast table. I think I would redouble my efforts to make sure grammar was impeccable and make sure jump lines were correct. Those little things really are annoying."
- From William Hilliard, former editor, *Portland Oregonian*: Lead bravely. "You have to be visible, let people know what your philosophy is and that as long as you're editor, that is the way you want things to go. Too many people run popularity contests, and that's a bad thing to do if you're a leader."[16]

4 The editor as decision maker in a multimedia age

It was just before midnight, deadline time at morning newspapers along the East Coast, when word came of an extraordinary news development. Twelve of 13 workers trapped in a West Virginia coal mine had been found alive. Or, more precisely, family members gathered at a nearby church had been told the miners were alive.

Imagine yourself as the editor on duty that night. The story was potentially huge, but it was also possibly premature, perhaps even mistaken. Given just a few minutes to ponder, what would you decide? What headline should go onto your newspaper page, whose permanent and unchangeable type would greet people over breakfast seven or eight hours later? Should you post the same headline, or something different, on your website, whose evolving and impermanent format could easily be updated if the early information proved wrong?

When this situation actually occurred in early 2006, many newspapers, including the *New York Times* and *Washington Post*, reported in at least some editions that the miners were alive. "Jubilation in West Virginia" read a headline in the *Boston Globe*. "Twelve miners found alive" declared some editions of *USA Today*.

Sadly, the early reports were wrong. Twelve of the 13 miners had died, not survived. But the correct information wasn't available until around 3 a.m., far too late for most Eastern newspapers to change their pages. On websites, the erroneous reports were updated within minutes, but for thousands of newspaper readers their morning editions contained tragically inaccurate information.

For editors, the episode was especially dramatic and the error was humiliatingly obvious, but the basic situation was hardly unusual at all. Editing, as we have seen, is about making decisions. Editors make hundreds of decisions every day, from what stories are credible enough to publish, to who has to work on weekends, to when to allow anonymous sources. Most decisions do not have the emotional impact of reversing the life and death of someone's loved ones. But all decisions have consequences.

Sometimes the consequences seem almost absurd. In some 20 years of working for newspapers, only once did I ever come close to a fistfight. That happened when another editor and I argued irrationally over where new furniture would go in our newsroom. We stopped short of throwing punches, but the incident stuck with me as an example of how everyday flash points can consume an editor's energy just as much as the grand moral quandaries.

As newsroom decision makers, editors regularly confront more nasty dilemmas about everyday operations than high-stakes journalism. Tempers flare over who will receive the new computer terminal or which copydesk will win the latest shipment of ergonomic chairs. On a given day, an editor may spend less time deciding news play than debating how to handle a budding romance between the police reporter and the assistant city editor. Updating a website feature package may take second place to placating readers irate about a rude comment on the web page.

Given the highly charged, heavy-stress climate of many newsrooms, these quagmires can be inflammatory and stomach-churning. Invariably, they wind up in an editor's care. When editors complain of being "nibbled to death by ducks," such are the pecks they have in mind.

While doling out the new furniture may provoke the *real* passion, editors also face more orthodox tasks. They make decisions about content, copy, and design. They manage staffs. They make judgments about legal issues, ethics, and policies of all kinds. Some fortunate editors take naturally to all these tasks, but many find at least some of them daunting.

Having a sense of humor helps. I worked with one editor who gamely espoused the "live toad theory." It holds that, if you swallow a live toad as soon as you arrive at work, nothing else that happens can seem quite so bad. On an especially sour day, another colleague of mine left a note in the office mailbox of a late-arriving editor. "Flee while there's still time," the note warned.

Hearty souls though they may be, however, editors also need training and practice at making decisions. Beyond journalistic and managerial skills, editing calls for sound judgment, analytical thinking, and old-fashioned horse sense. Most of us have these qualities—sometimes, in some quantities—but have trouble displaying them consistently in the face of newsroom crises.

Most editors, I am convinced, have good sides and bad sides. The good sides show at tension's low tide: early in the day after a good night's sleep, or in the local hangout after deadline, or at the podium before a local civic club. In those lucid and relaxed moments, editors can talk eloquently about the stresses of journalism, the importance of civility, and the necessity, not to mention the cost-effectiveness, of treating people with respect.

But editors' bad sides come slinking from their caves when the pressure needle soars. Eyes darken. Tone of voice turns snappish. Graciousness yields to drill instruction. At these moments, which may come regularly on deadline, episodes that would seem trifling a few hours earlier trigger angry overreactions. Situations that could at better times be calmly reasoned out give rise to testy, forced-march resolutions.

Can we avoid this unfortunate, good side–bad side duality? Perhaps not entirely, given the daily news business. But editors *can*, it seems to me, equip themselves to respond as positively as possible to the duck-nibbles and hair-pullings of life in the newsroom.

In this chapter, we look at how editors can prepare to confront a variety of issues, from substantive areas like libel and news values to policy questions like nepotism and scheduling. Without attempting to solve every problem, we can suggest some ways of thinking and planning that can help editors reach conclusions in the best possible settings. Then, in the chapters that follow, we examine in more detail the editor's role as decision maker in several more specific areas.

Making decisions: The foundation

Responsible decision making is, of course, partly a function of basic competency. But it can be enhanced by paying attention to the setting where decisions must be made and by studying how decision making works best for each individual.

Although newsrooms may never be ideal places for contemplative deliberation, some steps can be taken to smooth out the process. Knowing that the daily nibbles are adding up, editors can institute systems to keep from wasting time and to expeditiously handle arising dilemmas.

At the highest levels, management can help by laying a foundation of support for editor/decision makers. Newspeople make hundreds of choices a day, many of them under tremendous pressure. So mistakes occur. Under a top management that second-guesses too often, editors become gun shy and insecure. Under a top management that never critiques at all, they become lax. To achieve an optimum middle ground, publishers and senior editors can establish fair ground rules and procedures, select staff editors in whom they have confidence, and delegate authority to them to operate within the broad boundaries. Regular reviews should follow, but with a constructive tone and a goal of steady improvement, not finger pointing.

Even with their very tough jobs, editors can thrive in a supportive, team-oriented environment. Without the backing of their superiors, editors run scared, constantly looking over their shoulders. Decision making suffers. This principle holds all along the line: from publisher to top editors to section editors to line editors. At each step, support from above can free an editor to act with confidence and strength.

Properly outfitting the newsroom

As a young reporter many years ago, I was given a guided tour of a small one-person news bureau I was inheriting. To my surprise, I was handed a large gas mask and instructed in how to use it. Given the general turmoil of the times, I learned, it wasn't unusual to cover protests and strife where tear gas might fill the air.

Today's reporters are assigned masks for other reasons, including the possibility of biological and chemical attacks or accidents. In these and other cases, having the proper equipment can facilitate coverage, save time, and promote workplace health and safety.

Making wise decisions about staffing and news coverage becomes far easier if editors don't have to worry about basic operational necessities.

Here are some areas where planning and preparation pay off.

A safe workplace. On one occasion my newspaper ran a series on dangerous biker gangs. We received several threats, and the top editors actually hired shotgun-carrying private guards to sit outside the newsroom for a while. The biggest excitement came when one of the guards fell sleep and tumbled from his chair, making so much racket that reporters were convinced they were under assault.

Most news operations, but not all, take at least modest security precautions. I once visited a newspaper where outside doors were locked late at night but no security guard was in place. Instead, the duty editor on the city desk was responsible for watching a monitor located at the back door and buzzing in people with legitimate business. It disrupted the editor's concentration and supplied far from foolproof security. Because journalism requires 24-hour-a-day vigilance, people need to come and go at all hours. Newsrooms, building grounds, and parking lots should be adequately protected.

Reliable technology. For both everyday work and the many emergencies that arise in news gathering, journalists depend on available, operational equipment. They need working desktop and laptop computers, cameras, audio and video recorders, television and radio monitors with battery or generator backup, mobile phones, access to global positioning assistance, and of course spare batteries and rechargers. And they need readily available technical help when computerized systems blow out, as they all do from time to time, not only during daylight business hours but at the worst possible moments near deadline or on assignment.

Staple working materials and support. I have known newsrooms that rationed reporters' notebooks or locked away photocopiers. People who work hard and must respond quickly need prompt access to their tools. Journalists need pens, pencils, notebooks, maps, street directories, reference materials, research assistance, help with last-minute travel needs, and petty cash for cabs and sudden trips.

Organizing logistical support in advance saves innumerable headaches in emergencies. If journalists can count on the raw materials to do their jobs, they become far less likely to burden editors with a drumbeat of minor crises to settle, to the detriment of more important activities.

Strategically allocating time

William Shawn, a legendary editor of the *New Yorker*, once was asked by John McPhee, a legendary writer, how he could "afford to use so much time and go into so many things in such detail," considering his endless duties as editor. Replied Shawn, "It takes as long as it takes."[1]

It was a simple, even elegant, answer, but the effort behind the thought could not have been simple at all. Busy as he was, Shawn found ways to make time for an activity he considered vital: working patiently with writers.

Almost everything about journalism would be easier with more time, but time of course is finite. We cannot magically expand the day. So the pressure of time hovers as a chronic problem in the deadline-driven news business. Managing time, making the most of whatever moments are available, becomes an art that often separates that best editors from the also-rans. The overall goal is to spend more time on your highest priorities and less time on everything else.

To move toward this goal, consider the following 4 Ps of time management: priorities, percentages, pockets, and pleasures.

Priorities. There are two ways of approaching problems: the order in which they come to you and their order of importance. Editors should practice the second way. Inventory the tasks at hand, decide which are your highest priorities, and devote early and extra attention to those matters. Many issues take on urgency because of time. For example, a page must be designed or a deadline will be missed. Other issues are urgent because of their longer-run importance. A reporter must be counseled because she is at a crucial point in a key project. Most editors will focus on both kinds of urgencies each day. But the essential point is this. You should make deliberate decisions about how to divide your time so that as much energy as possible goes toward your highest objectives.

Percentages. Journalists generally spread their time among work that is short-term (to be published during the next 24 hours or so), mid-term (the next week or so), and long-term (everything else). The percentage of time contributed to each category will vary broadly from day to day. So a good strategy is to take a longer view. Think about, say, the next six months. By consulting with your supervisors and weighing your organization's needs, try to outline a plan for allocating your time over this six-month period. For example, your goal might be to devote 75 percent of your work to short-term demands, 20 percent to medium, and 5 percent to long. You cannot do this with mathematical precision, of course, but setting such a goal provides important focus and direction.

Put your plans into writing. The act itself helps fix objectives in mind. Obviously, an editor must allow plenty of flexibility and leave room for spontaneity. Think of planning your work in the same way you might plan a cross-country vacation. You do not want to lock in every hour's activity, but you do want a general road map and some overall goals. Then move toward your goals even as you allow room and time for the unpredictable.

- *Short-term goals.* Simply coping with a typical day's routine can exhaust an editor's time. One defense is to make a to-do list each day, rank the items, and make sure that at or near the top are activities that directly contribute to high-quality journalistic content. If at all possible, each day's goals also should include at least one thing out of the ordinary: a serious discussion with a writer, the planting of an idea for a great story, a breakthrough concept for online journalism. Challenge yourself every day.
- *Middle-term goals.* Do not settle for just making it to the weekend. Stretch. Setting modest, reachable goals each week can, over a year's time, for example, produce a body of significant accomplishment. An assignment editor's goal might be one outstanding article for each Sunday paper. A photo editor might rotate a half-day's free time among staffers each week to produce particularly artistic enterprise shots. A web editor might want to add at least one interactive feature a week. Be ambitious, but also make your goals realistic. "To produce six excellent projects this year" is a more helpful goal than "to win the Pulitzer Prize." Good goals are those that you can achieve and that you will be proud of achieving.
- *Long-term goals.* My experience suggests that most editors maintain at least short- and medium-term plans, but many overlook the long term. Football coach and TV commentator John Madden described the value of such planning in a striking way when he recalled a conversation with the great coach Vince Lombardi: "What is there," I said, "that separates a good coach from a bad coach?"

    "Knowing what the end result looks like," Vince said. "If you don't know what the end result is supposed to look like, you can't get there."[2]

Through long-range planning, editors can envision how they want their news operations to be and move step by step toward their visions. Most importantly, by specifying medium- and long-range plans and sticking to them, editors help keep the short-run emergencies from devouring all their time. They also reduce the perennial frustration of "never getting anything accomplished."

One final vital task is to set aside a small percentage of your time to *control as your own*. It doesn't have to be a huge fraction, but it should be enough to let you work on the projects that mean most to you, works that offer greatest depths of satisfaction. Just spending some time on them each week can do miracles for morale and, ultimately, for quality.

Pockets. Nobody can remember everything. Editors have so many things to do and to remember that they need a systematic approach for keeping track. Pockets are places to store, file, and organize information and materials so you have them when needed.

For most editors, staying organized begins with calendars: desk calendars, purse calendars, electronic calendars, or a combination. These calendars often also serve as notebooks for reminders, story ideas, to-do lists, phone numbers, email addresses, and other memos. Most editors, and reporters too, keep notepads handy at all times, even on their bedside tables. Some keep digital recorders in their cars. You never know when a good idea will surface.

Editors also need pockets for materials that are too big or bulky to attach to a calendar or notebook. For this purpose, many use old-fashioned manila file folders to create what is sometimes called a "tickler system," to tickle or remind them as necessary. A common system works like this: Assemble about 50 manila file folders. Label one "next year," and use it for any long-run reminders and ideas. For example, if after covering this year's July Fourth parade you are inspired by how you could have done better, then jot down the idea and put it in next year's file. You'll be delighted to rediscover it in time for the next go-around.

Next, label one folder for each month of the year. Use those folders to store material relevant to a given month. For instance, if in January your city hires a new school superintendent, you might put a note in the July file to remind your education writer to take a look at how the superintendent is doing six months into the job.

Then, label folders with the numbers 1 through 31, one for each day of the month. Use these folders to hold material you need during the current month. Check the appropriate folder daily, and carry over live material from one day to the next. At the end of every month, open the folder for the succeeding month and redistribute the contents as appropriate into your daily folders.

Finally, label one folder as your daily action file and place in it anything you may need immediately.

Pleasures. Every now and then, an editor should depart from the busy routine to do something important and satisfying that requires extra time. Take a couple days off to write a story yourself. Spend an outlandish amount of time coaching a reporter on a spectacular project. Devote an entire day to rummaging through your website and brainstorming how to make it sparkle. Whether you manage to achieve these pleasures once a month or once a year, they can provide just enough refreshment and rejuvenation to recharge you for the marathon.

Setting a tone for good communication

Walk into some newsrooms, and you instantaneously sense bad vibrations. Hostility and alienation leave a residue, almost an odor, that few people miss. In other cases, newsrooms seem warm and relaxed. Newcomers quickly spot these qualities, and old-timers never forget them.

Ironically, considering that journalism depends on communication, editors often show remarkable insensitivity to problems in their own domains. As an editor, especially a beginning one, do not underestimate the importance of the tone you set. The best editors nurture a demanding but pleasant atmosphere that encourages free communication and that keeps channels open, even in the throes of deadline overload.

Editors can act in several ways to foster better newsroom communication. One way is by scheduling regular meetings at which staff members can determine the agenda, question managers, and make suggestions. Another is by having open bulletin boards where staffers can display anything they like, from examples of good work to anonymous cartoons poking fun at management. A third idea is to distribute a newsletter every month or so, to which all the staff is invited to contribute praise, criticism, and general discussion of newsroom matters. Still another is to maintain online bulletin boards or chat areas for ongoing discussions.

However you do it, rule one is to make communication easy. Rule two is to make it happen. As an editor, you should:

- Communicate up (to your bosses), over (to your peers), and down (to your subordinates) every single day. The more you know about what people in the newsroom are doing and thinking, the better armed you are for helping them (and yourself) through the rough spots.
- Be clear about expectations—yours and theirs.
- Avoid surprises. Keep your superiors informed and insist that staff members keep you informed.
- Debrief each other after a day's work or a tough assignment. Learn from successes and failures.
- Cultivate the idea that handling crises should be a team effort, not an individual burden.
- Know where you can turn for help and who is likely to call on you.
- Strive toward consensus rather than conflict. Reward cooperation *and* constructive disagreement.

Sniff the air. Monitor the tone. In a divided, divisive newsroom, small complaints fester and decision making pays the price. In an open, team-spirited newsroom, petty irritants get swept aside, and even the tough decisions come easier.

Shaping an effective decision-making model

Editors make dozens, hundreds, even thousands of decisions per day. Most are made quickly and naturally, based on experience, expertise, and sound personal and professional judgment.

A few decisions, however, require extra work. One key trait of a good editor is recognizing which of the many daily decisions require slowing down and deliberating. Usually they are cases where:

- The stakes and consequences are exceptionally high
- The possibility of harm or embarrassment is especially serious, or
- The appropriate response is particularly tricky to discern.

I remember an editor visiting me to commiserate after her paper had published an article containing gratuitous racial stereotypes. She had read the story on deadline without appreciating its potential for offense. Then a firestorm erupted after publication, and the editor spent many hours in damage control. How much wiser it would have been, she said ruefully, to have noticed the potential problem before publication, debated it then, and arrived at a decision that might have prevented the furor.

The demands of deadline compel editors to work efficiently and often rapidly, but they can never excuse the neglect of serious issues. Few truisms are more valid than the one that says it is far better to avoid a crisis in the first place than to have to manage it after the fact. When these dilemmas are identified, editors should think through how they like to make decisions. Most of us have some scheme, whether we articulate it or not, that helps us resolve dilemmas. With some reflection, editors may be able to identify theirs and to isolate its stages. The more familiar they become with the steps in the model, the easier the model is to apply under fire.

Here, broken down into steps, is a simplified model for working through tricky issues.

A decision-making model

- *Collect* information and listen to all points of view. If possible, remain open-minded during the fact-finding stage.
- *Analyze* the information. Isolate and focus on the central issues. Set aside the secondary ones. Consider motives, values, and consequences. Try to summarize the issue in a way that gets as close as possible to its heart.
- *Weigh* all options, in light of your goals and values. Do not think only in extremes (for example, whether to front-page a gory news photo or leave it out altogether). Consider possible middle courses as well (whether to crop the photo and reduce the gore, to display it inside

the paper instead of on the front, to run it smaller than your first instinct, and so on). Try to think creatively, looking at problems from all sides in search of solutions.

- *Solicit advice*. Research the question as time permits. Others may have suggestions or experiences that apply. Sharing the problem also gives others a stake in solving it and, once a decision is reached, in making the decision succeed.
- *Decide* and specify your reasoning. Clarify to yourself and others the basis for your actions.
- *Explain and carry out* the decision as positively and flexibly as possible, without trampling on people you may have overruled. A tendency arises at this stage of the process, especially when the decision may be unpopular or have taken long negotiation, to become impatient and gruff. By now, you will be tired of the process. But try to speak evenly, tolerate a suitable amount of dissent, and avoid acting self-righteous or as if your decision is divinely inspired. This is a crucial stage, both in determining how enthusiastically the decision will be effected and in affecting whether people will remember your actions as fair and judicious or as arbitrary and divisive.
- *Follow up*. Gently but firmly make certain the decision goes into effect and is carried out (even if not necessarily liked) by the staff.
- *Move on.*

In summary, the steps are to *collect information, focus on the problem, consider the options, get appropriate help, make a decision, explain it, execute it, follow up* and *move forward.*

Consider how this model might have applied to the situation outlined at this chapter's outset. As many morning newspapers went to press, they learned that families of trapped coal miners had received preliminary word most of the miners were safe. Editors had to quickly decide how to play this new development.

Step one involved collecting information, especially about the sources and credibility of the information. Here, things were murky. It was clear that the families had been told the miners were safe, but by sources whose knowledge seemed indirect or secondary. Prudence probably called for considering the information to be unconfirmed.

Therefore, the central issue was whether to publish unconfirmed but blockbuster information that might, several hours later when the papers hit doorsteps, turn out tragically wrong. To publish incorrect information would be embarrassing to the news organization and hurtful to friends and relatives of the miners. But, if the miners were indeed safe, failing to publish that fact would be equally distressing to those awaiting word on the miners and would make the newspaper seem stale.

Options included trumpeting the development as big news; publishing it with qualifications in wording and presentation; deciding not to publish on grounds that the confusion was too great to permit a story meeting standards of accuracy and clarity.

It seems clear the brief consultation among key editors would have supported the middle option: reporting the late-breaking development but making certain that headlines and articles reflected its preliminary nature. For example, instead of a headline blaring "Miners Are Safe," a wiser choice might be to use smaller type to say "Early Reports Raise Hope for Miners."

On the web where changes can be made by the minute, a qualified headline could quickly be written and then updated as new development arrived.

These on-deadline decisions could have immediately been executed. By the next day, when the unfortunate truth was learned, editors could have spent a few minutes discussing their actions, reinforcing to the newsroom the importance of a sound deliberative process, and summarizing lessons that might apply to future dilemmas.

No single model can guide every decision, but by giving thought to their decision-making methods and applying them systematically wherever possible, editors can grow more comfortable with acting under pressure and can bring a consistency to their problem solving.

Conclusion

In journalism, *substance* should outstrip *process*. That is, what matters most is what gets published and presented to the reader, not the gyrations journalists go through to produce their reports.

It need not concern readers that a computer malfunction required reworking a front-page headline at the last minute or that a power outage blew out the website for an hour or that the sports editor and football reporter had a yelling match over the game story. All the readers notice is the unintelligible headline, the blank screen, or the lousy copy.

Results count. Therefore, I do not mean to overly encourage editors to lose themselves in the dynamics of decision making at the expense of concentrating on good journalism. Making plans, setting goals, and following models can, carried beyond moderation, generate unnecessary bureaucracy and create artificial impediments to a natural working style. No editor wants to spend all day shuffling paper and filling in forms.

But ignoring the process can carry high penalties. Good editors, generally not trained in making decisions and managing time, can save themselves terrible tribulation by understanding how and why decisions take hold. A small percentage of their time devoted to planning, thinking through objectives, and systematically attacking problems can keep an editor focused on the most important targets. If so, then time will actually be saved.

Of course, being prepared to make decisions does not necessarily produce wise choices. It can, however, dramatically reduce the stress and battle-zone nature of operating on deadline. Better substance should result.

In the next few chapters, we further explore the editor's role in reckoning with the full range of newsroom issues, beginning with the most pervasive of all: working with people.

Sidebar 4: Characteristics of editor-friendly newsrooms

As editor of the *Bremerton Sun* in Washington, Mike Phillips learned an unexpectedly pertinent lesson when he began studying with a master wood carver. The craftsman spent painstaking time perfecting his own tools before he ever started carving.

For Phillips, "being in control of my own tools" became a metaphor for being empowered in a newsroom.

One big stress factor for editors, he was convinced, involved equipment and hardware problems. The more that editors could control their tools, the more they, like other artists, could thrive. In training his paper's staff, Phillips pushed them to design their own systems and perform as much system maintenance as possible.

Acquiring a mastery of the tools and a sense of professional control can help new editors flourish and make better decisions under heightened pressures and complexities. Yet it can be a challenge to find news organizations that foster such development. Below are some signs of newsrooms that are editor-friendly. If you are an aspiring editor, look for work in such places. If you are an experienced manager, try to champion these best practices.

Editor-friendly news organizations have an ample staff of editors. How many editors should a newsroom have? Though most newspaper newsrooms follow a rough formula of one staff person for each 1,000 subscribers, I have found no consensus on what percentage of the total staff should be editors. It does seem apparent that, as editing duties have piled up, news organizations have not commensurately increased the number of desk people. So many desks are stretched thin, leading to higher stress, more errors, and less creativity.

A commitment to adequate staffing can help reduce turnover, improve quality, and save money in the long run.

They cultivate good editing. In these meeting-crazy times, editors often complain that what gets squeezed out is actually working with writers on stories, with artists on presentation, or with web producers on packaging. Working directly to improve content is the essence of editing, what most editors do best and like best, and what the audience benefits from the most. Managers should foster a newsroom climate where this kind of editing is expected and rewarded. Otherwise, it will sink on editors' priority lists.

They offer middle editors some real control. Many middle editors call themselves the "sandwich editors," squeezed between their bosses and their staffs. Too often they feel stranded, without adequate clout in roiling newsrooms. Their decisions may be regularly second-guessed by superiors. It is natural and appropriate for top editors to weigh in on important matters, but in the best newsrooms they avoid whimsical, last-minute intervention and respect the decisions made by line editors.

They promote solving problems early rather than late. Frantic editing flurries on deadline are the worst way to upgrade copy. In a healthy system, editors are involved all along the way as copy progresses from the idea stage toward publication. The earlier that issues and problems are debated and solved, the higher the morale, the lower the stress, and the better the journalism.

They support teamwork. Entire staffs can be demoralized by the jaded negativism of one or two newsroom sourpusses, or by toxic rivalries sometimes allowed to fester inside a news operation. Good news organizations promote collaboration and healthy competitiveness, but they don't tolerate levels of intimidation, sarcasm, or one-upmanship that can leave others embittered and unable to work together constructively.

They are centers of praise. Editors seldom get credit lines, and their work tends to be invisible. But over and over again, mid-level editors describe how much they cherish praise from managers who make it a practice to understand what line editors really do.

"People only know when you make a mistake," Steve Shender, a former editor at the *Santa Cruz Sentinel*, once told me. "They don't know all the mistakes I caught. You do 20 things right, and if there's one thing wrong you come in the next day, and everybody's all over you. . . . You have to make an effort to say, That was a great layout, or, That story came out very clean."

They encourage flexible schedules. Perhaps the nature of the news business and the pride of journalists make it impractical to expect routine seven- or eight-hour work days. Establishing three- or four-day work weeks for editors can work better. Long weekends can prove magically rejuvenating.

They provide escape valves. For editors who work very hard, a natural counterpoint is to want to play hard. But because the news never ceases, many editors find little slack time for such diversions. In many newsrooms, the senior editor routinely works 15-hour days, and junior editors feel they must outlast the boss. Yet driving yourself to your limit every single day, without relief, can eventually be brutally destructive.

Editors should take time off every week, not skip vacations, and seek scheduling that lets them follow a long day with a short one. Editor-managers should follow these principles and insist that others do so as well.

Their pay scales show that editors are appreciated. Low pay is a chronic issue, and most journalists resign themselves early to modest incomes. But the issue gains importance as editors progress up the hierarchy, accumulating duties and demands. Poor pay can make it harder to attract top talent and therefore can aggravate management problems.

They value fun. Listen to a newsroom's noises: Do you hear laughter? Camaraderie? Respectful tones of voice? It doesn't take long to detect whether a newsroom is cheery or cheerless, and the difference affects morale and quality. "This is never going to be life in a Paris cafe," the late Foster Davis, *St. Louis Post-Dispatch* managing editor, once told me. "But it doesn't have to be as tough as we make it."[3]

Vignettes

The afternoon news meeting at the *Newport News (Va.) Daily Press* limps into its 96th minute, and editors are still mulling various decisions.

It's a long meeting, but extended talk is not uncommon in newsrooms as editors grapple with issue after issue. Already on this day, the *Daily Press* editors have debated a range of issues:

- Whether it is fair, in a story about a killing at a local bar, to mention the last shooting at the same saloon nine years ago
- How explicit to be in a story suggesting that AIDS can be spread through oral sex
- How to respond to a reader's complaint about a complex graphic.

Their longest debate concerns whether to publish a business item with undeniable buzz: the names, as compiled by a private vendor, of more than 500 young local businesspeople who run million-dollar companies. Deciding that it had little real news value and might embarrass people on the list, they kill the item.[4]

5 Making decisions about people

Editing is by nature about working with others, and supervisory editing is by definition about teamwork and leadership.

For many if not most editors, nothing consumes more time, energy, and emotion than the endless challenge of dealing with people. Every move an editor makes, from hiring a trainee to rewriting a lead to assembling a web package to awarding days off, can ripple far into the newsroom and leave a trail that lingers incalculably.

A moment of brilliance, often even unwitting, can transform a person's life. I once received a letter profusely thanking me for "saving the career" of a young man years earlier because of a chance remark (which I had by then forgotten) that inspired him to rededicate himself to journalism. Yet a careless misjudgment, or just bad managerial luck, can bring trauma to talented staff members, their families, and the news organization.

Editors deal with all sorts of people: consumers, sources, subjects, applicants, subordinates, superiors, and many others. In this chapter, we focus on the area that seems universally relevant to the career editor: managing journalists in the modern workforce.

The challenge begins with management in the broadest sense, such as hiring, firing, and supervising, and continues into the specific responsibility of helping fellow writers and editors produce the best possible journalism.

Managing in today's newsroom

Not all editors manage, but most do. And the ability to manage—specifically, the ability to manage other *journalists*—stands among the most widely prized, yet difficult to come by, qualities in modern journalism.

As prior chapters have described, today's newsroom managers confront ever-more-complex circumstances. In part, they stem from changes in institutional journalism (centralization of ownership, declining readership and viewership, tightened newsroom resources, and the pressures that ensue), and in part from changes involving people (the evolving nature of the contemporary workforce). Kevin M. Kelleghan, in his book

Supervisory Skills for Editors, News Directors, and Producers, summarizes the problem as follows:

> Although you've been promoted to your position, or hired, because of your journalistic ability, you'll be expected to manage your department from your first day with the competence of a seasoned, professional supervisor. . . . [H]owever, you face a formidable challenge: The journalists you supervise are more independent than workers in other services or industries and often more difficult to lead with traditional management methods. The supervisory skills you practice must be adapted to the special needs of journalism.[1]

Unhappily, novice editors do not have a heritage of managerial excellence to draw on. Journalism's managers have never exactly won acclaim. In his excellent book *Newsroom Management*, veteran editor Robert H. Giles recalled noticing throughout his career that "we put out pretty good newspapers, but we don't give much thought to managing people." Over time, according to Giles, the problem became excessive:

> Insensitive management has driven thousands of talented, bright, hard-working journalists from daily newspaper jobs. . . . Publishers and senior editors were slow to recognize the features of newsroom life that were creating the talent drain: high stress, low pay, lack of opportunity for growth, uncaring management.[2]

A comprehensive analysis by Northwestern University's Readership Institute underlined just how widespread the management problems were. In a survey commissioned by the institute, journalists across the country were asked how their organizations rated on key practices such as hiring, training, performance management, and compensation. The results seemed to shock the researchers:

> 80 percent of respondents either disagreed or strongly disagreed that best practices were in use. It is highly unlikely that there are many other industries in the U.S. today where, as a whole, they have a similarly low self-report in this area.[3]

The Readership Institute found that newspapers in particular tend toward an "Aggressive-Defensive culture," where stress and confrontation raise conflict and impede problem solving. "Compared to other industries," it reported, "newspapers operate more as 'silos' both within and among departments, and produce lower-quality products and services." Instead, it suggested, for both morale and business success "the ideal culture would be Constructive," a more humanistic, achievement-oriented environment associated with "high levels of motivation, satisfaction, teamwork, service quality, and sales growth." Specific "opportunities for improvement" were suggested in the following areas:

- Giving positive rewards to others
- Encouraging others
- Helping others to develop
- Enjoyment of work
- Opportunity to think in unique and independent ways.[4]

Under these circumstances, moving into newsroom management would challenge even the best-trained executives. Journalists, however, tend to advance with little training in management, human relations, and organizational skills. Not even the current popularity of advanced business degrees solves the problem, because what is most needed is journalists who can manage, not managers who can learn journalism. Journalistic values and skills remain the most fundamental qualifications for editing. The task for the coming generation is to add to those basic values a far greater appreciation of the techniques and subtleties of managing other newspeople.

Where does an editor or aspiring editor begin in learning to manage? Many people possess natural leadership abilities, and many of those people gravitate toward editing. Experience helps; almost all new editors, especially supervisors, have served in the rank and file and carry forward personal memories of effective and ineffective management methods. Simple observation tells us that today's workers prefer autonomy, respond poorly to traditional top-down management, value time off and family considerations, and may have more complicated career and personal goals than workers of past generations.

All this experience and knowledge can feed into a new editor's management style, but it seldom substitutes for systematic training and attention to the complexities of modern organizational leadership. Fortunately, more resources are going into newsroom management than ever before. News organizations are investing more heavily in training and development, and a body of literature is accumulating to better prepare incoming managers.

Still, nothing can replace diligent study and preparation. In her autobiography, *Personal History*, Katharine Graham recalled her anxiety at taking over as president of the *Washington Post* when her husband Phil died. Graham felt unready, but she moved quickly to prepare herself and eventually guided her paper expertly through the contentious Pentagon Papers and Watergate eras. Here is how she started:

> I was always interested in what constituted good management, both within and outside our industry. In the same earnest way that I attacked many things, I began to do my homework in management. I

must have driven everyone around me crazy by studying everything so intensely, but I was compelled to know more. I traveled to several cities to observe newspaper operations. I spent a day at Texas Instruments, which had an excellent reputation at that time for its planning processes. I visited the headquarters of Xerox and NCR. I attended a week-long hands-on production-process school run by the publishers' association.[5]

It seems important, then, for incoming editors to more systematically develop their own styles and strategies as they cope with the range of management obligations such as recruiting, supervising, and dealing with stress. As a beginning point, Robert Giles, in his previously mentioned book, identifies five general principles at the heart of a philosophy of newsroom management:

- All people are different.
- There is no best way.
- Behavior can be changed but personalities cannot, and editors must deal with a variety of personalities.
- Perfection with people is impossible.
- Natural motivations (such as the drive to achieve) are more powerful than artificial ones.[6]

We examine some of these issues more closely in the following sections.

Developing a management style

Trust yourself

Managing, like so many other activities, begins with that Emersonian injunction. Like it or not, your management style will in all likelihood reflect your personality. So build on that. Be yourself and operate in a way that comes naturally.

Take charge. Make the tough decisions. Have the confidence and security to behave as though you actually believe you should be the boss. But do not become consumed or obsessive. Keep your sense of humor. Remain flexible. Do not bully others. Admit mistakes. Do not get your ego so engaged that every issue becomes a psychological tug of war.

Robert M. Stiff, a veteran Florida editor, once summarized his management style as follows:

I have no philosophy of management but I have a golden rule.

I try to manage with sensitivity and treat my staff as I wanted to be treated when I wasn't an editor. I praise in public and criticize in private—and do both frequently. . . .

My door is always open and even if it means staying very late to finish what I'm doing, if a staffer says, "Do you have a minute?" I always do.

I seldom lose my temper, insist on staffers having fun at their jobs, take a personal interest in them, keep them informed about what is happening, never lie to them, try to treat them fairly, try to pay them what they're worth within budget constraints and let them know they have disappointed me deeply when they screw up.[7]

A key concept in management is simply *respect*, for yourself and those persons around you. Everyone wants to be treated as an individual and as a professional, and belittling or patronizing people rarely makes sense. Editors have much to gain by remembering the proverbial golden rule of managing: Treat your employees as you want your boss to treat you. Of course, following that rule raises the obvious question of what today's journalists want.

What do journalists want from employers? As we discussed in Chapter 2, typically they want respect, trust, challenge, reasonable working conditions, clear direction, candid feedback, some say in schedules and assignments, and a sense of working someplace special. They want better pay and opportunity for advancement. They want more stability than newsrooms have traditionally afforded, so that they do not feel compelled to move on to a bigger organization every two or three years or to drop out of the profession when it comes time to pay children's college costs. And they want greater appreciation of their professionalism and less exploitation of their commitment to working 50- and 60-hour weeks without extra compensation.

Managers may or may not deliver on all these desires, but they should begin by understanding them and taking them seriously. Simply listening and noticing will help. In turn, managers have the right to their own expectations, and employees must respect and appreciate them.

What do today's managers want from staff members? They want commitment to a profession whose relentlessness leaves little margin for error or slack. They want hard, fast, accurate, thoughtful work. They want people who are both tenacious and flexible, creative and open to direction, tough and fair, individualists when appropriate and team players when necessary.

Nobody who has ever worked in a newsroom remotely expects utopia. But editors must face up to this hard-headed fact: Newsrooms can be managed more effectively than in the past and, whatever the obstacles, it is the responsibility of editors to do it. Whatever management problems exist in a newsroom may stem from inadequate resources, self-absorbed staff members, lack of support from ownership, or a host of other sources beginning with the unflinching dailiness of the job. But, as the newsrooms' problem solvers, editors have the duty of analyzing whatever problems they find and then working as constructively as possible to relieve them.

Take responsibility

If the first rule in management is trust yourself, the second is take responsibility. Forget pointing fingers or looking for scapegoats. Set aside, as much as possible, the excuse, "I didn't have time." Figure out what your goals are and what you can change or control to move toward them.

Here are some additional suggestions for managing effectively. They apply whether you are the assistant web editor or the managing editor or the head of the three-person Bumpkin County Bureau:

- *Forget both dictatorship and democracy.* Today's highly educated, self-aware journalists would not stand for old-fashioned authoritarianism, but they do not like drift and wimpiness either. They accept the authority of the boss, as long as they feel heard and respected. Make it clear that you are in charge but that you need and want their help.
- *Promote teamwork.* Cultivate the idea that everyone is in the game together, for the same goals. Harness collective energy, for example by convincing copyeditors, reporters, and web producers to be collaborators not antagonists. Or by giving employees a chance to help set policies on such things as weekend scheduling or how to allocate new positions.
- *Explain and discuss.* Have you ever, in jobs you have held or classes you have taken, felt you knew as much as you wanted to about what your boss or teacher was thinking? Neither has anyone else. Few management sins are as universal as underestimating how important a few words from the boss can be.
- *Praise people; criticize work.* Writing coach Roy Peter Clark often asks groups of journalists, "How many people here think they get *too much* praise?" I do not think anyone has ever raised a hand. At the same time, most journalists thirst for constructive feedback. For the manager, the most effective course can be to personalize praise and to depersonalize criticism: "*You* wrote an excellent headline yesterday," but "I'm not sure this lead is as effective as *it* could be."
- *Play fair.* Listen to complaints and recognize that people encounter personal problems. In your newsroom, try to set a humane tone. But keep an appropriate distance from staff members and make clear that you expect professionalism on the job.
- *Stay close to the action.* Be visible and talk privately to find out what is on people's minds. It is often said that one primary rule of managing is to get out of your chair.

- *Do not neglect "managing up."* Keep your superiors informed. Follow the "no surprise" rule and insist your staff follow it, so that everyone is kept informed about major developments, changes, and decisions. Nothing makes top editors' blood boil hotter than to get flooded with complaints about stories they did not even know about. Nothing riles reporters faster than not being informed of major rewrites before stories get published.
- *Watch the little things.* Is the parking lot well lighted? Does the company snack bar close while the copydesk and web producers are still hard at work? Does anyone ever put notes on bulletin boards praising good writing, clever headlines, intrepid photography?
- *Watch the big things.* Does the city editor play favorites? Does a key staffer have a drinking problem? Is sexism tolerated in the newsroom? Has your pay scale been the same for five years?
- *Give people an opportunity to influence you and your policies.* As my former editor Walker Lundy used to say, "Give an employee's ego a way out of every discussion." If you and a staff member disagree, for example, explain that she or he may be right but you are not yet convinced. Transfer to the staffer the burden of providing evidence to convince you.
- *Do not go it alone.* Consult with subordinates and superiors about key decisions. Use available resources such as company personnel specialists or psychologists, people with relevant experience in other newsrooms or elsewhere, outside experts such as university people.
- *Do not play God.* Do not try to convince subordinates that superior wisdom and infallibility underlie every decision you make. They will not buy it. A common management error, especially in newsrooms, is to phrase issues in terms of "right" and "wrong": "Your story is written all wrong, and I'm going to show you how to make it right." Instead, acknowledge that journalism is often subjective and explain that you take your responsibilities seriously and are doing what you believe to be best. Enforce your decisions, even unpopular ones, because that is your job. But don't presume that your decisions are necessarily any smarter or more correct than anyone else's.

Coping with management challenges

In any enterprise, journalism included, the range of potential problems may be unlimited. However, we can identify several newsroom issues that are universal enough to merit individual consideration. They include recruiting and hiring, supervising and evaluating, and handling the inevitable stress.

Recruiting and hiring. Not all editors participate in formal recruitment or hiring, but almost all can or should have some say in those processes. Whether it is in attracting an individual to the news organization itself or deciding which two reporters to pair on a special project, editors need the knack of appraising and positioning people. Here are some observations that may fit editors' needs:

- *Make recruitment an affirmative process.* Do not just wait for wonderful applicants to come to you. Create a network and work it regularly. Visit key journalism schools, read college newspapers and websites, track the best students, and encourage them to stay in touch with you. Cultivate contacts in other regions and work the grapevine to learn who the best journalists are at news organizations just beneath your own. Keep clear, complete files of good candidates.
- *Make sure you know the aspirations and abilities of existing staff members*, who often make excellent candidates for other jobs. Too many managers overlook the talent right beside them in their quest to fill desirable positions.
- *Stress diversity.* Take special pains to identify prospective candidates who broaden and deepen the variety of the newsroom. Avoid the old snare of favoring candidates who remind you of yourself. Diversity makes sense as both a moral imperative and a practical way to develop new ideas and fresh thinking. Pay attention to diversity in many ways: by sex, by race, by age, by background.
- *Always be ready to take advantage of an opportunity.* Despite your most systematic exertions, hiring often is a matter of timing and luck. One day a reporter quits, and the managing editor cannot decide whether to fill the position or to use the money to buy new digital cameras. If you have an appropriate candidate already in mind and have done the preliminary screening, your readiness can determine whether your section gets or loses the position.
- *Be thorough.* When considering an applicant, read clips, check references, and where appropriate ask nonreferences who might know the candidate. Consult information available from computer search engines. Ask staff members for advice. Involve several people in the interview process and value their impressions. Give tryouts wherever possible. Stay alert for issues of integrity or coded comments from references that hint of potential problems. Hiring someone can be a lifelong, hundreds-of-thousands-of-dollars decision, and it should seldom happen merely because an applicant makes a good impression over lunch.
- *Make job interviews revealing.* You want to get beyond stock answers and predictable situations. Ask applicants about the last time they got angry. Give them a tricky scenario and ask how they would handle it. Find out the biggest obstacle they have ever overcome, or their biggest fear, or the one story they would like to do over.
- *Hire brains.* Editors have an endless list of qualities they seek in

applicants. But few are more important than hiring smart people with a demonstrated commitment to journalism.

- *Listen for "bells."* I do not know whether this accords with orthodox personnel theory, but it used to work for me. More often than not, outstanding candidates will in some way set off special "bells" of excitement in your head, by the quality of their work, the pulsating of their minds, or just some intangible measure of personal electricity. Good applicants should somehow make a strong and arousing impression. Don't settle for the mundane. If you do not have a candidate you feel excited about hiring, keep looking and listening.

Supervising and evaluating. Managing journalists has often been compared to herding cats or goldfish. They are slippery little devils with cantankerous, independent natures. Managers who value journalists for their tenacity and skepticism outside the newsroom should not flinch when those same traits arise within it, often aimed squarely at management. To supervise such people requires what often has been called "tough love": thick-skinned editors who set firm standards, push relentlessly for excellence, relish the give-and-take of intellectual combat, know when to intervene and when to leave alone, and understand as if by instinct when to exhort and when to mollify.

The following advice is aimed at helping editors with motivation and oversight of subordinates and staff members:

- *Try to understand each staff member's goals and needs.* David McClelland has identified three fundamental motivations for workers: the need for achievement, affiliation, or power.[8] In short, some workers derive their top satisfaction from accomplishing a goal; others, from working and developing relationships with colleagues; still others, from leading the team. Recognizing which drive is motivating a particular individual can help you tailor a successful management approach. The adage "Treat everybody alike" certainly holds in terms of fairness, but it remains important to remember that each individual has different strengths, styles, dreams, and fears. As veteran editor Randolph Brandt says, "Treat people with equal consideration, which isn't the same thing as treating everybody the same."[9]
- *Listen carefully.* Whether you are making a photo assignment, revising a reporter's lead, setting standards for a blog, or transferring someone from one job to another, the person involved will probably have stronger feelings than you expect. People take almost everything personally. Listen to those feelings; think about them; put yourself in the employee's place. Many editors are so itchy to dispose of an issue and move on that they fidget, scowl, interrupt, and react in other ways that reduce their ability to listen. Try not to reveal your own

feelings until the staff member has finished. Then respond. Even if you stand firm, send employees away knowing they have received a fair hearing.

- *Set clear goals and offer regular evaluations.* Think of this point in both short-range and long-range terms. In the short run, you should make clear assignments and give employees routine feedback so they know how well they meet your expectations. Over the long run, you should provide periodic formal evaluations, in private, in which you review the standards and the employees' performance. Be specific, candid, and constructive, using examples to document both praise and criticism. Do not be cruel and do speak softly, but make certain that employees, including those who are failing, know where they stand with you and, vitally, what they can do to improve in your eyes. Most employees are willing to modify their work to better please their bosses, but they cannot make those changes unless they know what the boss wants.
- *Remember the Fourteenth Amendment.* That's the one that stresses "due process of law" and "equal protection of the laws." Treat all employees fairly. And follow an orderly process of dealing with problems. The two worst things you can do if people are not meeting your standards are, first, nothing (a festering problem only worsens) and, second, overreaction (such as firing without warning). Instead, devise your own systematic due process. Discuss the problem; develop a plan and timetable for improvement; offer assistance and monitor the employee's progress; and then, after a reasonable period, decide whether further action is needed.
- *Think carefully about your style of motivation.* Different situations and different workers call for different methods of inspiration. A good editor considers the options and consciously tries to match motivation style to the desired result. Kevin Kelleghan lists three common motivation styles: leadership by example, cheerleading, and spontaneous inspiration. Leadership by example (working diligently in hopes others will get the message) sets a good standard but may not provide enough personal contact and recognition for others. Cheerleading can create high levels of excitement over short periods but is hard to sustain long-term. "By far the best suited to journalism," he says, is spontaneous inspiration, which he describes as "brief, sincere, frequent, one-on-one encouragement, either verbally or in writing."[10]

Managing stress. We have already discussed how newsroom stress can breed tension, burnout, and health problems. As highly accountable managers in a harsh-deadline business, editors face constant stress. In addition, editors can also induce stress in others through their management styles. Author Bob Baker listed several ways in which writers and editors can experience such anxiety: deadlines, unpredictable overtime, night work, distrust of editors, lack of leadership or direction from editors, inability to meet or understand expectations, suspicion or hostility from sources or audiences, pressure for productivity at the expense of quality, and the need to play office politics in order to advance.[11]

Given the inherent pressures of the job, editors will never banish stress. In fact, a certain level of stress helps account for the exhilaration and excitement that make journalism so satisfying. What the good editor can try is to contain and manage unnecessary stress, to keep it within reasonable limits, and to help others cope.

The further away I have gotten from daily journalism, the more destructive and inexcusable the high-stress newsroom environment has seemed to me. Although the news process is inevitably pressurized, some editors pour on unnecessary fuel by condoning Stone Age management styles: cutting remarks, macho city-editor crudeness, contempt for family and free-time needs, and petty battles over space, time, resources, and assignments. Good editors can do a great deal to reverse much of the inattention and misplaced priority that aggravate the naturally high stress levels.

Because of their roles as decision makers, editors can be both victims and inflictors of stress. They need to fortify themselves with precautions against both spreading and absorbing it. Some suggestions, which editors can apply to themselves and recommend to others, include the following:

- *Live a balanced life.* Eat and sleep properly. Set aside time for relaxation, family, and social events. Exercise regularly. Develop a hobby. Steal a few minutes from a busy day to take a brisk walk or listen to some music.
- *Share.* Do not bottle up anxieties and frustrations. Do not feel responsible for every mistake and dilemma in the newsroom. Communicate. Delegate. Consider yourself part of a team, not the solitary sentinel.
- *Never lose your sense of humor.*
- *Set reasonable goals and work toward them systematically.* Do not constantly over-pressure yourself.
- *Solve one problem at a time.* Break large problems (the publisher's criticism of your news coverage) into a series of smaller problems that you can tackle one by one (setting new goals for local reporters; adding one new enterprise story a week; improving web coverage of high school sports).
- *Learn to manage conflict.* Conflict is inevitable in newsrooms, and how supervisors manage it can hugely affect morale and productivity. Edward Miller, a longtime editor and management consultant, believes that conflict should be confronted (not suppressed) in a positive, forthright manner. He suggests that editors deal with impacts,

not motives; focus on values and interests, not staked-out positions; and patiently repeat and rephrase their messages without rancor. If someone persists in perpetuating conflict, Miller advises, an editor should acknowledge the individual's position and then explain how the continuing conflict departs from newsroom values, has long-run disadvantages, may be hurting others, and can erode the staff member's own professional reputation.[12]

- *Imagine how you want things to be in a year, 5 years, or 10 years.* Then, as Thoreau said, move confidently toward your dreams.
- *Get away from journalism and journalists.* Have a separate social circle. Eat lunch with someone new. Take a course in philosophy or physics.
- *Be positive.* Accept your own anger and failings and those of others. Do not compromise your standards or settle for mediocrity, but keep life in context, expect some adversity, focus on what you can control, and do not dwell on the past.
- *Hold a long view.* Perhaps some problems *do* deserve major-league fretting (the $25-million libel suit filed because you misedited a story). But most do not. Journalists spend a great deal of time worrying over whether paragraph 6 should be paragraph 11, or whether a story should be 12 or 18 inches long, or whether the managing editor likes the city editor better than the features editor, or whether the print front page is less important than the web home page. A managing editor I once worked for would periodically cruise through the newsroom saying, "In a hundred years, we'll all be dead." That did help put things into perspective.
- *Think of others.* One of my favorite bits of advice comes from Scott Libin of the Poynter Institute, who wrote that, because editors are forever calling people at home at horrible hours, they should "know at least the names of the significant others in the lives you so routinely disrupt."[13]

A management checklist

While management can be considered a weak point in many newsrooms and for many editors, it also provides a relatively easy opportunity for improvement. Even slightly better management can dramatically influence people and enhance journalism. Shelby Coffey III, a respected editor and newsroom leader, spoke with numerous industry leaders to collect dozens of practical tips. In an excellent slim volume called *Best Practices: The Art of Leadership in News Organizations*, he compiled these and other suggestions:[14]

- *Treat each person as vitally important*—your number-one priority at the moment.

- *Make lots of time for "face-to-face management"*—helping make people's problems, large and small, a bit better.
- *Don't deliver criticism by email.*
- *Keep good debates going on among staff on key issues.*
- *Create an inclusive organization with mutual respect and honesty.*
- *Don't bear grudges.*
- *Reinforce to the staff that you win as a team*—or lose as a team.
- *Create an environment where mavericks can succeed.* The best innovations are disruptive, and so are their creators.
- *Remember your moods are contagious.* Show them wisely.
- *When a crisis gets hotter, get calmer.*

Leading other journalists

Author Thomas Kunkel, in his perceptive biography of Harold Ross, founder of the *New Yorker* and one of journalism's most illustrious editors, offers this insight into Ross's success:

> He believed that the same unique vantage point that made creative people insightful could also render them vulnerable, impractical, and maddeningly unreliable. . . . Ross's style had less to do with coddling his people . . . than with protecting them. . . . One cannot help but appreciate the staggering amount of his time Ross devoted to his sensitive, skittish charges.[15]

Editors do not manage in a vacuum; they manage in a newsroom. And although journalists have much in common with all other workers, today's reporters and editors also inherit a special tradition. By that tradition, they view themselves as creative professionals who exalt First Amendment values of independence and idiosyncrasy, elevate individualism, resist corporatization, and regard affiliation with an organization as a kind of loose confederation of kindred free spirits rather than a synchronized workforce under central command. They are not easily managed, but—crusaders and missionaries at heart—they stand ready to be led.

The editor tossed into a leadership role should remember at least three general (although not universal) qualities of the contemporary journalist:

1   Journalists typically choose the occupation for reasons that are non-material. While compensation and working conditions play a growing role in career calculations, most journalists are, underneath it all, reform-minded spirits who feel they have something important to say and who appreciate help in saying it.
2   They do not see journalism as only a business, or even as primarily a business. They see it as a public-spirited enterprise with special social

responsibility, in the words of A. J. Liebling "a privately owned public utility."[16]

3   They prize the creative aspects of their work and increasingly see themselves as empowered to express themselves in their individual voices, even inside institutional news boundaries. The rise of blogs, the growing premium on analysis, and the natural conversational style of interactive and online journalism all reinforce the value of individuality and erode the appeal of conventional detached newsspeak.

Editors, then, enter this equation at some peril, generally experiencing bittersweet relationships with those they supervise. Officially, they must carry the corporate mandate and the corresponding power to act as boss. Unofficially, having not forgotten their own rank-and-file sensibilities, they must captain their unruly shock troops with a deft combination of empathy, exhortation, and example.

Because journalists increasingly see themselves as professionals with growing independence, they expect to have a large say-so in determining their duties. Rather than hired hands to be ordered into action at an editor's whim, they prefer being considered specialists to whom editors turn for needed expertise and creativity.

Most often, this scenario plays out in terms of individual editor–writer relationships. Therefore, we now examine how editors can bolster their capacity to lead their colleague-subordinates.

The journalist as introvert

Here is one of the great ironies of journalism: Most writers are a strange combination of ego-incited prima donnas and fragile little flower buds. A writer who seems an invincible monument of vanity may in a twinkling metamorphosize into a crumpled lump of insecurities, all over an editor's sardonic aside or a reader's casual slight. Nearly all writers I know waver between expecting their next assignment to be a timeless Pulitzer-worthy classic and fearing that it will expose them, finally and for all, as a talentless pretender.

The editor's job is to help these people.

A useful starting point is to realize that many writers are *introverts pretending to be extroverts*. The exigencies of journalism require large doses of extroversion. Reporters spend much of their lives barging into chaotic scenes, confronting official tough cookies, schmoozing and charming reluctant sources. The very act of reporting involves a kind of on-stage performance artistry. Even writing, in most institutional journalism settings, becomes a risky semi-public act.

While aggressiveness and outgoingness come naturally to some journalists, to many if not most they are out-of-character qualities. Journalists develop such traits from necessity, but to see most journalists as naturally gregarious and expansive is to misjudge their true personalities. In real life, many tough-talking reporters and writers are merely playing a role or following a script that disguises their natural shyness.

"Most newsroom folks are introverts," explains editor and management authority Sharon Peters. "It has been documented by my own research at more than three dozen newspapers, where without exception, 60 to 65 percent of newsroom personnel have scored as introverts."

Being an introvert, Peters points out, is "not a disability," but does make people "predisposed to certain behaviors that can make open communication a challenge." Introverts often prefer written to verbal communication, avoid sharing themselves and their real thoughts spontaneously, favor one-on-one or small-group settings, and prefer working alone.

Therefore, their editors must work especially hard at connecting with all their staff members, especially those who may be introverts and possibly pretending otherwise. Peters advises editors to allow staff members time to process information and formulate responses; to provide multiple times and channels, both written and oral, for communication; and to engage staff members in regular, one-on-one, face-to-face discussions.[17]

The editor as helper

In journalism as elsewhere, managers should help, not hinder. That help can begin with how newsrooms handle issues of work–life balance. Jill Geisler, a leadership specialist at the Poynter Institute, examined what reporters and editors seek from their supervisors. Based on survey results, she found that the following qualities were associated with "supportive supervisors":

- Get to know their employees
- Praise as well as criticize
- Show empathy during times of stress
- Monitor workload
- Encourage needed time off
- Set clear expectations.

The surveys also identified some characteristics of "unsupportive supervisors":

- Don't know or care about workers' outside lives
- Cause extra work for others through poor planning or scheduling
- Make workers feel guilty about being sick or having family responsibilities
- Favor employees with families but "dump" on single people

- Treat workers who finish their assignments within regular hours as showing a "lack of commitment."[18]

Beyond these matters, editors also must help journalists produce better content. In a classic volume called *How I Wrote the Story*, writing teacher Donald Murray and staff members of the *Providence Journal-Bulletin* shared their insights into how editors should and should not treat writers.

Among the problems cited were inflexibility in assignments, unrealistic deadlines, overly preconceived story ideas, failure to listen, unnecessary tinkering with copy, condescending or defensive approaches to the writer, mistakes inserted into copy, and editing without conferring with the writer.

"Remember," they wrote, "that psychologically bad editing is far worse than technically bad editing. An editing mistake may be remembered by the writer for a week; a mistake in handling the writer may be remembered for a lifetime."

These journalists recommended that editors:

- Listen open-mindedly to writers
- Ask questions and stimulate ideas
- Let writers know, without nagging, that the editor is available to consult
- Suggest approaches without demanding them
- Challenge writers' assumptions
- Change copy only when change is needed.

Heeding some of these suggestions, the Providence staff members concluded, could help at "achieving a lasting truce between these natural enemies of the newsroom."[19]

Similar words could be written about the relationships editors have with other constituencies: subordinate editors, designers, photographers, web specialists, and others. Utmost concern must go toward establishing positive bonds that promote both better people treatment and better content.

Coaching and teaching

Donald Murray, the late Pulitzer Prize winning writer, teacher, and newsroom guru cited earlier in this chapter, is credited with a rich legacy: what came to be known as the newsroom coaching movement. Murray often called it "consultive editing." His influential ideas and methods have been advanced and further popularized by Roy Peter Clark and Don Fry, two sensitive and thoughtful writing coaches associated with the Poynter Institute.

All three equate the editor with the "coach," an apt metaphor conjuring up the image of a demanding but loving teacher and taskmaster. In their outstanding book *Coaching Writers*, Clark and Fry explain, as I mentioned in Chapter 2, that coaching is "the human side of editing." It is a process that involves "nothing more than talking with writers in certain ways," especially in ways that help writers identify and solve one key problem after another as they advance from assignment to publication.[20]

Interestingly, the authors trace the history of coaching back to an academic rather than athletic origin. In the 19th century, they write, British university students used the word to describe their out-of-class tutors.[21] Murray then adapted the term to refer to editors or visiting teachers who became tutors inside the newsroom.

Today's view of coaching imagines a collaborative process in which editor and writer work as near equals more than as boss and underling. This wasn't always the protocol, of course. A more traditional view, of the editor as tyrant, was grippingly if sensationally expressed by Heywood Broun in a 1920s column. Broun wrote of covering a small story, writing it painstakingly ("as I settled down to my machine playing it as some of the masters play Chopin"), and then turning it over to "the big man at the desk":

> The copy reader took out a long, keen knife and sharpened several pencils. . . . Yawning slightly, he got to work. . . . He lingered over this opening sentence. I wondered why. . . . Finally, the man drew his thickest pencil and throwing all the power of his back and shoulders into the stoke he slashed my copy. Probably it was my ears alone which heard the horrid sound of blood dripping to the floor. . . . "I did it for *The World*," I murmured and fainted quietly upon my desk.[22]

As Broun's column vividly conveys, editors should never forget that every writer feels a trembly, sweaty dread in relinquishing beloved copy to an editor's hands. Much of this fear can and should be offset by better reporter–editor consultation, and today's good editors operate far differently from their fiercer predecessors.

What do modern coaches do? You will find a step-by-step guide in Chapter 8. For now, we can say that in general the editor-as-coach works collegially with a writer (or artist, photographer, web producer, or other journalist) from start to finish of an assignment, offering support, an open mind and listening ear, and advice where needed.

Murray advised editors to consult with reporters at several key points in the writing process: at the assignment, during the reporting, before the first draft, at delivery of the draft, and after publication.[23] Such close communication helps ensure that neither reporter nor editor will be surprised as the process plays out.

Many of these conversations can take place quickly. Extended, sit-down discussions, although often helpful, are not always practical. A two-minute dialogue focused on a specific problem ("What's the point of the story?" "Can you help me with this second paragraph?") can pin-point key issues and align the thinking of both parties. Through such continuing conversations, editors and writers develop mutual trust, make each other's lives easier, reduce strains, and lower the likelihood of error or misunderstanding. They build the bonds that can last far beyond today's passing story.

On individual projects, coaches help writers with everything from improving storytelling technique to navigating newsroom politics. Over-all, as Clark and Fry write, coaches hope to better the craft of journalism, build the confidence of journalists, and contribute to a newsroom culture of "listening, learning and collaboration."[24]

At this point, you may be asking, "How is coaching different from editing?"

The answer, of course, is that it isn't different at all. Coaching *is* editing. Or at least coaching is one central aspect of editing. Few if any editing duties are more essential than helping writers produce better journalism.

What Murray, Clark, Fry, and many others noticed, though, is that, as editors' roles grew in complexity over the years, their new duties began to usurp time once devoted to working directly with writers. As we have discussed repeatedly, editors' administrative and management functions seem ever expanding. Editors operate in increasingly corporate cultures. They spend more time in meetings. They grapple with large legal and ethical issues. They combat competitive and marketplace challenges more serious than those of previous generations. For these and other reasons, editors now split their time into more and more slices. While few would disagree that producing great content should come foremost, many find themselves distracted and their energies redirected. A constant in the many newsrooms I visit is reporters' fervent desire for more coaching time with their editors.

The coaching movement, then, reminds editors of this primary obliga-tion. Almost nothing is more important than developing superior con-tent. Teaching and coaching contribute directly to improving talent, which improves content, which improves a news organization's prospects for success.

In short, we should see coaching as an inherent aspect of every editor's job, not as a separate function performed by specialists or visiting con-sultants. If you are not a successful coach, you will in all likelihood fail as an editor.

None of this advice is meant to lessen the editor's responsibility to take charge where necessary. For all the sensitivity that editors need, they also require decisiveness and determination. Not everything is negotiable. Entrusted with responsibility for all or part of important business activities, they cannot shirk the burdens of production and performance. Inevitably, editors will occasionally disappoint, anger, and overrule others.

But these top-down tactics should be occasional not routine. It is not *that* an editor must lead that is at issue, but *how* the editor does it. Like good coaches and teachers, good editors realize they are not operating democracies, but they strive to execute their responsibilities with respect for, and the maximum involvement of, their colleagues.

Conclusion

In this chapter, we began by considering management in a rather broad sense: What are some strategies for the supervision of employees by a designated superior? Then we added some particular considerations for managers within a newsroom: What makes journalists peculiarly hard to manage, and what methods help?

Effort has intensified over recent years to remedy some longstanding newsroom management problems, but as we have seen much work remains. Developing strong management techniques must continue. They can give any editor an important head start, clear time and energy for the more enjoyable aspects of the job, and reinforce strong relationships and teamwork for long-term success.

As a good manager, however, the aspiring editor is only partially equipped for duty. As important as people skills are, editors need equally strong journalistic skills as well. The next chapters spotlight the most basic requirement of all: competence at delivering quality copy under pressure.

Sidebar 5: My first editor

Your first editor seems immortal, or at least too tough to die, so I was shocked as well as saddened when my first editor, Annie Laurie Kinney, died at age 96.

No editor ever terrified me more or yelled at me more or—how do you say this?—loved me more.

But it is what she taught me that sticks in my mind.

I met her when, with her husband William Sr. and her son Bill Jr., she ran the twice-weekly *Marlboro Herald-Advocate* in my home town of Bennettsville, S.C. One day when I was 14, I showed up at her doorstep and announced I had come to be a reporter.

She didn't flinch. "Sit here," she said, and she lectured me for half an hour on community journalism. Then she assigned me to cover my first story (a baseball game) and two days later gave me a front-page byline. For the next five or six years, I wrote stories, took pictures, edited and proofread copy, handled circulation complaints, inserted section B into section A, stamped the finished papers with address labels, and drove them to the Post Office. Eventually, I was actually paid for some of that.

She taught me many lessons but two stand out:

1   Never, ever, for any reason, get anything wrong, or else.
2   Fill the paper with as much news as you can, especially the human stuff people really care about.

Here's how I learned Lesson No. 1.

I had been proofreading copy for a week or two when I handled an ad for a local furniture store. It featured a color television set on sale for $399.99. But when I finished proofing the ad, the price mistakenly read $39.99.

Early the next day the phone rang. It was the manager of the furniture store. "You want to come down here," he thundered, "and see the line of people outside my store waiting for their $39 television!"

Mrs. Kinney gave me the tongue-lashing of my life. Then she taught me something else: how to use a piece of paper to cover up everything in the copy below the line you're proofing, so your eye concentrates on it and doesn't wander. It is a great editing tip, and I use and teach it to this day. You can even do it online, by reading each line of copy at the bottom of your screen.

Lesson No. 2, to go after news all the time, was reinforced every day. Mrs. Kinney regularly would give me names of people in town and order me to call them and dig up some news. She was the master of this tactic. She could dial someone up, chat for a minute, and in no time know that Uncle Earl was recovering from gall bladder surgery, Buddy and Janelle and the kids were spending the week at Myrtle Beach, and Buddy Jr. had just gotten his acceptance letter from Clemson. All of which went into the next issue.

Seldom have I handled a touchier assignment than my first high-society wedding. Our ace social correspondent, Miss Harriet Jackson, was away, so I was drafted to cover the big event, under the meticulous and relentless supervision of the bride's mother. Soon I was immersed in descriptions of bridal gown bodices and floral center-pieces, in recording which great-aunt presided over which reception punch bowl.

I wrote the story, quadruple-checked everything, proofed it (naturally, using a piece of paper to underline each line), and patrolled the backshop to ensure the printers didn't chop off the story in mid-sentence, as often happened in those hot-type days.

The day the story ran, my heart froze as I saw the Mother of the Bride locomoting into the newsroom with a look of grim determination. I considered fleeing but that would have violated another lesson I had quickly absorbed: In small-town journalism you cannot escape the people you write about. So I trembled and stood my ground.

The Mother marched toward me from one side as Mrs. Kinney closed in from the other. I was a dead man. Then Mother smiled and took my hand. "Thank you for the lovely story," she said warmly. "I just hope you know how much people appreciate it when the paper takes time to treat them right."

Another eternal lesson of journalism took hold.

It won't do to sentimentalize Mrs. Kinney, of course. Like most editors, she was both guardian angel and tormentor. She could be difficult, and her paper was far from perfect. But for me she exemplified tough love.

Never, from the first day I set foot in her office, did Mrs. Kinney treat me as the Kid Playing Reporter. She respected my ambition, and she demanded performance and discipline, on the fundamentals, every day. No excuses. No slack because I was a kid.

Respect your colleagues and readers. Get the news. Get it right. Or else.

Could you have a better start in the business than that?[25]

Vignettes

William Shawn edited the *New Yorker* for 35 years. He was beloved by writers for his low-key, thoughtful approach to both people and copy. On his death, the magazine published a section called "Remembering Mr. Shawn," including these recollections:[26]

- Calvin Trillin: "Shawn was that rare bird, an inspirational listener. For 35 years, writers emerged from his office buoyed by the belief that at least one other human being in the world understood precisely what they were trying to get at. . . . His approach to editing involved what amounted to a conscious denial of ego—a characteristic so startling in the writing trade that it was, ironically, one of the bases of his fame."
- Arlene Croce: "He seemed to know how much farther I could still go in a piece and how not to interfere with the process. I would say that this sympathy, this restraint, was the essence of his editorial gift."
- Roger Angell: "Journalists like to think of themselves as tough birds, old pros. . . . But Shawn . . . knew better. He had somehow perceived that writers are desperately in need of praise for their work—wild for it. . . . Praise makes them grow and go on."

6 Making decisions about copy
Editing for content

Content matters most.

Almost everything editors do, almost every decision they make, should be viewed through this prism. Will it help make the content better? Journalists' work is judged most decisively by the outcome, the product that goes to the reader or viewer. In the end, good editing equals good content. Good content equals good editing.

For that reason, the success of editors rests largely on their effectiveness in helping writers, photographers, designers, producers, and others to approach excellence in every assignment.

Whereas previous chapters have stressed that editors perform a range of duties besides processing copy, it is inescapable that, ultimately, the ability to edit copy is a touchstone quality of editors. Few will succeed without it. The editor who gains a reputation as a helpful "copy doctor"— able to take copy apart, examine it, and put it back together without the writer or reader seeing anything amiss—will win the allegiance and trust of a staff and the appreciation, if not the recognition, of the audience. The editor regarded as a "butcher" faces resentment and resistance and drives away readers.

In this chapter and the next one, we spotlight the editor's role in helping writers reach toward excellence, one piece of copy at a time.

Like so many creative enterprises, editing is in part natural talent. Some people have more of the gift than others. Like almost everything else, however, editing ability can be improved through practice and attention to technique. So this chapter rests on the following two propositions:

1 *Editors should be as systematic as possible in dealing with copy.* A systematic approach, that is, a set of procedures that are regularly and consistently employed, offers at least two benefits. First, it saves time, that most precious newsroom resource. Like following a recipe or playing the piano, the more you repeat an operation, the faster and more proficient you become at it. Second, a good system helps editors approach copy methodically instead of haphazardly. One of editing's biggest challenges is that any piece of copy offers an infinity

of potential problems. A system can help organize the editor's diagnosis. Think of how searches are undertaken for people lost in forests or the wilderness. Searchers don't simply drift randomly in all directions. They divide the area into grids, starting with the ones considered highest priority, and approach them in a deliberate and meticulous manner.

2   *Each editor's system should be personal and flexible.* On the other hand, every editor is different and every piece of copy is different, and no one editing system fits each situation. Your best bet as an editor is to develop a reasonable system that works efficiently for you and to adapt it thoughtfully to each task at hand. It is true that musicians practice and practice until they can, almost by muscle memory, play fluidly and consistently. It is also true that they develop a feel for when it is time to improvise, add an unexpected flourish, or alter the routine. Editors, similarly, should be systematic, but not compulsive, methodical but not mindless. Like other creative endeavors, good editing combines the discipline of craft with the occasional decisive moment of inspiration.

In this chapter, I will share a system that represents a sort of consensus method drawn from conversations with hundreds of editors. But it is offered as a starting point, not an end-all. For an editor who has never considered having a system, it provides a default to get started. Most editors, in my experience, use some version of the system but tinker with it, personalizing it to their tastes and needs.

Editing for content and structure

Examine the following potential lead for a news article. What problems do you see?

> School Superintendent Audrey Smith held a press conference Monday and said that, despite conflicting advice from school board members she plans to implement new teacher accountability measures for city schools next Autumn.

An alert copyeditor quickly can spot several problems: failure to abbreviate *Superintendent*, improper capitalization of *Autumn*, a missing comma after *members*. But those are the easy catches. They do not capture what is most wrong with this lead: It is off base and out of focus.

First, it is long, cumbersome, and loaded with fuzzy words like "implement" and "measures." Second, it backs into the point. And, third, it offers superfluous information, such as "held a press conference," at the expense of what the audience truly needs to know.

A lead I prefer:

School Supt. Audrey Smith promised Monday to fire teachers whose students don't meet county goals next fall "even if it costs me my job."

If you are like many editors to whom I have shown this and similar leads, your attention may have locked immediately onto the style and usage problems. Given what former *Miami Herald* reporter Edna Buchanan once described to me as their "itchy cursor fingers," editors often plunge right in and begin correcting such obvious errors.

Too frequently, they overlook the more important, but less glaring, deficiencies in an article's basic message or focus. To avoid such problems, I recommend *subdividing your editing into two separate phases: editing for content and editing for structure.* Content refers to matters of conceptual substance, the facts, images, and ideas, and their selection and arrangement. Structure means form, the language, usage, grammar, spelling, punctuation, and style.

Each stage requires a different style of editing and a different way of thinking. I often call content editing the "telescope" work. You are viewing copy from a distance in search of larger meaning and impressions. Editing for structure uses the "microscope." You must scrutinize every mark on the screen. Trying to do both at once produces incomplete, inconsistent editing, the kind of headachy blur that would result if a scientist kept bobbing between the microscope and the telescope.

To treat both the big picture of content and the details of structure necessitates using both sides of the editor's brain: the logical, sequential left side, which facilitates close reading, and the intuitive, creative right side, which is more attuned to rhythm, style, flow, and overall excellence. Good editors, as well as good writers, should cultivate both realms to realize the optimal blend of craft and creativity.

Editors have historically been left-side dominant. The ability to move methodically through a piece of copy is a classic left-brain trait. More and more, though, journalism requires right-brain thinking. From the advent of television to the rise of the Internet, journalism has evolved from a word-dominated, beginning-to-end communication pattern to one featuring images and graphics, shorter and multiple bursts of copy, and quick cutting from one segment or link to another. Today's editors must have, or work diligently to develop, full use of their right-brain faculties.

Still, for many, content editing raises more difficulties than structural editing. With structure, editors have well-defined rules and styles to follow. A news organization's style is either to capitalize the word *autumn* or not, and editors can look it up. But content editing requires dealing with intangible qualities such as fairness and relative significance or with subjective measures such as taste and literary merit. These areas are trickier, rooted less in memorized regulations than in professional judgments and experience. They are negotiable and disputable.

In this discussion, we first consider content editing. Then we turn to structural editing. That is the most common order followed by the pros. The editor looks first at content and takes whatever steps are appropriate to help writers tailor it to fit their intentions for the audience. Then, it is time to edit for structure.

There are three reasons for this order: First, if you painstakingly edit the structure before dealing with content, and then your content editing produces major revisions, you will have to repeat the structural editing anyway. Second, content and structural editing, as distinct processes requiring different ways of thinking, are best done sequentially rather than simultaneously, moving from broad conceptual thinking (content) to fine-tuning (structure). Third, editors who begin with structure may wind up spending all their time on it, never getting to content.

Some editors do prefer to edit first for structure and then for content. They reason that editing the structure goes relatively quickly and easily, allowing them more time to think about how to handle the larger conceptual matters.

I would not be dogmatic about the order. What is vital is to see editing for content and for structure as necessarily separate ways of thinking, impossible to do simultaneously. An editor concentrating on each comma and apostrophe may well overlook a fatal flaw in reporting or logic. Likewise, an editor zoned in on overall story flow may well miss typos and careless errors. The best course: Use separate reads, in whichever order works better for you, for content and for structure.

The RECESS model for editing

Editors, like writers or chefs or football coaches, develop personal work habits ranging from the cerebral to the idiosyncratic to the weird. Although you will find considerable variety in how editors operate, what follows is a brief model that sketches how editors typically proceed through a piece of copy. I call it the RECESS model because its key steps include:

> **R**ead
> **E**dit for
> **C**ontent
> **E**dit for
> **S**tructure
> **S**ign off

The model also includes a preparation stage to gain the concentration and focus needed for careful editing. First, we will outline the model, and then treat each step in greater detail.

Prepare to Edit. Remember that you are handling the copy of a fellow human being, a writer who is probably both proud and nervous about the work. Respect the effort. As editor, you have responsibility for the copy, but it does not *belong* to you. Make yourself concentrate fully and remember the three cardinal rules:

- *Never make any important change without consulting the writer.* Writers word their work exceptionally carefully to be precise and, sometimes, to tiptoe around missing information. A small change in wording can add serious error or misinterpretation.
- *Don't change anything unless you have a specific reason that you can explain to a neutral observer.* The editor's job is not to arbitrarily convert all copy from the writer's style to the editor's. Everything being equal, the writer should prevail on questions of style and wording. The editor's job is to seek out those instances where everything isn't equal, where there is a definable need for correction or improvement.
- *Never add an error to someone else's work.* Nothing humiliates a writer more than trying to explain to a skeptical source or a reader that errors in the story carrying the writer's byline were really someone else's fault. Sure, the sources always seem to be thinking. Whatever you say.

Read the copy completely before editing anything, to get its overall effect and to see how it strikes you, cold, as a reader. Reading a story all the way through also shows respect for the writer. Few acts are more irritating than when an editor dives into the first sentence or two, barking questions and furiously changing things. Instead, good editors take a moment to read the copy and to try to understand the writer's goals and intentions. What was the assignment? Who is the audience? What special circumstances surround the story? What does the writer seem to be attempting? How will the story be played? Has it already gone through other editors?

Edit for content. Check the story for accuracy, fairness, clarity, consistency, logic, taste, and thoroughness. Focus on the lead: Is it clear, interesting, meaningful, and based on the most compelling point? Are sources named and reliable? Is evidence adequate? Does the piece pose legal or ethical problems? Is something important omitted? Is the copy interesting? If you encounter questions or problems, discuss them with the writer. If major changes are necessary, try to give the writer responsibility for making them.

Edit for structure. Inspect the grammar, punctuation, spelling, style, and usage. Guard against wordiness and muddy writing. Think of style in its literary sense. Strive for polish and sharpness. To the extent you can, make your editing consistent with the writer's style. Finally, let the writer see the finished copy.

Sign off. Re-read the story, for final effect. Make sure you haven't inserted errors. Double-check any changes you have made. Look for glitches that can occur off-screen, when the computer is justifying margins or scrolling out of your sight. Is there anything at all whose accuracy is in question? Is anything crucial missing? Will you vouch for this story?

Although following this model might seem to require large chunks of time, that is not necessarily the case. The key point is that, using whatever time is available, the editor should attend to each step in proportion to its relative importance. Thus, a rough schedule might go as follows:

- *Preparation*, 5 percent of available time
- *Content editing*, 60 percent
- *Structural editing*, 30 percent
- *Signoff*, 5 percent.

Such an allocation can work if the editor has 10 minutes or 10 hours for a project. And it gives precedence to content, allows time for structure, and leaves room for a good beginning and a clean finish.

Now, we can develop the model in more detail.

Preparing to edit

The most important single step toward better editing is fuller concentration. Editing needs your total attention. But by the nature of the job, many editors must juggle numerous thoughts and duties. Often they catch themselves putting their brains into a kind of editing autopilot while they also ponder some separate issue. This, however, is no more advisable for editors than it is for air traffic controllers. Far more editing errors stem from inattention and carelessness than from incompetence or stupidity. For rookie and veteran editors alike, few steps produce better payoff than training themselves to devote complete attention to the project at hand.

Many editors devise elaborate warm-up rituals for this purpose. Once, old-timers adjusted their green eyeshades (used as shields against the glare of harsh newsroom lighting) and carefully sharpened five fat copy pencils before even glancing at the story. Today, web-trained editors adjust their ergonomic chairs, slide a favorite pillow underneath, set the contrast button to their personal satisfaction, limber their fingers like a pianist, and then, at last, peer in at the copy. Others simply stare into space for a few minutes, clearing the mind. One editor I knew would roll up his sleeves, wring his hands, and walk around the newsroom saying, "Scrub me up, nurse."

At best these rituals, whether products of rational planning or magical incantation, serve to bring editors into something akin to a state of self-hypnosis. Almost nothing is more important than learning to get yourself into this intense zone of concentration.

Thus prepared, editors should spend a moment contemplating their task. Read through the story. Consider the writer, the assignment, the circumstances. Is it news, or feature? A story alone, a print package including photos and graphics, a multimedia presentation with a slide show and audio clips? Culmination of a six-month investigative project, or a bulletin for the web? Intended to convey some specific message to the reader (such as tomorrow's weather forecast), or open to experimentation (such as how area farmers are coping with a season-long drought)?

The editor's goal here is to become oriented to the story and everything that has preceded it, from conception, through reporting and writing, to any judgments already made by other editors. All this can happen in just a few seconds or minutes, but it is important. The more that editors know of this history, the more sensitive they can be in handling the copy and sidestepping potential land mines.

Editors should never forget a central difference in point of view between themselves and writers: To the writer, the turned-in copy represents an *ending*, the finished product of a creative professional. To the editor, it may seem the point at which work *begins*.

Although the reporter may view the story as the equivalent of perfectly grilled steak ready for the palate, editors may see it as raw hamburger meat, available for shaping in the hands of a master. At this point, some common courtesy is called for. The writer should understand that editors are charged with taking a broad view and that it is duty, not simply their itchy trigger fingers, that compels them to scrutinize, challenge, and sometimes rework copy. Editors, on the other hand, should respect the writer's work. Nothing is gained by patronizing writers. Instead editing should be the time for two professionals to have a constructive, respectful conversation about work in which both have an active stake.

Editing for content

Before plunging into detailed wordsmithing, editors often start by addressing two crucial ingredients of copy: *its overall impact* and *the effectiveness of the lead*. If they have fundamental questions about either the overall direction or the specific approach, this is the time to iron them out, before either the editor or the writer gets too invested in a given viewpoint.

First the editor evaluates the copy taken as a whole. Is it important, interesting, and compelling? Will it stop a busy reader, viewer, or surfer? Does it make sense? Is it of value? Does it make a significant point, or will it leave the reader saying, "Who cares?" Is there anything at all, in the reporting or the writing, that could be a fatal flaw?

The lead is the most important element in answering these questions. It is, of course, the reader's starting point. If the lead doesn't induce the reader to continue, then the entire story is lost. A good lead is like ice, so slick that before they realize it readers find themselves sliding flat on their backs into the middle of a story. Nothing else within a story (we will discuss the role of design and headlines later) comes close to the lead in having the power to sell readers or send them fleeing.

In analyzing the overall impact and the lead, editors draw on the same two questions the should have guided the writer from the beginning: "What is my purpose, and who is my audience?"

- *Purpose*. Traditionally journalists tended to see their purpose as either informing (via news stories) or telling stories (via features). However, that way of thinking may be overly simplistic in today's age of round-the-clock, multiplatform, multimedia coverage. For example, news stories now unfold in quick stages: a bulletin on television, a few early paragraphs in a web report, an online update featuring audio and video, interactive additions of words or clips from audience members, comprehensive writethroughs and analytical pieces for the printed newspaper, and so on. At each point, the writer and editor must share an understanding of the precise purpose of a particular piece of copy.
- *Audience*. A second key point is the audience. At whom is the story directed, and in what format is the audience receiving the copy? If the article is aimed at the mass newspaper or online audience, then the writer must keep in mind the distracted, hurried, heterogeneous nature of the group, and must write accordingly, for example employing clear, simple, direct language. On the other hand, if copy is intended for certain specialized audiences—say, magazine readers or niche websites aimed at young trendsetters—then certain assumptions about the audience can be made that will affect the writer's tone and style. The editor's duty is to help ensure that the writer, in choosing a lead and basic framework, tailors them to the appropriate audience and format.

The lead: The all-important starting point. Once the overall assessment is completed, then content editing begins in earnest. For most editors, the lead is the logical place to begin hands-on editing. It is a crucial starting point, and, for too many readers, the quitting point as well.

Aside from ensuring accuracy, which is always the editor's most important concern, the single most important contribution an editor can make to the lead is as follows: *Ensure that the meaning is in the lead.* An article that is totally accurate and that conveys meaning effectively to the audience is well on its way to succeeding. If either of those conditions goes unmet, then the article will most likely fail.

In reviewing leads, it is wise to remember how people read. In fact, viewing today's audiences as "readers" is only partly correct. Some consumers, but fewer than in the past, are primed to read in a leisurely, beginning-to-end fashion, with a hearty appetite for, and full attention to, detail and depth. But others, especially those reading online, may be less readers than scanners. Scanners typically read rapidly, skimming everything, turning pages quickly or jumping from web link to link, making hasty and cut-throat decisions about what to read and what to ignore. They read and surf while watching television, eating and snacking, listening to music, or interacting with friends and families. They may take only three or four seconds to decide whether to read an article or visit a site that a writer has spent hours, days, or weeks preparing.

However, this harried speed reading may not be the setting being imagined as the writers go about crafting their articles. Instead, writers are more likely to envision an idealized audience of attentive, hungry news devourers, ready to drop everything in order to read to the very last word of every story.

How easy it is to forget the differing perspectives of writers and readers:

- *Writers begin to write at the point of peak interest in their stories*, after hours or days or even weeks immersed in discovering what is interesting in the lives and events of their subjects.
- *Readers begin to read at a point of relatively low interest*, without knowing (as does the writer) how the story will come out, without the context to quickly grasp the relevance of every description or foreshadowing anecdote.

A problem, then, is that writers, knowing what is to come, may want to build to their climax, as an organist builds toward a crescendo. But readers, not knowing or even necessarily caring what is to come, may be unwilling to stick around past a slow-moving prelude. Into this equation comes the editor, who must help writers reconcile their literary aspirations with the knowledge that so many readers are skimmers who must be hooked quickly or not at all.

Types of leads: News, news-plus, and feature. As we have already noted, the lead flows from considerations of purpose and audience. As we have also mentioned, good editors will have discussed these matters with writers long before the copy is submitted. Remember the coaching model: The editor and writer should have a clear conversation, at the writer's organizing stage, of how to approach the piece. So the lead should not come as a surprise to the editor.

Sometimes, however, it will, and in all cases the editor must once again carefully review whether the lead, at this near-final point in the process, is the best it can be.

Even in today's information-saturated society, many articles still exist simply to convey important new information to the audience. If this is the purpose, then the *news lead*, a simple, direct statement of the most important point, may be the most effective lead, especially if the information will be truly new to the audience. The mission may be simply to convey the point from one place (the writer) to another (the reader), as efficiently as possible. For this kind of writing, the inverted pyramid structure works quite well: Begin with the most important point and proceed with points in descending order of importance.

If you are standing at an office window and see a tornado approaching, for instance, you would not turn to your colleagues and say, "Today dawned bright and sunny over the city but before long the clouds began to roll in. . . ." You would say, "A tornado is heading this way and we'd better take cover."

For such stories, an old saw generally works: Base your lead on what you would say if you were summarizing the story for your mother.

However, for many journalists a more common task is writing about situations where the audience already has some basic information. For example, if a bad storm has indeed struck, then it does little good, in a web report hours later or in the next day's newspaper, to simply rehash the basic facts. These circumstances may call for the *news-plus lead*, an approach that summarizes the basic event but builds on it, adding information or angles that are new or previously unknown. Often, such leads offer what is called *future spin*, a look ahead rather than behind. In the case of a storm, for instance, a news-plus lead might say something like, "Utility crews have developed a three-day schedule for restoring power after yesterday's tornado that injured 15 people."

Similarly, if a writer is covering a school board meeting where a new superintendent is hired, the fact of the hiring might lead the writer's first blurb for the web. But the story for the morning newspaper might begin with some backstage insight, such as, "Intensive behind-the-scenes lobbying by teachers' union president Marilyn Beemer proved crucial in last night's hiring of a new school superintendent. . . ."

With a news-plus lead, the reader receives the news, but additional value as well.

If the purpose is to tell a story as a feature or a narrative, then the direct statement may not work best. In storytelling, the idea is not necessarily to rush to the ending as quickly as possible, but to create the best dramatic effect using characterization, plotting, scene, description, emotion, and other such devices. This process is akin to telling a joke: You do not begin with the punch line, nor do you drag out the story to such elaborate lengths that it loses its edge.

A good *narrative lead* should accomplish at least these goals: introduce the key character or idea of the story, illustrate the main point, and intrigue the reader.

In all these cases, the editor must understand the writer's purpose and help analyze whether the lead best serves it.

Attributes of good leads. In working with the writer, the editor can often ask a series of questions that can help guide the writer to tweaking or recasting a lead that needs work:

- Is the lead accurate in every way?
- Does it convey the meaning?
- Is it clear? Nothing besides accuracy and meaning is more important.
- Is it appropriate for the format?
- Is it focused firmly on the most compelling point?
- Has the writer chosen the most effective possible way of engaging readers?
- Is it magnetic? Does it grab readers, lock them tightly to the story, and make them want to read on? Does it offer enough tension, irony, drama, or seductiveness to promptly engage the reader's curiosity?
- Is it vivid? Does it use direct, concrete words and images that readers can readily visualize?
- Does it answer the questions "Who cares?" and "So what?" Does it demonstrate, through the power of fact or narrative, why the overall story is important enough for readers to care?

In some ways, writing an article for the public is a supremely arrogant act. Writers dare the audience, in effect, to stop everything else, to reject every possible alternative use of time, in order to read what they have written. Consequently, a heavy burden falls on writers (and their partners, editors) to make readers consider this sacrifice worthwhile.

As helper, the editor should not merely criticize. We have said that the editor's job includes offering expertise. So, while it is not possible or even desirable to promote any precise lead-writing formula, it may be useful to offer some general guidelines that editors can share with writers struggling over their leads. Here then are 10 qualities to share. In my view, most good leads should:

1   Take less than 25 words and fit into one sentence.
2   Express a single thought. Roundups, over-generalized summaries, and leads that try to skip through several elements confuse readers.
3   Begin with the single most tantalizing point and write it crisply.
4   Be direct. Go to the heart of the story. Usually, the subject and verb of the lead sentence should reflect the main figure and the main action of the story.
5   Use active voice and action words. Stories should be dynamic. They need movement. If they stand still, so does the reader. By the end of the lead, something should have *happened* or *changed*.
6   Avoid the verb "to be" and passive introductions like "There is."
7   Place the dominating idea—the single most crucial point—as near the beginning of the lead sentence as possible.

8   Avoid the nonessential. Leave out extraneous circumstances ("took the witness stand today and said . . ."), acronyms, jargon, unnecessary titles, and names of government agencies, unless they are required for clarity or accuracy. This material can come later.

9   Give the reader some worthwhile new fact, feeling, or image, in understandable, easily pictured terms. Consider the lead: "A local woman is a hero tonight after rescuing her husband from an auto accident." What does the reader see here? What woman? What is a hero? What kind of rescue? What kind of accident? Instead, substitute stronger words and say, "A 76-year-old local woman dragged her disabled husband from their flaming car tonight, seconds after a tractor-trailer rammed it on Fifth Street." In your mind, you can see the difference.

10   Move the reader smoothly to the second paragraph.

In all this, the editor's job is to help the writer, not to replace the writer. So the role remains to analyze and evaluate, and then to discuss reactions (and the reasons for them) with the writer. If revision is needed, editors can point out why they think so, and then, wherever possible, let the writer do the revising.

And remember this key point: Some leads need no changes at all. If the lead seems splendid, point out why, say so out loud, and leave the writer feeling good.

Other content issues

By this point, the editor should have become acquainted with the copy and the writer, considered its overall impact, and scrutinized the lead. Now other content areas await. As a warm-up exercise, I recommend reading the massive collection of news media errors, gaffes, goofs, and apologies collected by websites such as regrettheerror.com. Not only will it humble almost any editor, but it will permanently reinforce the importance of never-ending skepticism and alertness.

Accuracy. Nothing is more important than accuracy. The editor should make sure (and this can be surprisingly tedious) that every assertion or fact is sourced and documented. Look for careless errors, hasty conclusions, unwarranted assumptions. Do not hesitate to ask the reporter, "Are you certain?" or "How do you know this?" If a reporter complains that your questions show disrespect or lack of trust, explain that everyone makes mistakes and your job as editor requires examining everything. Even major publications including the *New York Times* and *USA Today* have faced fabrication scandals in recent years, underlining the vigilance incumbent on all editors.

Logic. Stories should make sense, so editors should check for gaps in logic and reasonableness. In one newsroom where I worked, we frequently invoked the "two-minute-mile rule," which held that if someone makes a claim that is too good to be true (such as having run a mile in two minutes, half the world-record time) then it probably is not true. One example from regrettheerror.com: A Milwaukee newspaper's recipe that, according to the subsequent correction, "misstated the length of time for baking the pudding. The recipe calls for baking it for 40 minutes, not 540 minutes."[1]

Organization. Does the body of the story flow smoothly from the lead? Try to outline the story. Typically, you should find a lead that introduces the main theme, followed by about three secondary themes, covered in some logical and orderly way, and a suitable ending. If you cannot detect an outline or order, then the story may ramble or seem blurry. The equivalent of turning the focus knob on a television set is to ask a writer to reexamine the organization to make sure it flows smoothly.

Directness. Read a newspaper or online news source and notice how easy it is to find stories that never directly demonstrate why they exist: articles about obscure cabinet changes in faraway places or subcommittee haggling inside Congress or microscopic fluctuations in business indices. Unless a story's importance is inherently obvious (such as when a plane crashes and people die), copy needs a concise, straightforward statement of the point. Sometimes the lead serves this purpose. Often, it comes in the second paragraph, where the lead expresses the newest or most dramatic development and paragraph two puts that development into perspective.

Writers have many words for such a paragraph: the nut graph, the billboard, the catholic graph. My favorite description is to call it the "why-are-we-at-this-party" paragraph. If you cannot find one, ask the writer the age-old question: How would you sell this story to me in one sentence? That sentence, quite often, can become the telltale explanatory paragraph.

Sources and documentation. In checking for accuracy, the editor should independently consider whether sources and documentation are authoritative, adequate, and reliable. For almost two generations, many editors have invoked the "two-source rule," popularized during coverage of the 1970s Watergate scandal. It requires separate confirmations of any point that may be disputed. Reporters, in their haste and eagerness to locate someone willing to talk, may exaggerate the importance of a source or whether a source is truly in a position to know. A red flag for the editor should be phrases such as "a Defense Department employee" or "a company executive." Even when such sources are named, it does not necessarily follow that they are authoritative. Similarly, sourcing should be especially solid on material with a high potential for embarrassment.

In short, sources should be clear, named, and dependable. Readers should know, from the story, where information came from, how the writer got it, and why the sources were in a position to know it.

Completeness. Stories need context, background, and definitions of unfamiliar concepts. I can remember as a youngster reading news articles about the Vietnam War and wondering who was fighting whom and why. While it is not practical to give detailed explanations in every story, it is important that sufficient historical background be present so readers can comprehend each story. And it is worth remembering that new readers (newcomers to town, young people, people who usually read the competition) constantly enter the news flow without the same frame of reference journalists have. The obsessive fear of repetition is a journalistic bugaboo that should be laid to rest.

Omissions. The editor not only must critique what reporters have written but also what they have not written. What pertinent questions have not been asked? What information is missing? What angles are not covered? What arguments or points of view have been slighted? What alternative approaches might work better? For some, editing what is not there proves the hardest editing of all, because it requires imagination and distance, two elusive editing qualities.

One simple, time-tested technique is to explicitly search for the five Ws and the H in every story. You may surprise yourself at how often one is missing.

Another method is to compare the existing copy against an imagined ideal, and see how close the two can be made. This is one area where dealing with the writer can get dicey. An editor who insists on new material is directly challenging the reporter's thoroughness. So move cautiously here, but do move. Instead of demanding, "Why didn't you call the defense lawyer?" try saying, "What if we added a quote from the defense lawyer?" Instead of complaining, "This is a one-sided story about pit bulls," try saying, "What would you think about calling some dog owners?" In almost every case, reporters recognize a good suggestion and are eager to add material that will improve stories, if they do not have their backs up because of the editor's style of challenging.

Fairness. Unfairness shows itself in many ways: in choice of what sources to interview and what material to include, in the judgments of reporters and sources alike, in the ignorance or distortion inherent in sources' and reporters' points of view, and in word selection, among others. As a relatively impartial reader, the editor tries to sniff out unfairness or apparent unfairness and to inform the reporter when it seems present.

A common example occurs in police stories, where officers assume the guilt of an arrested suspect and announce something like, "This arrest clears up 47 burglaries in the northeast of town." Too seldom do we hear the position of the accused, or of his or her lawyer. A good guideline is to see that any people criticized in an article are given a chance to offer their very best defense *within the same article.* Saving that for a follow-up story is not fair.

Another fairness problem occurs when writers adopt the terminology used by one side of an issue (using words such as "pro-life" in the abortion debate, or "tax reform" in the political arena).

Stereotyping. Stereotyping, as when racism, sexism, or ageism finds its way into copy, can be blatant or subtle. Be careful of racial identifications. In descriptions of suspects, for instance, do not fall into the trap of signaling that people are assumed to be white or male unless you tell the reader otherwise.

Double entendres. Nobody has dirtier minds than journalists, except perhaps readers. So an editor must watch for both the dirt that almost every reporter will at times try to slip by and for the dirt that no one notices until it is too late. Beware of obituaries of the sort that begin, "Bessie Sanders, 54, died Saturday shortly after assuming a missionary position." Watch headlines, where the devil seems to get loose most often. Everybody enjoys reading the headline gaffes as reprinted in the *American Journalism Review* or the *Columbia Journalism Review* ("Loose Dogs Tie Up Police"[2]), but no one wants to personally contribute to their collection.

Pranks. Be extremely cautious about typing jokes or sarcastic comments onto copy with the intention of deleting them later. Far too often, they find their way into print or online, where they can be captured and saved for embarrassing eternities. The *Philadelphia Inquirer* invited readers to submit responses to its editorials, and then added, "The Editorial Board members will roll their eyes and chuckle at your remarks." It was meant as a gag, not for publication, but it somehow made its way into the paper.[3] A Danbury, Connecticut, news organization fired a copyeditor who was "goofing around" and posted an offensive caption on its website; under a photo of a high school girls' soccer team celebrating a victory, the caption said the group was enjoying a teammate's decision "to come out of the closet as a lesbian."[4] A good rule: If you don't want to see it posted, don't write it.

Taste. Sex. Nudity. Blood. Gore. Death. Violence. Profanity. Blasphemy. Taste issues abound, in copy, headlines, photos, audio, and video.

Although this issue is covered in more detail elsewhere in the book, its applicability to content editing is obvious. In most such cases, the editor's job is not necessarily to impose taste decisions on reporters but to raise them for discussion. Different publications will have varying standards. What is most important is for editors to regard themselves as early warning signalers, programmed to respond when they see a potential taste issue, so that the ultimate publish-or-not decision is reasoned and deliberate.

Law. This subject, too, has its own chapter later. But it cannot be overlooked in the context of content editing. Few duties surpass the editor's responsibility for producing legally sound copy. The editor must look for potential libel, invasion of privacy, contempt of court, plagiarism, and trademark or copyright violations. As with taste questions, the editor may not be a lone decision maker and should not simply reflexively snip out any potentially offending item. Instead, the editor should trigger whatever procedure a' news organization has (and every newsroom should have one) for deciding legally troublesome questions.

Having listed all these categories, I find myself wondering what kind of paragon will have the time, judgment, and brain capacity to police them all. Clearly, so much can go wrong with stories that not even the world's best editor can possibly guard against everything.

How do editors deal with this problem? Some editors, like those reporters who always seem to be nearby when the big story breaks, do it with instinct, with some sixth sense that nudges them about an approaching defect in copy. Part of that intuition, I think, comes from a life of constant reading and writing. Eventually they come to sense good and bad work, in the same way that, after years of listening to music, one can tell when a disk is warped or an instrument is out of tune.

Other editors do try to question everything, cross-examining reporters with one indiscriminate question after another with no sense of priority. I think this approach is a mistake. The best editors do not simply think of every possible question and then suffocate reporters with them all at once. Instead, they *rank* their questions, asking the most crucial ones first and moving down the line as time and reasonableness allow. Most questions fall into one of four categories:

- *Fatal.* These are questions that must be settled or else the story cannot be published. Example: in an investigative story on corruption in the mayor's office, what to do about possibly libelous material not adequately attributed or documented.
- *Important.* Questions that need answering and must either be settled or written around. Example: in the mayor story, how to resolve a conflict on the spelling of a source's name.
- *Marginal.* Questions worth settling if there is time, but of less consequence than the above. Example: background information on what previous mayors have faced investigations.
- *Picayune.* Questions of esoteric interest or little interest at all, which suggest an editor is simply showing off an ability to ask *something*. Example: what the mayor was wearing when interviewed for the corruption story.

Overall, one good rule is to consider what is most likely to go wrong and what areas have the potential for most damage. Then, pay priority attention to these areas. On my list of code-red areas would be the following:

- *Identifications.* Names should be checked and double-checked. Errors here ruin stories, destroy credibility, and invite lawsuits. Once—

following the rule that, in controversial stories, full identification is best—my newspaper published a story about Maurice H. Wilson Jr. The next morning, I heard from the *other* Maurice H. Wilson Jr. in our town. Be careful and be consistent. Make sure stories and cutlines match. Make sure the newspaper and website agree.

- *Numbers*. Face it. Many journalists turned to writing only after they realized they could not pass math. Always double-check numbers. Make sure stories and headlines are internally consistent. A headline said 19 men were arrested at a shopping mall on sex charges. The story listed 16. All over the area, people wondered who was left out, and why. Triple-check phone numbers. An editor I know was once assigned to go answer the nonstop calls coming into a local bank, after her paper mistakenly listed the bank's phone number as the place for citizens to call to request the city's fall leaf pickup.

- *Claims*. Recognize that people take special glee in trying to catch the press in errors. So verify any special claim such as a superlative (the county's biggest tomato ever, the largest drug bust in state history, the first woman to hold a certain job) or historical citation. The *New York Times* reported that no Nobel Prize existed in math because gossip had it that Alfred Nobel's wife had been involved with a mathematician. Subsequently, a reader informed the *Times* that Nobel was a bachelor.[5]

Conclusion

Make no mistake: Both content and structure influence meaning.

With experience, editors may learn to examine many content areas automatically. But it normally proves safer and more thorough to do so explicitly, thinking through each issue and consulting with the writer. Using a systematic approach can save time and help with discipline and priorities.

Once content seems secure, the editor can move confidently to structure. Far more than a preoccupation with technicality, structural editing seals the final impressions copy will leave. Writers connect, or misfire, because of scores of accumulated decisions about spelling, grammar, punctuation, and usage. That explains why careful attention to structure is the next step—and the culmination—of good editing.

Sidebar 6: An editing checklist

Reminders can be helpful. Many editors keep lists of tips and techniques taped to their computers or posted near their desks, consulting them from time to time as refreshers or inspiration.

Here is a checklist that elaborates on the RECESS editing model.

Preparation for editing:

- Focus intently on the copy, blocking out distractions.
- Understand the assignment and what other editors have done to the copy.
- Remember you are dealing with the finished work of a fellow professional. Show respect to your colleague by respecting the work.
- Read it through once, cold, as a reader, making few if any changes.

Editing technique:

- Don't change anything without a good reason, a reason you can explain to a neutral party.
- Check all major changes with the writer, and let the writer make the changes where possible.
- Never add errors or distort meaning.
- Solve problems in order of importance, from *fatal* to *important* to *marginal*.

Presentation and format:

- Art and graphics.
- Online considerations.
- Multimedia considerations.
- Reader service or interactive material.

Editing for content:

- Clear theme, with *meaning* conveyed early in story.
- Compelling lead, based on the theme, underlining *twist* that makes story special.
- Lead that is short (25 words or less) and direct (key thought in main subject and verb).
- Second paragraph that flows from lead, amplifying most important or compelling point of lead.
- Clarity.
- Fairness and balance.
- Taste and ethics.
- Legal issues.
- Solid evidence based on credible, named sources.
- Good quote in first few paragraphs.
- Human examples and voices.
- Concrete detail.
- No important omissions.

Editing for structure:

- Grammar, especially subject–verb and noun–pronoun agreement.
- Punctuation, especially commas, apostrophes, and quotation marks.
- Spelling.
- Style.
- Usage and language.
- Active voice, action verbs, precise words.
- Wordiness:

  Too many prepositional phrases
  Too many long sentences or paragraphs
  Too many sentences beginning with *A, An, The*
  Too many "to be" verbs
  Redundancy
  Jargon and bureaucratic language
  Long separations between subject and verb.

Signoff: The final read:

- Errors possibly added during editing.
- Any final concerns.

Vignettes

"Nobody's perfect," began a *New York Times* article compiling some of the paper's most peculiar corrections.

Among the most embarrassing examples:

- "An article about the Central Asian lands whose names end in 'stan' referred incorrectly to Kafiristan. It is the former name of a region of northeastern Afghanistan, not an imaginary place invented by Rudyard Kipling."
- "An article about decorative cooking incorrectly described a presentation of Muscovy duck by Michel Fitoussi, a New York chef. In preparing it, Mr. Fitoussi uses a duck that has been killed."
- "An article about the town of Washington referred incorrectly to the Revolutionary War travels of its namesake, George Washington. He could not have visited the town by railroad; steam-powered locomotives came to the United States in the 1820's, some 30 years after his death."[6]

7   Making decisions about copy
Editing for structure

A schoolchild became upset after discovering a pea in milk at lunchtime. Rumors flew, and reports hit the Chicago media: Urine had been found in pupils' milk.[1]

A *pea* or *pee*? As the message was passed along, the substitution of one tiny letter turned the meaning inside out. So it goes often in the process of communicating. Success rests on sustaining the fragile bond between writer and audience, a bond possible only if both parties heed the structural conventions of language.

Once content editing is done, the work enters the structural editing stage. Where content editing calls for viewing copy broadly as through a telescope, in structural editing we slide it under a microscope, analyzing each mark on the paper or dot on the screen. Every comma, period, and space; every word, phrase, and clause; every sentence, paragraph, and link requires scrutiny. Clarity, accuracy, and precision compel the pickiest attention to this fundamental architecture of writing.

The good editor finds it axiomatic that "there's no such thing as a small error." Consider the headline that forms the title of the *Columbia Journalism Review* collection of press missteps: "Squad Helps Dog Bite Victim."[2] Here, all meaning hinges on the humble hyphen.

Or take an example cited by editor Roscoe Born: "Use a *which* for a *that*, and your readers may have to have their stomachs pumped." He illustrates with the following sentence: "If you eat ashtolaka nuts which come from the groves of the Portmanteau Islands, you may die within hours, for they are deadly poison." Are all ashtolaka nuts poisonous, or just those from Portmanteau? The answer lies in whether the clause is restrictive (essential to the meaning, not set off by commas, introduced by *that*) or nonrestrictive (incidental, set off by commas, introduced by *which*).[3]

Such hairsplitting necessarily occupies at least some time of most editors, and it often dominates the work of copydesk rim people. As the last newspeople to see copy, editors stand responsible for ensuring the clarity and correctness of everything that is published and posted, down to the finest details.

Why does structure matter?

First, structure affects *meaning*. Language is a code that depends on consistent, mutually obeyed rules.

Second, structure affects *credibility*. The audience includes people who understand structure, and they rate the press. Sloppiness in structure breeds suspicion and mistrust that can compromise the overall integrity of writing.

Third, structure adds *convenience* for the reader and writer. It provides a consistent model. It gives writers some helpful substitutes for the voice modulations, facial expressions, hand gestures, and other techniques that complement spoken language.

Finally, structure contributes to *artistic value*. It indicates pride in craft and finished professionalism.

To begin structural editing, editors should take time briefly to adjust their vision. Inspecting each individual item requires utter concentration. And still, no editor will see everything. So, as one essential element in structural editing, good editors try to cultivate an instinctive awareness of the danger zones where defects most likely lurk. Then they pay extra attention there.

Among the most common danger zones are spelling, grammar, punctuation, style, and usage.

Spelling

Andrew Jackson once supposedly snorted, "It is a damn poor mind indeed which can't think of at least two ways to spell any word."[4] What's worse, for writers and editors, is what we might call the Journalist's First Law of Spelling: The longer you stare at any word, the less certain you are whether it is spelled correctly.

While the occasional genius arrives on the desk knowing how to spell *will-o'-the-wisp*, most of us struggle to sort out *principle* and *principal*. Doubtlessly, much can be done in school to improve spelling, but, given the infinite aggravation spelling inflicts on almost everyone, I prefer a purer, quicker method to wipe out most spelling errors: Buy a good print dictionary and bookmark one online; then use them *any time you are not certain a word is spelled correctly*.

Use a dictionary 25 times a story if you need to. Looking up dozens of words takes only a few minutes, and it replaces countless hours lost in memorizing "i before e except after c" rules that do not apply to *seize* in the first place.

Then, of course, liberally use your computerized spelling checkers. Although these programs can assist the editor, they do not replace careful copyediting, for obvious reasons. Their style choices are sometimes idiosyncratic and not in keeping with journalistic preferences. And of course they may not recognize misusages such as "it's" for "its" or "affect" for "effect," where the error involves a variant that might be correct in other circumstances.

Because spelling is a universal problem, it is also wise to identify certain letter combinations that pose more hazard than others. They include:

- *-able, -ible endings* (such as permissible and allowable)
- *-ant, -ent endings* (consistent, descendant)
- *ie, ei* (weird, wield)
- *doubled consonants in the interior of a word* (harass, embarrass)
- *-er, -or endings* (regulator, propeller)
- *words subject to careless misspelling* (it's/its, their/they're, who's/whose)
- *all-time favorites* (use mnemonic devices to remember that the principal is your *pal*, or that accommodate has two m's just like commode, or that consensus relates to consent, or that stationery is with an e when it means letter and with an a when it means standing).

Despite its perpetual capacity to bedevil us, spelling is, more than any other structural consideration, solvable. I have deep sympathy for students, writers, and editors who have trouble spelling, but I have little sympathy for those who cannot use a dictionary and turn in copy free from most misspellings. Use a dictionary. Look up words.

It doesn't really matter whether you can spell. It matters mightily whether your copy has the words spelled right.

Grammar

You cannot remedy grammatical problems by consulting a dictionary, but you can and should attack them systematically. Grammar can be mastered. It usually takes about one year's tough drilling. For some, that comes in Mr. Smith's or Mrs. Whitner's ninth-grade English course. Others are not so fortunate. If you still find yourself spending excessive time struggling with grammar, then act promptly. Take a demanding grammar course. Buy a grammar handbook. Use a computer tutorial.

As a teacher and editor, I find some grammatical issues crop up regularly and sometimes can be headed off early. Among the most common are subject–verb agreement, noun–pronoun agreement, and modifier placement. For reasons of both carelessness and confusion, writers make these errors often enough that they should be checked faithfully in each piece of copy.

Subject–verb agreement. Many grammatical mistakes stem from inattention rather than ignorance. Because both kinds of errors occur regularly, checking all agreement makes sense. The basic rule is simple enough: Singular subjects require singular verbs, and plural subjects require plural verbs. But enforcing it can be confusing. Frequent errors are cited here:

- Incorrectly using a plural verb with a subject that is singular grammatically but logically seems to convey the idea of more than one person. Often, this error involves *collective nouns*, words that are singular in form but that name a group, such as *team* or *committee*. Such words usually take a singular verb.
  Wrong: "The team *are* winning the game." It is *is*.
  Right: "The couple *has* two children."
- Mistakenly letting a prepositional phrase confuse your thinking. In the sentence, "John as well as Minnie is going," the subject is singular (*John*). *As well as Minnie* is a phrase that doesn't affect the subject–verb relationship, so the verb is correctly written as singular.
  Wrong: "Not one of the 15 students *are* failing." Use *is*.

Noun–pronoun agreement. Similar to subject–verb agreement. Check pronouns to be sure they match their references in number. A typical problem involves *institutional nouns*, words singular in form but representing an organization composed of many parts. For example, an increasingly common mistake is to write "The company has begun advertising *their* new product." Again, the rule for collectives applies. Most take singular pronouns.

Wrong: "The Supreme Court will reveal *their* decision." Use *its*. If the expression strikes you as awkward, then try "The Supreme Court justices will reveal their decision."

Dangling and misplaced modifiers. Every modifier needs a specific word to modify. Beware of incorrect formulations where modifiers have no such word, or where they are placed too far apart from the words they actually modify.

Wrong: "Majoring in journalism, his writing immediately improved." There is no word for *majoring* to modify.

Right: "Majoring in journalism, he took courses that helped his writing." Now *majoring* correctly modifies the word *he*.

Confusing: "She scolded her dog who was barking loudly while text-messaging with her husband."

Clear: "While text-messaging with her husband, she scolded her dog, who was barking loudly."

Punctuation

These tend to start with commas. Why this tiny mark should so confuse us remains a mystery, but comma problems plague us all. On this issue, more than most others, writers guess, often inserting commas into copy seemingly at random: "When the alarm sounded, there was mass confusion as frightened people ran for the exits, and jammed the stairwells." The first comma belongs. The second one, after "exits," does not. A good beginning rule for a writer: Do not use any comma unless you have a reason and know the reason. The editor's corollary: Check every comma to make certain you know why it is needed.

Among the most common errors are:

- Confusing *restrictive* and *nonrestrictive* clauses. As we saw in the earlier example from Roscoe Born, restrictive clauses are vital to a sentence and are not set off with commas: "The book that you're looking for is on the sofa." Nonrestrictive clauses are parenthetical and do need commas: "The book, which I found interesting, is on the sofa."
- Using only one comma where a set is needed.
  Wrong: "She is driving from Washington, D.C. to Baltimore." A second comma should come after *D.C.*
  Wrong: "The player, 42 plans to retire." Commas should come both before and after the parenthetical *42*.
- Using a comma before *and* in a series. Most grammarians (and book publishers) prefer this comma, known as the *serial* comma, but journalistic style traditionally has shunned it as unnecessary. The preferred way journalistically: "They own sheep, cows and goats."

Period usage. A rule to live by: Use fewer commas and more periods. Someone wise once said, "Write as if you get paid by the period." Use a period to end a sentence. Use a period, not a comma, between two independent clauses not connected by a conjunction such as *and*.

Wrong: "The mayor has been working in favor of the bill's passage, city council members have not." Put a period after *passage*.

Apostrophe problems. The most common use of the apostrophe is to denote a possessive, but writers often confuse where the apostrophe should be placed. Here are some basic rules:

- For a singular or plural noun that does not end in *s*, simply add an apostrophe and an *s*: "the president's speech," "the women's room."
- For a plural noun ending in *s*, simply add an apostrophe: "the three judges' ruling."
- For singular nouns ending in *s* or for other unusual variations, consult your news organization style guide. Some prefer only the apostrophe; others prescribe the apostrophe and *s*. Apostrophe usage can get very esoteric (for example, in single common nouns that end in an *s* but are followed by words that begin with *s*), so you should always follow the editor's default creed: When you have any doubt at all, look it up.

Punctuating quotations. I see several areas where writers seem prone to confusion:

- Uncertainty over placing quotations marks. Several rules apply.

  First, use quotation marks when, and only when, you know for certain that the material within them is directly quoted, that is, when it is exactly what the speaker said.

  Second, quotation marks always go *outside* commas and periods.

  Wrong: She enjoyed watching "American Idol". Make it: "American Idol."

  Wrong: She called the movie "a genuine classic", but her companion disliked it.

  Right: "We're first going to play 'The Star-Spangled Banner,' " the director said.

  Third, do not use quotation marks at the end of a paragraph if the direct quote continues into the next paragraph. Do use them at the beginning of every quoted paragraph.

  Right: The speaker said, "We will do everything necessary to accomplish our goal.

  "We will contact every legislator and every senator. We will write the White House. We will go to court.

  "We will march on Washington. We will be heard at the ballot box. We will not be denied."

- Confusion over use of commas and periods surrounding attribution. To recapitulate briefly: Use commas between the end of a quote and its attribution. Use commas after the attribution if the quoted sentence continues. Use periods after the attribution if the quoted sentence has ended. Examples:

  Wrong: "The home team is winning." he reported.

  Right: "The home team is winning," he reported.

  Wrong: "The meeting will be held next Thursday," she said. "unless you hear otherwise."

  Right: "The meeting will be held next Thursday," she said, "unless you hear otherwise."

Style

Journalists use the word "style" in two ways. Broadly, it refers to the literary qualities of writing, as when we speak of the spare, potent style of Hemingway. More narrowly, style designates journalists' policies governing recurring matters of abbreviation, capitalization, and usage that formal grammar may not cover.

Newspapers, magazines, wire services, websites, and others adopt style rules for several reasons. Style contributes to consistency, credibility, and clarity. It provides standard guidance for the thousands of tiny issues that arise daily. It settles endless questions that linger over such issues as whether to abbreviate the word "Street" in addresses or whether to use numerals or words to indicate someone's age.

But keep in mind that, while enforcing style is an important beginning point for the editor, it should never become an obsession or an ending point. I have known some editors so compulsive about style trivia that they get consumed by questions such as whether "coroner" is an occupational title (and therefore not capitalized before a name) or a formal position (and therefore capitalized).

Rather than memorizing a particular stylebook that might or might not be used on the job, it is preferable to learn to *think* about each potential style issue and to enforce whatever policies hold sway within an organization. What matters is not whether one capitalizes the word *president* but whether one recognizes the editor's duty to understand and enforce some reasonable style.

Few newsrooms would suffer (and I suspect readers would gain) if editors spent just a bit less time mulling over matters like whether "5-foot-7" should have hyphens and more time editing for content, logic, and clarity.

Nonetheless, many editors swear by style proficiency, so the incoming editor should probably be familiar with at least the most common rulings from that most-used reference, the *Associated Press Stylebook*. Among the entries worth remembering are those for abbreviations, addresses, ages, numerals, and titles.

Usage

Here is a small quiz. Read the following statements (adapted from an exercise I first encountered from the late Prof. William L. Rivers), and then answer the questions that accompany them. Give one *specific* answer for each question, reflecting as best you can what image comes to your mind.

1   "Mayor Smith won re-election by an overwhelming majority." What percentage of the vote did the mayor receive?
2   "She comes from a well-to-do family." What is the family's annual income?
3   "I watch an average amount of television each week." How many hours do you watch every week?

When I pose these questions to my students, they often express surprise at the extraordinary range of answers. For Question 1, answers have defined "overwhelming majority" as everything from 50 percent to 90 percent. For Question 2, estimates of the family's annual income range from $30,000 to $1,000,000. For Question 3, average television watching is listed as anywhere from 2 to 40 hours a week.

Students quickly grasp the point: If a group of relatively similar students does not have common understanding of such everyday terms as "overwhelming," "well-to-do," and "average," then imagine how much more difficult communication becomes when journalists present far more subtle material to a heterogeneous mass audience.

For that reason, questions of *usage* have far more riding on them than one might at first think. *Usage* refers to how we use words. As journalists, our object is to move a message from sender to receiver, maintaining the meaning as precisely intact as is humanly possible. We falter in the mission with every example of vague, fuzzy, distorted, imprecise, ambiguous usage.

Writers know what they intend, and this knowledge taints their ability to read their own copy dispassionately. Their intentions ride piggyback on their words, so the writing may not be sharp. It falls to editors, then, to guard against wording problems that may confuse or confound readers.

In journalism, writers often serve as, in effect, translators. They take technical language used by sources in government, law, medicine, sports, business, the arts, and elsewhere, and "translate" it into clear prose understandable by a mass audience of nonspecialists. This must be done carefully, so as not to distort the meaning. The editor's job is to backstop the writer, angling both for pristine prose and for maximum precision. You take the wordiness, insider terms, and circumlocutions and turn them into plain English. Then publish the English.

Caution: In all these matters, editors should tread cautiously, for hasty or sloppy editing too often introduces errors. Various studies have found that from 10 to 25 percent of errors in the news media are introduced by editors. To reduce the chance of errors, good editors approach copy with firm knowledge of the rules, regulations, and policies. But they need other qualities as well: an "ear" for good writing, a sensitivity to individual style, and a judicial carefulness.

Here are several categories where editors can often help.

Wordiness. Fat writing abounds. The best editors become sure-footed wordsmiths, constantly sharpening and focusing. Common symptoms of word flab include the following:

- Excessive prepositional phrases. "The friends were on a boat in the middle of the lake for four hours on Friday." Instead, try replacing the phrases with single adjectives, adverbs, nouns, and verbs: "The friends spent four hours Friday sailing on the lake."
  Often an adverbial phrase can be turned into a one-word adverb: "The soldiers fought with great courage" becomes "The soldiers fought bravely." Likewise with adjective phrases: "The golfer with the suntan" becomes "The suntanned golfer."
- Lame "of" phrases. "All of a sudden" becomes "suddenly." "She is in favor of endorsing the mayor" becomes "She favors endorsing the mayor." Other examples where the "of" can be pruned: a number of

(several), in spite of (despite), in process of buying (buying), each of the women (each woman).

- Clauses that can reduce to phrases or even words. "We voted at the meeting that was held yesterday" becomes "We voted at yesterday's meeting."
- Clauses and phrases that can come out entirely. "He is a man who loves peanuts" becomes "He loves peanuts."
- -ion words. "Take action" becomes "act." "Make a decision" becomes "decide." "Reach a conclusion" becomes "conclude."
- Weak verb constructions. Whenever it takes several words to form a verb, consider whether one word will do. "Took the witness stand to testify" becomes "testified." "Held a press conference to announce the firing of her deputy" becomes "fired her deputy." "Arrived at a verdict" becomes "convicted" or "acquitted." "Walked unsteadily because of the injury" becomes "limped."
- Tag-along words. These words can trail behind a phrase or sentence, adding nothing. "Here are the latest traffic conditions" becomes "Here's a look at traffic." "Let's plan ahead" becomes "Let's plan." "Canned food items" becomes "canned food." "To fight low enrollment problems" becomes "to fight low enrollment."

Redundancies. A subcategory of wordiness, in which the thought is repeated. Common examples include "dead body," "10 a.m. in the morning," "12 noon," "lift up," "free gift," "male prostate," "female vagina," "past experience," "between the two of us," and "set a new record." Perhaps less obvious is "personal habit." And what about "the working press"?

Abbreviations and acronyms. Using abbreviations and acronyms may suggest an intimate acquaintance with the elite. But, to consumers, they can be baffling. Who outside of Washington would recognize such constructions as "FERC" (the Federal Energy Regulatory Commission) or "NIOSH" (the National Institute for Occupational Safety and Health)? One reporter's copy referred to the purchase of MICUs by local government. Careful deciphering revealed that "mobile intensive care units" were, in fact, special ambulances. Editors should root out abbreviations that too many people will not recognize.

A simple test can help here: If most people use the abbreviation in routine speech ("FBI," for example), then editors should accept it. Otherwise, strike the abbreviation, and use a generic term like *agency, organization*, or *commission*.

Jargon. Experts in many fields, including science, medicine, law, business, technology, and journalism, often depend on highly specialized language. Journalists, particularly beat reporters, often spend so much time around these groups that they adopt the groups' vernacular and forget the rest of us do not speak it fluently. Sometimes, jargon is merely annoying ("Police apprehended the perpetrator"). Too frequently, however, it poses a barrier to communication. When economists refer to "leading economic indicators," for example, they do not mean indicators that are "important" but those that are "early," providing advance clues about economic direction. Jargon should be avoided where possible. When it must be published, it should be explained.

Euphemisms and doublespeak. Sometimes confusion or obfuscation seems the very goal of jargony expressions. English professor William Lutz wrote about various ways companies try to deflect the jagged impact of firings and layoffs, by calling them *workforce adjustments* or *census reductions* or by using verbs such as *dehired, surplussed* or *rightsized.*[5] For years the National Council of Teachers of English has given an annual Doublespeak Award for "a glaring example of deceptive language by a public spokesperson." Among the winners: labeling body bags for dead soldiers as *transfer tubes*; referring to a bombing mission as *visiting a site*; and describing torture as *the excesses of human nature that humanity suffers.*[6]

Signing off: One final read

Whew. Editing can seem grueling. So many items to consider, so many potential pitfalls. Sometimes you tire out and simply want to get rid of the copy as soon as you can.

Be careful!

In editing as in horseracing and brain surgery, finishing strong is essential. A careless slip at the end can ruin hours of work. Practice maintaining maximum concentration until this final stage: the last read, the point at which you sign off on copy as certified for publication.

Carefully read the copy one more time. Especially scout for problems or careless errors that have been added during editing. At this point, you are editing not only the writer's work but your own additions as well. Also be on guard for a scarily common occurrence. Amazingly, you will routinely find that your final trip through a story unearths something you had overlooked all along. You had read a sentence a dozen times without noticing a blatant comma error that had been there from the start.

So take a break if you can, then approach the copy with one last revitalized examination. You will be surprised how often you make one last game-saving catch.

Helping writers with style and form

In their ongoing relationships as well as their work on individual pieces of copy, editors can serve writers immeasurably by helping them evaluate and improve the underlying structure of their work. Over time, editors perform a teaching function that, when successful, helps writers grow, improves copy, and saves future editing time.

Here are some ways editors can help with various writing challenges.

Helping with leads

- Answer the question, "Who cares?" A good lead makes a reader stop and care. It should provoke some kind of emotion: curiosity, anger, amusement, sadness, sympathy. Help the writer identify the element in the story that reflects the main point in the most stimulating way, and you have probably found your lead.
- Let the writer tell the story to you or someone else. The point the writer seizes on in talking about a story may be best for the lead.
- Have the writer read the lead aloud. Listening to one's own writing provides insights that merely reading it silently will not supply.
- Ask the writer to supply a budget line or web blurb for the article. Most editors compile a daily budget listing each available story and a one-or two-sentence description of it. Having writers produce these descriptions forces them to distill their stories to the essence—and often helps bring the leads into focus.
- Prod writers to limit their leads to one thought, expressed directly. A common problem is that writers get so excited by all their good material that they want to tell everything first, to cram all the good stuff into the first two sentences. That seldom engages the busy, distracted reader. Do not let writers settle for roundup leads. Force them to focus.

Helping with clarity

- Make certain the subject and verb of a sentence express the main point the writer wishes to make. Do not bury key thoughts in dependent clauses and phrases.
- Reduce the number of words and ideas in a sentence. Slow the pace of information, and it becomes easier to process.
- Avoid long separation between the main subject and verb in a sentence. The more words between them, the harder it is for the reader to hold the thought.
- Eliminate jargon and clichés. They confuse.
- Supply examples or illustrative quotes at the key points of the article.
- Avoid words that do not convey direct meanings. Words such as "mother," "love," "car," "prison" create strong visual images for readers. Words like "program," "proposal," "legislation," "reform" create fuzzy mental pictures and require still more words to make good sense. Good writing specifies.

Helping pep up flat writing

- Use a strong quote within the first three paragraphs. Quotes enliven copy by introducing human beings and new voices. But insist on a strong quote, one that adds fact, feeling, or insight. Rule of thumb: Use good quotes at dramatic high points.
- Use anecdotes, examples, and illustrations. Concrete detail does more to make writing sparkle than any other single thing. Many good sentences begin with the words "for example."
- Use action verbs and the active voice and reduce reliance on the verb "to be."
- Use colorful nouns rather than flowery adjectives and adverbs.
- Maintain a strong fact-per-paragraph ratio, with few sentences containing no new specifics.
- Write with drama in mind, selecting imagery and details that help readers feel why an article is special.
- Recommend re-reporting. Often, a writing problem isn't really a writing problem at all. It is a reporting problem. If the writer does not have sufficient quotes, details, and facts, then it is time to stop writing and do more reporting.
- Encourage revision, as often as is necessary. Revision seems anathema to many students and professionals, who chorus almost universally, "There isn't time." Occasionally time does run out, but in fact most journalism is not written hard on deadline and most writers can find time for reworking. Editors should routinely ask writers, "Does it really make sense to publish your first drafts for all the world to see?" Good writing is, almost always, rewriting. As John Kenneth Galbraith once said, "There are days when the result is so bad that no fewer than five revisions are required. In contrast, when I'm greatly inspired, only four revisions are needed."[7]

Preparing yourself to help

As we have discussed so often along the way, facility with language is in part natural and in part developed through practice. In their evolving roles as wordsmiths, editors can take several steps to develop their fluency.

Read hungrily. Reading helps develop the ear for good writing . . . and for bad writing. The editor who learns to "hear" the copy will occasionally get a timely nudge from the subconscious that something is out of whack. Similar nudges also clue editors to cases where copy should go untouched even when it appears to violate some rules.

Know yourself. As an editor, make a mental checklist of your own trouble areas, of the structural flaws you most often overlook. Then compensate by spending more effort in areas where you seem weakest.

Develop routines. Some items should be checked every time they occur: subject–verb agreements, pronoun references, use of math. Even in the writing of professionals, you will spot enough such errors to pay for the time spent.

Forget the third grade, or at least that part of it where teachers encouraged you to read rapidly, comprehending entire lines and thoughts at once. That facility betrays you in editing. It leads your eyes to see, not what is actually in front of them, but what they expect. For example, the quick reader tends to overlook the error in the phrase *the Pananamian Canal,* because the error does not prevent easy comprehension of the overall meaning. In structural editing, reading slowly is more productive than reading rapidly, but you probably will find that doing so takes conscious effort.

Conduct an editor's final fact check. Many writers make their last step a methodical examination of every fact and assertion for accuracy, evidence, and sourcing. Editors can take a similar step, by reviewing each change they have made. Modern computer programs, which often highlight the differences between the writer's and editor's versions of copy, can make this easier.

Read backward. When all else is done, many editors read copy backward, from the last word through to the first. This process, which seems agonizingly tedious the first time you try it, works because it breaks down the logical connections. Instead of reading for sense (and therefore taking in entire phrases and ideas at a time), you force yourself to read item by item. Consequently, you see small errors you might otherwise read past.

Better editing by computer

For a couple of generations now, writers have benefited from using word processors and computers. Their advantages are well known. Computers let you write fast, revise easily, and correct painlessly. They reduce one of the largest psychological barriers to relaxing as a writer: the need for immediate perfection. In the old days of writing by hand or using a manual typewriter, the result looked so permanent and was so hard to change that writers labored over every not-quite-exact word and phrase. The ease of composing fast and perfecting later has revolutionized writing.

Editors, too, gain something from this revolution. On-screen editing is quicker, neater, and easier to undo than on-paper markings. A growing number of editors also apply the power of computing in a variety of innovative ways. They include:

- *Increasing type size* on the screen, which can make it easier to concentrate on individual words and phrases and to spot careless errors

- *Formatting copy into narrow columns* rather than viewing the full width of the computer screen, another way of focusing the eye on smaller segments of type
- *Using split screen effects*, for example to display both the original copy and the edited copy side by side for comparison
- *Using the editing-history functions* to monitor how a succession of writers and editors modifies copy
- *Using word processing tools* such as spelling and grammar checkers, search-and-replace functions, and keys dedicated to repeated tasks (for instance, headline formats or common style changes)
- *Strategically placing the cursor* to help keep the editor's eye and brain coordinated on the same spot in copy. Some editors move the cursor from left to right and line by line, running it over each word. Others key it down the left side line by line rather than word by word. Still others program the cursor to jump from paragraph to paragraph. Many others I have encountered can't even remember how their cursor moves. Think about your own editing: How can you use the cursor to help focus on copy and prevent your thoughts from drifting to other things?
- *And of course using the vast research powers of the web*, to check everything from spelling and geography to full-text public records or news archives.

In these and many other ways, editors build new tools to make their own jobs easier and the copy they handle better.

Conclusion

Call this the sine qua non of journalism. Working with writers and other colleagues, the good editor must produce accurate, clear, interesting copy, suitable to its purpose, audience, and format, under deadline.

What needs to be stressed, however, is that doctoring copy one item at a time, while an essential skill, is only a beginning. Both content itself and the smooth working of the newsroom are also directly affected by actions editors take both in preparation for receiving copy and after they have processed it. Now we will turn to those other duties: coaching writers, coordinating coverage, overseeing presentation, and dealing with the variety of legal, ethical, and policy issues that arise in any newsroom.

Sidebar 7: 10 survival tips for the time-deprived

When I was an editor at *USA Today*, the sports department set up a small electric train that encircled the copydesk. As deadline approached late each evening, someone revved up the train and it went flying around the track a few times, sending out the familiar toot-toot that signaled the final drive toward deadline and the urgency of "railroading" the copy.

To railroad copy means to process it as fast as possible while maintaining quality control and meeting standards. Newsrooms should try to avoid situations where editors have to rush, but every editor needs to become adept at the survival art of copyediting under pressure. For example, as news websites try to post copy as soon as possible, they sometimes resort to various "fly-by" editing systems: having writers or web producers take turns editing each other's copy; asking the nearest editor or colleague to quickly scan copy before posting; putting unedited or lightly edited copy on the web, and then reading it more carefully and making instant corrections.

It should be stressed that none of these systems or situations ever excuses errors, misjudgments, or hasty publication of unready copy. A news organization's credibility hinges on its reliability, and a good editor should refrain from moving any copy that could embarrass or blemish the organization.

Still, good editors need to know how to move fast. Here are 10 tips for doing your best when time is limited:

1   *Ensure accuracy.* Nothing outranks accuracy, from the largest editorial conclusions to the spelling of a local street name. Just as the standard for doctors is "first do no harm," then the corresponding imperative for editors is "first get everything right."
2   *Get the meaning into the lead.* What's the most important step after ensuring accuracy? Make certain the lead conveys the *meaning.* Answer the questions, So what? Who cares? Who wins? Who loses? If a story is fully accurate and quickly communicates its most important message, it will succeed at a threshold level.
3   *Think subject–verb–twist.* Most news stories report that someone did something newsworthy or something happened that made news. The strongest way to drive home these points in a lead is to put the story's *main doer* as the grammatical subject of the lead, its *main action* as the lead's primary verb, and its *main twist,* whatever makes it most unusual or compelling, as the rest of the lead.
4   *Use powerful words.* One tested way to lure readers is to see that the lead has an action verb and at least one other interesting, unusual, engaging word. Where possible and appropriate, you want to charge up the language of the lead, with colorful, powerful, precise nouns and verbs that crackle and sizzle and tickle. The words need not be precious, fancy, or sesquipedalian, just sharp, original, clear, and energetic.

5   *Have a punch line in the first three or four paragraphs.* A punch line is a catchy kicker to a little anecdote or quote, sometimes a small story within the story that helps induce readership. Often it follows a small scene that sets the tone or shows the key point.

6   *Shorten sentences.* Aim for one main idea per sentence and for an average length of no more than 25 words.

7   *Streamline the first three or four paragraphs.* Try to streamline every paragraph. But under time constraints, at least make the first few paragraphs sparklingly clear. Reduce the number of clauses and prepositional phrases. Clear out dense language, redundancies, and clutter. If you can snare readers for several paragraphs, you hugely multiply the odds they will keep reading.

8   *Enliven the verbs.* Look at every verb in the copy, asking, Can this be stronger or spicier? A caution: Avoid sensationalism and exaggeration. You want the most interesting verb possible—as long as it is in keeping with the tone and context. You can often replace to-be verbs, an unnecessary passive voice, and weak constructions such as "made a decision" or "came to a conclusion."

9   *Spotlight something memorable.* Whether it is in the copy itself (the lead, a great anecdote, the ending) or in the way it is presented (its headline, blurb, art, audio clip, or slide show), find some memorable element and make certain readers will see and appreciate it.

10 *Apply one last trade secret.* This old editor's trick almost always helps. Glance paragraph by paragraph to see that beginnings are varied. If you see too many consecutive paragraphs beginning with *The* or the same speaker's name, then introduce variety. Paragraphs can start with articles, nouns, and pronouns but also with participles, phrases, clauses, quotes, and transitions. Varying paragraph structure can dramatically improve flow.

Vignettes

Grammar and punctuation can generate surprising passion.

"The semicolon is an ugly bastard, and thus I tend to avoid it," declares veteran copyeditor Bill Walsh in his excellent and amusing style guide, *Lapsing into a Comma*.

Walsh also fulminates over what he calls the "abomination" of spelling *email*, a shortening of electronic mail, without a hyphen. "No initial-based term in the history of the English language has ever evolved to form a solid word," he writes. "I find it hard to fathom how anyone ever *thought* of writing *email*."[8]

Such spirit doesn't just rear up within editors. President Franklin D. Roosevelt had what biographer Jonathan Alter called an "obsession with punctuation." He hated commas so much that, when an aide inadvertently inserted some into a speech draft, FDR was driven "to gently upbraid her for 'wasting the taxpayers' commas.' "[9]

8 Coaching writers

Once when my son Jeff was young, I was absorbed in watching television when he came into the room and wanted to perform a magic trick. I watched indulgently but kept one eye on the TV. He asked me to pick two cards, look at them, and return them. Then he tossed the entire deck into the air, reached out, and grabbed two cards—the exact two I had chosen. "Wow!" I exclaimed, genuinely astonished, forgetting the TV. Jeff just grinned and strutted out of the room, murmuring to himself, "That one made Dad say wow."

The writer's goal is to capture the attention of busy, preoccupied readers and make them say wow. The editor's job is to help.

In this chapter, we expand the outlook from dealing with a specific piece of copy to dealing with writers over time. We look at tools and techniques for guiding reporters on assignments large and small. When successful, they will help produce not just better stories in the short run but also better writers and reporters in the long range. At its best, good coaching has the profound cumulative value of increasingly saving time, raising morale, leading reporters to higher levels, and, best of all, upgrading content.

As we discussed earlier, good editors coach writers throughout an assignment, beginning at the earliest points to help overcome problems and find solutions. The goal is to have copy arrive at the editor's desk in the best possible shape. Typically, as Donald Murray and others described it, coaching occurs during several decisive points before the copy is turned over to the editor, including at the idea, reporting, organizing, drafting, and revision stages. Later, coaching takes place after publication as well, to review the work and make any needed adjustments for future success.

In all these coaching conversations, here is what the editor offers: *expectations* and *expertise*.

These can be seen as intangible and tangible services, equally useful. Intangibly, the editor seeks to motivate the writer by raising expectations, confidence, and determination and by nourishing a relationship where the writer sees the editor as a helpful teammate in a positive collaboration. Tangibly, the editor offers knowledge, advice, and technical and professional assistance.

The coach's method. Individual styles vary, but the most commonly recommended coaching method is to hold, at each key step in the writing process, a short, focused conversation with the writer. Conversations can last as long as time is available, but in busy newsrooms they typically can be conducted in one- or two-minute bursts.

Each conversation has the following goals:

1   To help the writer identify and concentrate on the most important single problem at the current stage.
2   To help set the writer on the road to solving the problem now so the editor doesn't have to solve it later.

The coach's model. Each conversation often follows what has been called the Jeopardy! rule, in homage to the long-running television quiz show. Like Jeopardy! contestants, coaches phrase their remarks in the form of questions. Another convention is for editors to leave their own desks and go onto the writer's turf, where conversations may be more comfortable.

The editor's questions can be casual ("How's it going?") or specific ("What are you thinking of leading with?"), depending on the editor's experience and relationship with the writer in question.

In most cases, the editor should open the conversation, then listen carefully to the writer, help locate the one or two key issues at this stage, and efficiently move the writer toward focusing on their solutions. No system works every time, of course, but it should be obvious that good-faith efforts to solve problems along the way almost always prove preferable to trying to solve them after the writing is completed. My colleague, the late editor Foster Davis, once put it this way: "It's a lot easier to rearrange ideas in someone's head early than to rearrange paragraphs in a story later."

The coach's manner. Coaches should rarely dominate or intimidate reporters, but they should also avoid the equally risky error of ignoring them. Remember: The editor's job is to help. So the editor should be a collegial presence at each step from idea through reporting, focusing, writing, revising, and editing.

Coaches should also remember that writers are human beings and fellow professionals. They deserve respect. They should not be patronized or treated like children. Good coaching—which is to say, good editing—works best not as top-down domineering by some God-like omniscient figure, but as constructive interaction between professional colleagues, each with a vital but different role in the creative enterprise.

Like a good teacher, the coach should both challenge and encourage, yielding to the writer when possible but holding firm when necessary.

Or a writer might think of the difference between being interrogated by a prosecutor and a defense attorney. Both will ask you the same tough questions, but you take comfort in knowing that one of them has your best interests directly at heart. No matter how much pushing and prodding, gentle or otherwise, a coach delivers, writers should always know this as a certainty: The editor is on their side in seeking the best possible work.

The starting point: Coaching for great ideas

Great stories start with great ideas. Every editor should internalize this basic lesson: *Your single biggest point of influence on any story comes at the idea stage.*

Suppose, for instance, that you supervise an education reporter, who stops by your desk one day to announce she is heading to a school board meeting. What's on the agenda, you ask. Approving raises for substitute teachers, she replies. Okay, you say. Give me a blurb for the web and 500 words for tomorrow's paper.

Or, suppose you reply in a different way. Suppose you ask, What else is going on besides the meeting? Well, the reporter answers, I got a tip that the local high school didn't order enough books for its top math classes this semester. So students are having to double up, and they're falling way behind, with the big achievement tests coming up soon.

Which idea has more potential? Obviously it is the textbook shortage. But if you had not prodded the reporter, you would have ended up with a pedestrian meeting story.

A writer who begins working on a great idea has a high probability of producing a great story. But a writer who sets out with a mediocre idea will need unusual luck or good fortune to produce anything other than mediocrity. In many if not most cases, the idea stage sets a kind of quality ceiling for what follows.

Editors, therefore, should give special attention to helping writers embark on the best possible assignments. It is vital to remember, of course, that the assignment is only a starting point. You cannot lock yourself in, inflexibly, at the idea stage. Almost all assignments change as the writer digs into the reporting. It is a mistake to overcommit to one specific version of an idea too early. The point, instead, is to send the writer off with the best possible story in mind, and then adjust as necessary during the course of reporting and writing.

Here are some tips for building better ideas:

- Encourage reporters to offer several ideas at a time, not just one.
- Don't merely acquiesce when a reporter floats the first idea; ask probing questions and make sure reporters know they need to convince you the idea has high potential.

- Take time each day to have "creative conversations" in which you and a writer brainstorm for the best possible ideas to pursue.
- Involve as many people as possible in idea discussions; a colleague will often know someone or some fact that contributes importantly to an idea.
- Involve sources; make sure reporters are pumping sources every day for good tips.
- Involve readers; take their phone calls; interact with them online; make it easy for them to notify you when something interesting happens.

Too often, under pressure of time, a reporter will opt to pursue the first story idea that meets the minimum requirements, such as covering a meeting. Your goal as an editor is to set higher expectations and engage in sufficient give-and-take so the writer doesn't settle for something so ordinary. Your ambition should be higher: *Settling on the best possible idea that can be developed given the available time and resources.*

Coaching during reporting and writing

Once a writer launches into the reporting, the editor's job diminishes but doesn't vanish. Editors should not take over the assignment or hover too much over a reporter's shoulders. But they still play a key role.

The biggest mistake, at this point, is to lose touch with the writer from the assignment stage until the writer turns in copy. Not only does the editor lose essential information about the progress of the assignment and any unexpected problems that may be arising, but the editor also loses crucial chances to help ensure that the final copy is in the best possible shape.

Again, the central principle at work here is as follows: *The earlier you confront problems, seek solutions, and make decisions, the more time you save and the more impact you have.*

No matter how brilliant they may be, editors cannot rehabilitate bad ideas or cover for poor reporting at the final editing stage. There isn't enough time. They can fix typos and make relatively small adjustments, but the closer they get to deadline, the less time and flexibility they have. Like cement, a story hardens as time passes, making last-minute changes less and less practical.

So editors need to optimize their efforts during the key early stages. They can make specific contributions at three points: during the reporting, before the writing, and after the first draft.

Coaching during the reporting phase. The editor should not take over the assignment, overly invade the writer's space, or browbeat the writer to complete the work as the editor would have done it in her or his reporting heyday.

Instead, the chief contributions here are to be available as a sounding board, as a source of advice, and as a lookout for unanticipated shifts of story direction. In the first two cases, editors are mostly helping the reporter. But in the final one, gaining early warning of changes, editors can learn all-important early information to make their own jobs easier.

For example, suppose a reporter sets off on the idea we mentioned earlier: a textbook shortage at the local high school. Perhaps, by the kind of coincidence that seems routine in news coverage, the needed textbooks arrive that very day. The entire tone of the story will change. Instead of a critical look at an ongoing failure by the local school system, the writer will probably focus on something much more positive: the relief and re-energization students now feel as they prepare for their achievement tests.

Now many reporters would notify their editors immediately when a story takes such a turn. But some will delay, for one reason or another. Editors should do their best to insist that reporters keep in close touch. But editors should also make it their own jobs to consult with writers periodically during the reporting phase, just in case there are late developments. Armed with the new focus, the editor can recalibrate how to pitch and play the story, both online and elsewhere.

Coaching, then, often has selfish value for the editor. But the reporter also can benefit during this stage.

First, the reporter needs to know the editor is available. Many reporters are reluctant to seek help during reporting because it seems to suggest they are failing at their duties. Often they will simply stay out of the editor's way and hope that fate or good luck rescues them. Far better is a relationship where the writer feels free to confide in the editor and to discuss problems early, while there is time to work together to solve them.

Second, the reporter also benefits from the simple principle that two heads are better than one. The editor, with a different perspective and set of experiences, may well be able to offer advice about sources, documents, or reporting methods.

In both these ways, the editor serves as a *resource* during the entire reporting phase. Your top goals include:

- Helping ensure that the reporter has comprehensively and resourcefully located the best possible sources, evidence, quotes, examples, and details
- Motivating the writer to go beyond the obvious, to dig deeper toward material that genuinely surprises and engages the reader
- Serving as a backup to keep the writer from overlooking obvious or less-than-obvious resources, or from any failings of completeness, fairness, and balance.

At minimum, the editor should make a point to hold at least one coaching conversation, about midway through reporting, using the techniques we have discussed. Approach the writer, ask how things are going, move the focus to the most important problem at the moment, and set the writer along the road to resolving it.

Coaching during the pre-writing phase. Left alone, many writers shoot too quickly from reporting to writing. Time pressures tempt them to skip or skimp on organization. Yet taking just a few minutes to focus and plan a story can make the difference between a coherent narrative that hooks and holds readers, and a mishmash of miscellany that fails to engage.

Almost always, focus works best when done with a responsive colleague, preferably an editor. In two-way give and take, an editor offers the writer something impossible to get alone: fresh perspective.

So the coaching conversation can begin with a simple editor's inquiry, maybe something such as, "How are you thinking of approaching this story?" As the writer responds, the editor listens to make sure there is a *clear theme* and a solid idea for a *lead* that will develop the theme.

This is a tender stage for the writer, who presumably has taken a good idea and reported it thoroughly and now has high hopes, but the usual insecurities, about producing a story that lives up to its potential. Editors should be encouraging and constructive. If the writer seems awash in material, then the editor should try gentle guidance toward one main point. Good questions at this stage include:

- What should the main point be?
- What will people remember about this story a month from now?
- What do you think the story is really about?
- If you could tell someone just one thing about this story, what would you say?

If the writer lacks confidence in an approach, then the goal becomes settling on the most appropriate form and formats. Relevant questions might be:

- Would a hard lead, news-plus lead, or narrative lead be more effective?
- What if you tried writing several leads to see which one seemed best?
- What would make a good ending?
- How do you see moving from the lead to the ending? Are there three or four key points to make along the way?

This stage also provides a good opportunity to reinforce several administrative matters, including:

- How long should the story be?

- Should there be multiple versions for online and print?
- Do we have the needed auxiliary materials such as photos, graphics, audio, or video for various media platforms?
- Are we on schedule to meet deadlines?

If you have time, this phase merits an extended session with the writer. But under deadline, your minimum goal is a brief coaching conversation that helps the writer settle on a main theme and a basic approach to carrying it out.

Coaching after the draft. You will contend again with tender feelings at this stage. Few aspects of writing generate more terror than the necessity of turning over fresh copy to the editor's glare of judgment. Even hardened veterans still quake at this scary prospect.

Still, the editor owes the writer (and the news organization and ultimately the reader) a candid, straightforward, professional response. So remember this: *How you respond can be even more important than what you say.*

Have you ever noticed how, in a friendship or a romantic relationship, someone can blow up over something that seems very small? Or, by contrast, some good friends or lovers can deliver an especially critical judgment in a way that seems positive and non-offensive?

The key, of course, is sensitivity. Make your point, but do so with respect and diplomacy. Avoid the stern posture of a judge or the impatient irritation of a parent. Try to come across in the balanced and even tones of a colleague genuinely trying to help.

Remember, crucially, that a draft is a *draft*. It is not yet finished work. The worst two mistakes at this stage are (1) overreacting to small glitches that the writer can easily correct in the final version and (2) overstating concerns in a way that conveys lack of confidence in the writer's ability to fix them.

Remember, also, that the writer may well see the same flaws that the editor sees. One of the most bedeviling truths in the business is that writers often clearly see the problems but, after their very best efforts, can't make the actual copy match the idealized vision. That point, of course, is exactly where the editor should come in, because the editor's job, as we know, is to help. Useful steps at this point include:

- Listen to the writer first. Ask what the writer likes most and least about the draft.
- Read it through quickly but as carefully as possible.
- Praise where possible.
- Decide on one or two key points of emphasis, based on their importance. Often they will involve the organizational framework, the lead, or something unclear or uncertain about the first few paragraphs. Phrase your comments honestly but courteously, often as inquiries.

For example, avoid saying something unproductive like, "This lead doesn't work." Instead, try, "The lead seems a little confusing to me. What if you moved down the stuff about the truck pulling up with a load of new textbooks and focused on the reaction of the kids in the classroom?"

Where possible, take time to read the copy carefully and open an extended dialogue with the writer. But, as always during coaching, at least meet the minimum requirement at this stage: Identify the one or two sections of the story that can be most improved by revision and help the writer see ways of making them better.

Coaching the end game

Soon the final copy arrives, and it is perfect.

Or perhaps not. The objective here isn't to raise unreasonable and unattainable expectations. No matter what the editor does, few pieces of copy will be problem-free. But here is the point to stress: *If you have followed the coaching model, the copy will almost certainly arrive in better form than if you have not.*

Recall what you and the writer have done together:

- Brainstormed toward the best possible idea, rather than the first available one
- Worked as a team toward thorough, resourceful reporting
- Collaborated to resolve key issues of focus and approach
- Identified priorities for revision and worked on them.

Here, then, is what you should have: a well-reported, well-organized, polished story with surprising and interesting material about a compelling topic. To whatever extent you have succeeded, the final editing will go faster and the final version will be better. At this point, you edit carefully for content and structure, a process that should take less time because of the coaching you have already done.

Where possible, it is wise to edit with the writer sitting alongside you. This maximizes teamwork and communication. You can pose questions to the writer and discuss, rather than impose, needed changes. The writer in turn can question you and alert you to any problems that editing may introduce. You can also make teaching points or, if there is time, explain the thinking behind your editing. Over time, these sessions should serve as tutorials that help writers grow. Sometimes side-by-side editing can be exasperating, especially with writers who want to resist every single point. But generally the benefits for accuracy and collaboration outweigh the downside, and you can gently explain that there isn't time to debate everything.

Overall, good coaching is, in almost every way, a win–win enterprise.

Once the editor has completed final processing and the story has been published, broadcast, or posted, one more coaching moment remains. Editors and writers should have a debriefing conversation *after publication*.

Often, this conversation can take place, circular style, at the beginning of the next assignment, when you embark on a new round of coaching. Try not to neglect the final stage, however. You don't want a writer to go away wounded, or issues to lie festering. Now is the time to make points you need to convey to the writer and to listen to what the writer needs to tell you.

So the minimal goal here is straightforward:

- Let the writer talk first, and then make your own points.
- Discuss the last assignment, what went well, and what disappointed.
- Absorb any complaints the writer might have about others, for example, the headline writer or the web producer or anyone else who might have, in the writer's view, hurt or helped.
- Listen for any lingering issues that need attention, such as the writer's fatigue or failure to hear your message.
- Note any suggestions about what should be different next time and aim for improvement.

Final observations about coaching

Coaching should come across as authentic. You can't fake it, and you shouldn't try to imitate someone else's style. Genuineness, honesty, and good will win the appreciation of almost all writers if they are presented in a mode of helpfulness.

Here are a few final points that characterize good coaching:

- *Look for things to praise.* Few writers ever feel they get enough of it.
- *Talk less and listen more.* This takes discipline. Practice it.
- *Rehearse your vocabulary and tone of voice.* Especially on deadline or under stress, editors often lapse into drill-sergeant mode. Don't forget how personally everyone takes comments from a supervisor, so strive for a suitable tone.
- *When criticizing, offer alternatives.* Be reasonably specific but make your points as questions or suggestions. "What would you think about this?" is usually better than "Here's what I want you to do."
- *Negotiate, don't order.* Let writers defend themselves, and try to avoid defensiveness.
- *Let writers win some.* Stand firm when you need to, especially on matters of principle or ethics, but don't be the kind of editor who has to win every single point.
- *Keep the burden of problem solving on the writer.* Listen and offer a

few, high-priority suggestions. But people learn more when they take
responsibility.

- *Be tough but not mean.* Think of your best teachers in grade school
  and college. They almost always pushed and challenged you, but they
  also made you feel valued and special.
- *Make coaching part of your everyday routine.* Repetition and pre-
  dictability are potent weapons for an editor. If writers know you will
  be regularly following the coaching procedures, they will be better
  prepared and take things more seriously. If coaching comes across as
  an occasional gimmick, few writers will give it their best effort.

Conclusion

Editors teach every day, whether they know it or not. Writers read editors' words and body language, trying to decode the messages they should
take most personally to heart. So editors should be as deliberate and open
as possible about what they want writers to know and do.

Coaching—which, as we have discussed earlier, is just another word
for good editing—provides specific techniques for conveying these messages. Good coaching helps reporters grow, makes editing faster and
easier, saves everyone time and aggravation, and best of all makes copy
better.

Now we turn to a still-broader aspect of newsroom leadership: organizing and coordinating coverage.

Sidebar 8: Coaching—the good (?) old days

They made you swear and they made you cry, and some days you
despised their copy-slashing guts, but generations of writers owe their
careers to the city editors who broke them in.

They're dying away now, almost extinct, a Neanderthal league of
the politically incorrect, a dwindling herd of inky-fingered, whiskey-
breathed, tyrannosaurus wrecks, edged aside by the Suits and the
Slashes, the Assistant Managing Editor/Locals, manicured managers
for modern times.

Once they were kings.

The title resounded with glory. City editors bestrode the newsroom
with the supremacy of Zeus and the swagger of Civil War generals.
Hardened journalists cringed at their lacerating sarcasm, but a city
editor's wink could render the coldest-blooded writer sniffly.

Stanley Walker of the *New York Herald Tribune*, perhaps the most
famous of them all, captured the legend this way in his book *City
Editor*.

He invents strange devices for the torture of reporters, this mythical agate-eyed Torquemada with the paste-pots and scissors. Even his laugh, usually directed at something sacred, is part sneer. His terrible curses cause flowers to wither, as the grass died under the hoofbeats of the horse of Attila the Hun. A chilly, monstrous figure, sleepless, nerveless, and facing with ribald mockery the certain hell which awaits him.

Yet, looking back, journalists tend to remember them at least somewhat fondly, to miss their incendiary personalities. For all their pitiless bluster, old-line city editors were leaders and teachers, immovably loyal and unforgettably inspiring, and consumed constantly with mad, delirious pursuit of the latest three-alarm news story.

Most were men, but one who wasn't—Aggie Underwood, who became city editor of the *Los Angeles Evening Herald-Express* in 1947—held her ground. "I don't take any back talk, insulting loafing, or smart-aleck insubordination," she announced in her book *Newspaperwoman*. But she also observed, ahead of her time, "I know about the school which holds that 'all city editors are sonsofbitches'. . . . The period is passing when a city editor may whip reporters and photographers like dogs."

They included characters like Clem Lane of the *Chicago Daily News*, who "ruled the city staff . . . in fiery justice" from 1942 to 1958, described by James McCartney, who broke in under him, as "the archetype of the old-fashioned city editor, an Irish-Catholic, reformed alcoholic with a high school education, a great mane of white hair . . . irascible, immensely honest, tremendously talented, the personification of the newspaper . . . and very, very difficult to work for."

Even after McCartney headed the high-powered Washington Gridiron Club and covered premiers and presidents for over 40 years, he still referred to Lane as "Mr. Lane," and he still remembered his third day on the job, when he was two minutes late for work.

"Mr. McCartney," Lane told him, "if you want to work here, when I tell you to be somewhere at 9 o'clock, you'd better be there at 9 o'clock."

Later that year, McCartney and his wife were driving to work one morning when their car overheated on busy Lake Shore Drive. McCartney bolted into the street, hailed a cab, and abandoned his wife with the steaming car.

"I'm sorry to do this, honey," he yelled back, "but I've got to be in the office by 9 o'clock."

Jane Hadro grew up to become a legal editor for the Bureau of National Affairs, a Washington publishing company. She also grew up with a city editor for a father.

Poppa Ed Hadro was city editor of the *St. Paul Pioneer Press* from 1964 to 1982. A colleague once said he represented "the World War II type" of city editor: stubborn, principled, and earnestly attached to the community.

What Jane Hadro remembers is how he would edit her homework— and "read the riot act" to teachers who gave her poor grades for it.

He also edited her letters home from college.

"I came home once and saw one of my letters on his desk," she recalled. "There were things circled, and spelling errors marked. I just started to cry. . . . He had been giving them to my mother and telling her, 'Send them back to her.' But my mother couldn't do it."

City rooms and city editors seem different now, more businesslike and less whimsical, and that is mostly for the better.

"I think of [old-school Baltimore city editor] Lou Linley, and I think of the smells of the city, and I hear the fire engines going outside," said reporter and editor Amy Eisman. "They knew their cities like the back of their hand.

"I do think something has been lost, but I don't think it should be brought back. Lou was like the captain of the ship, a father figure in the newsroom. You did what he said. That was an era that has passed. It shouldn't come back."

Good riddance to the rascals. And thanks.[1]

Vignettes

Jack Hart, a longtime editor and coach at the *Portland Oregonian*, compiled a lifetime's wisdom about helping writers into his book *A Writer's Coach*.

Here are a few Hart insights:

- "Don't stall on the first line. The most important thing is to get moving, not to write the perfect opening before you write anything else. If an acceptable lead doesn't pop into mind, simply jot down your core idea and keep writing."
- "Be bold. Avoid little qualifiers such as 'somewhat,' 'rather,' and 'a little bit.' If the boor in the theater seat next to you talked through the entire performance, he was rude. Not *somewhat* rude."
- "Write the way you talk. Read your copy aloud. Does it sound like you? If not, try making your writing vocabulary more like your talking vocabulary. You want to be as appealing to readers as you are to face-to-face listeners."[2]

9 Making decisions about coverage

Several young journalists once shared with me their impressions of their own local newspaper and website. Too often, they complained, coverage seemed targeted toward readers much different from themselves. For example, they found garden columns that assumed people lived in houses with yards instead of in condos and apartments; food sections geared toward family meals not singles' grazing; entertainment guides previewing symphonies and museums not clubs and rock music.

To their credit, the young journalists acknowledged their own narrow perspectives. But they still had a valid point. How can the news media expect to attract under-30 readers if those readers don't see themselves and their lifestyles reflected regularly in the coverage?

Multiply this perception by the huge number of demographic categories and groupings the media try to reach, and you quickly see a problem of major magnitude. Deciding what to cover is complicated. Obviously no medium can satisfy everyone, but it must satisfy someone, and in most cases many groups. Making coverage decisions is a job vital to the success, in some cases the very survival, of news operations.

If you think of a website as a cyberspace of infinite size, it might seem that the media could conceivably cover everything. Even a 48-page newspaper or a 22-minute newscast offers a lot of room, with another opportunity the next hour or day for material that cannot be included now. Closer up, however, editors stare at a grimmer reality. Every issue or program, even the web, confronts space, time, resource, and audience-attention boundaries that require editors to make constant, sometimes brutal priority decisions among volumes of material competing for inclusion. It is no exaggeration to say that a huge (and, to the audience, invisible) part of editing is deciding what not to publish and post.

Every day, editors must kill ideas, half-done stories, even finished copy. Functioning like triage officers at a disaster scene, editors reach rapid-fire verdicts about which story tips to pursue and which to dismiss, which reporters to count on and which to suspect, which projects to accelerate and which to drop, which articles to publish and which to delay or withhold, which blurbs to banner on the home page and which ones to bury at the bottom of the screen.

Typically, we call this *gatekeeping*, or the exercising of *new judgment*. Bear in mind that not all editors deal in news in the strict sense. Some manage feature desks or sports sections or editorial pages or contributor blogs or online slide shows, where content definitions differ. In all such editing jobs, however, the gatekeeping responsibility remains the same. Editors must understand the demands and standards of their part of the news operation and then make choices that most likely will produce copy that complies.

In this chapter, we will deal with covering news in a broad contemporary sense. The word *news* itself is hard to pin down, of course, but our attention here will be focused on the mixture of journalistic content produced by the mass news media.

Editors are crucial to compiling this mixture. To exercise gatekeeping authority most effectively, they need steady decision-making and decision-enforcing skills. The following attributes can serve as points of departure:

- Knowledge of what news *is*, both in general and as specifically defined by their sections, sites, or publications
- Knowledge of what news *is not*, of what reasons may require that some apparently worthy material be rejected
- Capacity to organize and direct staff efforts to find, cover, and present the desired content.

What news is and isn't

Practically everyone has tried to define news, and practically no one has succeeded completely.

In *A History of News*, Mitchell Stephens supplies one definition of news as "what is on a society's mind."[1] Melvin Mencher's *News Reporting and Writing*, a staple reporting text, provides a two-part description:

- News is information about a break from the normal flow of events, an interruption in the expected, a deviation from the norm.
- News is information people can use to help them make sound decisions about their lives.[2]

Other definitions tend toward the droll. One of my favorites, often attributed to a longtime newspaper editor named Creed Black, is that news is anything that happens to or near publishers and their friends. Most commonly, when stuck for a satisfactory definition, we resort to characterizing news. Most reporters and editors will be familiar with the following standard list of attributes of news: timeliness, proximity, prominence, conflict, magnitude, unusualness, and human drama.

My own definition is that news is *fresh information of public value.* Over time, the definition has broadened rather than narrowed. A few generations ago, front pages and newscasts were dominated by news of big government and big business. Today, we find far more front-page coverage of cultural and lifestyle topics such as health, science, relationships, arts, leisure, transportation, and consumerism. These developments tell us that news is a *dynamic* concept, evolving with the audience's shifting needs and interests.

News, therefore, is a *commodity*, a product that is traded to the audience to satisfy a need or desire. That means news is *transactional*, or negotiated with the audience. So news consumers have a role, which has greatly increased in the online age, in determining and placing a value on news. News also is *relative.* The news value of a given item may vary from day to day, depending on what else is going on, what resources are available for gathering and presenting the news, what competitors are doing, and so forth. For example, a small fire at a local shopping center may be top news on a so-called "slow news day," when not much else is happening, but it might not even make the front page or web home page on a day when a plane crashes or a local professor wins the Nobel Prize.

Editors need to confidently and competently recognize news when they see it, even if precise definitions remain elusive. Beyond that, what often distinguishes the best editors is an ability to make discriminating judgments between various grades of newsworthiness and to recognize, and efficiently dispose of, material that does not merit publication. Determining what to kill, and when and how to kill it, calls for more rigorous judgments than simply knowing how to reflexively follow the trail of a valid news story.

For example, I was editing copy on deadline one day when one of my best reporters phoned in breathlessly. He had been standing by at the courthouse while a grand jury considered whether to indict a prominent public official. As he waited in the corridors, the jury room doors had opened, grand jurors strolled out for a coffee break, and several began discussing the case openly and loudly. My reporter had ambled over, without identifying himself as a journalist. Apparently thinking he was a court official, the jurors talked on, revealing specifics about evidence in the case and their desire to indict the official. Eventually one juror blurted out something like, "That man ought to be in prison." What a story, my reporter exclaimed to me: grand jurors outraged by the conduct of a public official.

The story had all the attributes of news: timeliness, proximity, prominence, conflict, unusualness. Yet it never ran.

Why not? Our reporter's information had come under ethically ambiguous circumstances, involved sensitive private opinions not being offered knowingly for publication, and would most likely, if published, compromise a complex case and require disbanding the grand jury. In the editor's judgment, the price was too high for a little juicy, careless conversation.

In short, situations such as this one fall into several categories of what might be called potential *disqualifiers* of news, attributes that make information less likely to be published even though it appears to meet the requirements of newsworthiness. The following paragraphs discuss categories of disqualifiers.

Legal problems. Editors may withhold information for a variety of legal reasons: because it raises potential libel or invasion-of-privacy problems, because it poses plagiarism or copyright concerns, because it involves stolen documents or national security, because it could provoke a contempt-of-court citation. Editors should not be intimidated to the point of knuckling under to every hint of a legal risk. But legal considerations do apply, and they sometimes result in decisions not to publish interesting material.

Ethical problems. Often, editors choose not to run material they consider incomplete, one-sided, unfair, tainted by improper news-gathering methods, or otherwise in violation of professional standards of conduct. Information can be contaminated in many ways. Most news organizations, for example, decline to pay sources for information. Editors usually reject stories if they know reporters have lied or misrepresented themselves to get them. A reporter who based an article on stolen documents would face a heavy burden to convince most editors to publish the material.

Taste problems. Particularly with photographs and video, editors often decide that good taste rules out running material of high interest, such as gory disaster scenes, bodies from car wrecks, shots containing nudity or obscenity. Written copy, too, often generates questions of taste, especially those involving use of explicit language. Taste problems have re-emerged for discussion in the past few years with the rise of online publishing and its often more adventurous tone. In general, but with numerous exceptions, editors tend to be most cautious in selecting material for broadcast, somewhat more permissive for print, and edgiest of all on the Internet.

Privacy problems. Here, we should distinguish between the legal notion of invasion of privacy and a broader ethical concern that can be called *disregard for privacy*. This involves the publication of material that may be perfectly legal to use but that seems unduly intimate, personal, or private. Many arguments occur over such issues, simply because they become quite subjective. But examples abound. Many newspapers do not publish the names of victims of sex attacks, for example. Suppose you learn that the married mayor is having an affair, or once had an affair, or is involved with someone 30 years younger, or is having a bisexual affair. Is any of that news? None of it? Clear guidelines remain elusive, but nearly every editor will at some time invoke a standard of compassion and privacy to withhold otherwise newsworthy material.

Danger to individuals or groups. My phone rang on deadline once and I heard a federal law enforcement official asking me to kill a story that, he said, would unmask an informant in a drug case and possibly result in the informant's death. In such cases, editors face an anguishing calculation: to publish and risk harm, or to withhold and fail in their obligation to bring the truth, whatever its consequences, to the audience. Here, editors consider such issues as the value of the information to be published, how widely it already is known, whether it involves public officials or the public trust, and whether it will emerge elsewhere. They also must evaluate the risk, knowing that some threats are deadly serious but that others are bluffs or manipulative attempts to stifle legitimate coverage. Editors also should look for reasonable alternatives to the stark poles of publishing as is or killing a story. There are other choices: delaying publication, taking precautions to avert the danger, or under some conditions "trading" for a better story. For example, in the case just described involving the drug informant, we agreed to withhold publication for a few days in exchange for an exclusive interview with the informant when he was out of danger.

Timing problems. This category of concerns is intensified by the emergence of the 24-hour news cycle. Editors face increasing pressure to post developments fast. But confirmation often comes slowly. You may have one source telling you there is a hostage situation at a local office, but what if the source is wrong, or lying, or exaggerating? Does it matter if the source is the police chief, or a tipster who insists on anonymity, or a caller who is willing to go on the air or online live? What if a competitor has already published the report? Editors have an old saying that probably still applies: Get it first and get it right, but first get it right.

In these and other situations, editors regularly must weigh the apparent news value of information against a range of potential delays or disqualifiers. So editors conduct journalistic cost–benefit analyses in which individual qualities of judgment, compassion, experience, courage, and discretion play as important a role as their professional understanding of news and audience interests.

In addition to the predispositions of editors themselves, what qualifies and disqualifies material for publication can be affected by social, institutional, and organizational factors.

Many decades ago, the sociologist Herbert J. Gans studied how several national media assembled news content. He isolated what he called eight enduring values "which can be found in many different types of news stories over a long period of time; often, they affect what events become news." Most if not all continue to have pertinence:

- *Ethnocentrism:* the tendency to elevate the United States and to evaluate other countries on how well they live up to American ideals
- *Altruistic democracy:* the notion that democracy is superior to

dictatorship and that ideal domestic conduct pursues public service and the public interest

- *Responsible capitalism:* an optimistic faith that most people and businesses behave as responsible citizens
- *Small-town pastoralism:* a stress on the virtues of the small and rural
- *Individualism:* the idealization of the rugged individual struggling against adversity
- *Moderatism:* the discouragement of extreme or deviant conduct
- *Social order:* the value placed on order and, in news stories such as disasters and scandals, the concern for restoring order
- *National leadership:* a reliance on and deference to civic leaders.[3]

Although these factors do not directly define news, they contribute to how the press in general, and editors in particular, view society and set expectations regarding news. They also underline a central point: News is not an absolute, objective phenomenon, and news coverage does not in some pristine way precisely reflect reality. News is a product constructed and reconstructed by journalists and sources, based on a range of values, expectations, motives, and ideals and directly affected by interaction with the audience. All these issues influence editors as they go about activating their newsrooms in the search for the desired content.

Organizing coverage

Assume that you, as an editor, have developed a working familiarity with what coverage is expected. Now you face the duty of searching each day for real-life examples of news within your area.

Where do you start?

Let's consider three aspects of the process:

- Organizing to gather news
- Making assignments
- Coordinating the flow.

Organizing to gather the news. Beginning reporters learn that there are only three ways of finding out anything: seeing it yourself (or *observation*), hearing about it from someone else (*interviewing*), and reading about it (*documents research*). Editors can put this truism to use in organizing their newsrooms or departments to seek news.

First, much of the news is predictable and observable. Reporters can be assigned to see for themselves such events as baseball games that begin at 7:30, city council meetings every Thursday, or theater openings and rock concerts on specific evenings. Second, reporters and editors can hear of news by plugging themselves into various beats where news can be expected to occur and by developing a broad network of sources willing to supply news tips. Third, journalists can use a host of written and electronic sources, both predictable (for example, lawsuits filed each day) and unexpected (for example, a reference on a website to a new product being manufactured in your area). Fourth, some news happens spontaneously, unpredictably, and outside the usual zones, and journalists need to be resourceful, flexible, and enterprising so as not to overlook it.

In a pioneering work on news gathering, sociologist Gaye Tuchman concluded that news, whatever its definition, "is a product of specific ways of organizing newswork."[4] Content, in other words, grows directly out of the methods journalists use to generate it: where they look, what sources they consult, how much time they invest.

I was reminded of this insight recently as I stood at the ocean's edge. My eyes were drawn toward the horizon. Dozens of birds hovered about 100 yards offshore, parallel to the beach in a nearly straight line as far as I could see both north and south. As the minutes passed, the birds, almost in formation, backed farther and farther from the shore. From time to time a bird would dive toward the ocean. It quickly became clear that they had located a school of fish and were tracking and raiding as it moved out to sea.

Journalists act in a similar way as they try to home in on the newsworthy and cast their nets where the yield will be most plentiful. As with fishing, it seems obvious that the day's catch will vary broadly with where they choose to cast the net. (It also seems clear, as my seashore observation suggests, that journalists like birds too often congregate in the same spots, compete for the same pickings, and ignore potentially fruitful sources elsewhere.)

In organizing coverage, editors need to pay special attention to how, when, and where they deploy their limited resources. As Tuchman and other researchers have documented, many variables can affect the outcome:

- *Place.* Where journalists are influences what news they produce. For example, if an editor assigns a reporter to Suburb A and does not assign one to Suburb B, then Suburb A is likely to get more coverage than Suburb B. That does not necessarily mean more news actually occurs in Suburb A. It simply means the news outlet is *better organized* to find the news there.

  Typically, editors assume that readers have high interest in news from specific locations (Suburb A), from specific institutions (city hall), and about specific topics (health). So they disperse their staffs accordingly by *geography, specialty,* and *topic* in order to acquire this high-interest news. As a result, readers are more likely to get news from these established, predictable zones than from elsewhere. They are less likely to get news that isn't territorial or beat-specific, that is intangible or abstract, or that falls between the boundaries.

For example, few news organizations cover university research laboratories, neighborhood gathering places, or online forums about local bands, despite the potential for finding interesting ideas there.

- *Time*. When events take place influences whether they get coverage. For a morning newspaper or an evening television newscast, the earlier in the day something happens, the better its chances of appearing, because journalists have more time to notice and cover it. News that happens on weekdays, when staffs are at full strength, is more likely to be noticed than events on weekends, when a skeleton staff may be overworked. Even online news operations, which could conceivably run round the clock, tend to staff up and maximize coverage during prime working hours.

  In a much broader sense, time favors the coverage of events over issues. Events (a trial, a ball game) have discrete, observable beginnings and endings. They are easy to find and to cover. Issues (changing cultural tastes, falling educational standards, coalescing concerns about environmental damage) evolve beyond the conventional news nets, without scheduled occasions that lend themselves to coverage.

- *Sources*. Whom you ask determines what you learn. In the ordinary news net, journalists routinely turn to centralized sources (government officials, industry spokespeople, celebrities) more often than to sources not as easily located or encountered (neighborhood leaders, rank-and-file workers, the disenfranchised). The result is a kind of legitimization of the status quo and a potential overrepresentation of middle-class, professional values in the news.

For editors, one important goal is to cast the news net as widely and as fairly as possible, bearing in mind critiques such as those by Tuchman and Gans. A key function becomes assessing how best to organize their staffs to achieve this goal. Simply recognizing the power of routines and patterns can help. Among other steps that editors can take are:

- *Creating beat systems that look beyond the obvious.* As many researchers and critics have pointed out, under most beat systems news will be gathered reliably from such places as the state legislature or city hall. Editors, then, must take special steps to acquire news from places where reporters are not regularly stationed, such as a university policy center or a tiny ethnic neighborhood. Designating beats such as "research" or "neighborhood issues" can fling the news net beyond the usual topical and territorial boundaries.

- *Matching beats and lifestyles.* Instead of defining beats by institution, try to define them in ways that overlap with how people live. For example, a beat described as "recreation" will produce broader coverage than one described as "Department of Recreation." Defining "workplace issues" as a beat, instead of "labor unions" or "Labor

Department," will do likewise. Paying attention to "personal shopping and spending" should bring broader, more relevant coverage than calling it "economics."

- *Expanding sources.* As we have seen, a reporter is more likely to rely on bureaucrats and officeholders (who have accessibility and a certain legitimacy and are thought to be in positions to know things) than on private citizens or interest-group leaders (perceived as biased or untested). Consequently, coverage tends to favor established groups and to neglect newcomers, fringe groups, or others outside the mainstream. Try to offset this tilt by suggesting that reporters develop sources from all segments of society and by making sure that official sources don't dominate your copy. A simple exercise: List all the sources on your front page or the top 10 stories on your website. How many are public officials? How much diversity do you find?

- *Reading your own print and web offerings, as well as the competition,* to look for new ideas or stories that need follow-ups. Classified ads, agate calendar listings, letters to the editor, online comment boxes, and news briefs often provide starting points for much larger stories.

- *Monitoring local news on community websites, citizen blogs, cable, television, radio, and other media.* Vast amounts of information float through real space and cyberspace these days, and the earlier you intercept it, the sooner you can identify emerging issues and stories.

- *Interviewing colleagues* about interesting goings-on in their lives, neighborhoods, clubs, schools, churches, and other social groups. Quite often, even your own staff members will neglect to mention something interesting because they assume editors already know about it. An exercise I recommend: Every week or so make the rounds of your newsroom and other departments (especially advertising and circulation, where contact with the public is high), asking people what potentially newsworthy items they heard over the past few days.

- *Scanning wire services, magazines, websites, and the national media* for stories that may have local angles or for trends that your community may be a part of, or, perhaps more interestingly, an exception to.

- *Reading the mail.* Most newsrooms get bag loads of paper mail each day and endless streams of email. Most of it is dull. But stay alert for the occasional great idea or juicy morsel.

- *Checking the archives* of your paper or site from last year or 10 years ago to see what was going on then. Surprisingly often, you will notice something worth following up now.

- *Doing your own reporting.* As an editor, develop your own source networks, both informal and formal, and work them diligently. Call friends and acquaintances. Find out who the area's best (and most reliable) news gossips are. Locate the best-informed people about the areas your news organization covers and stay in touch with them. And get out of the office. Have lunch with a source (preferably a new one) once a week. Drop in on meetings, events, activities. Make sure you and your reporters are chasing the news, not waiting for it.

- *Encouraging sources to come to you.* Make it easy to find your office or business cell phone number. Pay stringers and correspondents for usable tips. And, crucially, make sure that you and everyone else on your staff (especially people who answer the phone, take messages, or monitor voice mail and email) react with courtesy and appreciation to callers with story ideas.

- *Involving ordinary citizens.* One of many transformative changes brought about by the Internet is the empowerment of those on the receiving end of the media. What was once a one-way, producer-dominated system has become a busy two-way semi-democracy. No longer do journalists funnel information down the pipeline to passive audiences. Today's audiences want to participate, and the interconnections of modern technology make it easy. So journalists should capitalize on the audience's desire to contribute and be heard. Wherever appropriate and practical, make audiences a part of discussions about ideas, sources, reporting methods, and presentation techniques.

- *Reading and insisting that staff members read*, everything from popular magazines to trade journals to blogs in each beat area, from alternative publications to house organs to official websites, from municipal budgets to inspection reports on local restaurants to online rants, from the minutes of meetings you can't cover to every incident report at the local police department to online listings of neighborhood festivities.

The bottom line is to make the search for news an aggressive and generative process, not one that is passive or locked into stale and predictable routines.

Making assignments. As any editor can tell you, selling yourself on an idea does not ensure it will see publication. Editors do not write stories. They work indirectly, through others. So the hardest work often comes in selling those others on the idea. I can remember countless times when what I thought was an inspired vision for a wonderful story came back mangled and unrecognizable because I failed to effectively convey that vision to a reporter.

In making assignments, strive for:

- *Clarity.* Be clear about the idea and about the ground rules of the assignment. Most of the time, it is advisable to give a reporter as much autonomy as possible. If you want a feature story on this year's

Fourth of July parade, select a good reporter, talk through your own ideas, offer suggestions, and help the reporter see the end product you have in mind, but leave as much room as possible for the writer to put her or his mark on the assignment. If, as will happen occasionally, you have reason to insist on a particular approach, then be honest about that too. Make sure the reporter understands what you are asking, how much if any leeway exists, and why and how you want it done. One of the most common errors I encounter in newsrooms is a too-brief assignment conversation that leaves the reporter and editor with differing understandings of the mission.

- *Helpfulness*. Be an editor whom reporters count on for help. Reporters can tell the difference between an editor who bullheadedly dominates every point and one who offers steady counsel and useful suggestions. Offer your ideas and the wisdom of your experience in a constructive, not patronizing, way. Be ready to suggest sources, documents, or other steps that can help get a reporter unstuck.

- *Flexibility*. Try to avoid clinging to preconceptions that aren't borne out by reporters' research. Some reporters, of course, will dawdle on unwanted assignments and find countless reasons to pooh-pooh them. Learn to distinguish between a bad idea and an unmotivated reporter.

- *Balance*. Most mainstream news organizations operate on the food court model, trying to present a little something for everyone, from nutritious entrees to luscious desserts. Editors call this a good mix, and achieving it generally requires an openness to ideas from others, notably including ideas not to your personal taste. Recall the example cited at the beginning of this chapter, where young journalists complained that too few stories reflected their interests and lifestyles.

- *An overall strategy that sees beyond the daily grind*. Related to balance, this point involves making sure your assignments go beyond the next posting or the next issue of the paper. Make sufficient short-range assignments to cover the news, of course. But do not neglect medium- and long-range needs also. If possible, make sure that a portion of your resources is always devoted to medium-range projects (such as a weekender looking into hiring practices in the mayor's office) and long-range ideas (such as a look at the health effects of the local power plant).

Coordinating the flow. You have flung your news net, snared some nifty story ideas, and crisply assigned them to your crack staff. Time to relax, check out your email, and wait till the golden prose flows in?

Not exactly.

Far from relaxing, the editor is now more likely to resemble a harried police dispatcher, routing units from one scene to another, analyzing each situation to determine where resources are needed most, and juggling false alarms, unexpected bulletins, and logistical logjams. Here, again, an ability to make swift, defensible decisions, under fire separates the successful editors. Like quarterbacks calmly surveying downfield receivers as 300-pound behemoths lunge maniacally toward them, editors must bring knowledge, experience, hunch, and luck together to make a procession of snap, all-important judgments.

For some editors, these activities still take place within one medium, for example, a daily newspaper. Increasingly, though, editors work across several media or platforms, each with its own schedules, routines, and demands. Editors act as master coordinators in directing and distributing reporters and their stories in multiple formats and with almost constant deadlines.

A given assignment may find a reporter filing a few paragraphs of breaking news, with an audio clip, for the web; then contributing to a blog or a web chat, followed by a brief interview for cable television news; and finally assembling a story for the next morning's newspaper, complete with photos, graphics, and various sidebars. In most cases, several different editors and producers will assist, but one editor, usually the reporter's direct supervisor, will serve as overall case officer overseeing the flow.

These dynamic situations call for editors who are nimble, flexible, and hyper-efficient. They will benefit by bearing in mind the following points:

- *Plan, plan, plan.* Today's nonstop news cycle requires editors to get involved early, plan and coordinate each stage of the cycle, and keep careful track of each medium's deadlines and demands. Sometimes this can be as simple as improving the paperwork. For example, daily story "budgets" should be formatted to note whether each item is meant for print, broadcast, and/or the web; whether it includes photos, graphics, audio, and/or video; whether you anticipate any special reader-service extras, such as links to full texts of court decisions or slide shows of the county fair; and what the tentative deadlines and lengths are.
- *Monitor reporters' work.* Consult at several key points of the reporting and writing process, to help the writer as a coach, to remind the writer of impending deadlines, and to ensure that key details are not neglected. As we have stressed, you should not hover pantingly over a writer's shoulder or butt in unnecessarily. But good editors keep abreast of how stories and projects are developing, in order to offer suggestions at timely moments and to avoid being taken by surprise.
- *Think photos, graphics, audio, and video as well as words.* Multimedia journalism requires a good ear and eye and a broad focus. Make clear, complete, early assignments for art or multimedia elements. As stories rise and fall during a cycle, keep a running checklist of

audio and visual needs and coordinate fully with other relevant editors and producers. Good visuals and audio take no less time than good writing, so start early and plan carefully.

- *Think time and space.* At the point of assignment, give the writer a preliminary idea of what kind of treatment you have in mind, from a one-paragraph brief to a lead-the-paper package; from a full-fledged web, broadcast, and print extravaganza to a one-time-only web notice that will be gone in a few hours. Then, constantly re-think space and time allocations as you monitor variables such as how the story actually develops and what competing demands for space and web play may be. Ask the reporter to alert you immediately if the preliminary idea seems unworkable, and for your part keep the reporter posted on any changes in newsroom plans for the story. Avoid the kind of newsroom anarchy that results when every reporter writes to a self-chosen length and a personal deadline heedless of what others are doing or planning. It is much easier to write a coherent 10-inch story if you conceive and organize for 10 inches to begin with than if you craft a 20-inch article and then have to cut it in half. It is much easier to produce a coherent audio clip if the reporter knows about how much time will be devoted to it.
- *Coordinate with others in the newsroom.* This may call for a range of political, diplomatic, and negotiating skills. Keep superiors informed about sensitive stories or those needing unusual treatment. Try to avoid overlap among reporters or duplication with other sections or departments. Pass on tips that may be relevant elsewhere in the newsroom. Lobby when necessary for the extra time, space, or handling that key projects deserve. Especially in multimedia newsrooms, it is vital to work together smoothly and to avoid isolation and turf squabbles.
- *Stress surprise and creativity.* Journalism exists for many reasons, among them to inform and to delight. The awesome powers of contemporary media let you do both, and more, in ways unimaginable even a generation ago. Whether a particular project involves the ultra-serious (such as dramatic live war zone images transmitted by satellite) or the ultra-funky (such as homemade video of a pet dog who can open the refrigerator on her own), stretch your imagination for exciting and absorbing ways to both educate and interest your audience.

Conclusion

Not long ago, editors made decisions about coverage in a comfortably sequential fashion, moving step by step from conception to publication. This left-brain linearity has now yielded, for the most part, to a nonstop, kinetic, right-brain, multimedia tumult. Deadlines come faster. Demands for words, images, and sounds are more insistently complicated. Switching among media requires swift shifts in mindset. In the interval after articles are assigned, editors face new challenges and thrilling opportunities, all calling for full attention to the details of space, time, and flow. Making good coverage decisions helps the editor keep ahead of these careening news processes, anticipate problems, and smooth the way for what comes next: the final stages of packaging and presenting the material.

Sidebar 9: Elevating your editing career

Steve Buttry

Wherever you are as an editor and wherever you want to go, you can elevate your career by working on personal and professional development. Teachers, editors, colleagues, and training programs will help you move to a higher level, but nothing will help as much as your own commitment to improvement. As training consultant Alan Weiss notes, if you can improve by just 1 percent each day, you will be twice as good a journalist in 70 days.

Start with this assessment: *Where do you want your career to take you?* Clarify your ambitions and decide what steps might move you toward them.

- *Set goals.* Consider where you'd like to be in a year or two or five. Look at the others who are where you want to go. What skills do they have? What experience do they have? Decide what skills, personal characteristics and experience you need to reach your goals and make a plan to grow in those areas.
- *Take responsibility for your own growth.* Invest what it takes to grow into the kind of editor you want to be.

Here are some ways to move forward.

Improve your skills:

- Think visually.
- Think online.
- Master numbers.
- Develop your computer skills.
- Address your weaknesses.

Encourage your staff and colleagues:

- Praise good work.
- Encourage early writing.
- Encourage new story forms.

- Encourage authoritative writing.
- Encourage reporters to zig when others zag.
- Respect reporters' authorship and don't rewrite unless necessary.

Challenge your staff and colleagues:

- Challenge instead of criticizing.
- Develop story elements.
- Read aloud.
- Emphasize rewriting.
- Challenge leads.
- Develop self-starters.
- Review and share the best work and techniques.

Communicate clearly:

- Keep the boss informed.
- Be candid.
- Control your anger.
- Use humor but beware of sarcasm.
- Praise your peers.
- Show interest in the budget and other important administrative matters.
- Seek solutions in conflict.

Be a newsroom leader:

- Mentor those more junior than you.
- Share your experience.
- Pass tips to colleagues.
- Promote yourself but without becoming annoying or boastful.
- Lead, serve, and volunteer in your newsroom.

Learn from others:

- Seek a mentor.
- Attend courses and training programs.
- Follow up on training.
- Seek advice.
- Connect with other editors and join editing associations.

Expand your vision:

- Explore your campus or community.
- Read the best.
- Take on a bigger project or challenge.
- Put local stories into a national context.

- Follow up on earlier stories and issues.
- Remember the reader as you assign and edit stories.

Pursue opportunities:

- Voice your ambitions without whining about current complaints.
- Consider a new assignment.
- Be yourself, honest and upfront.

Grow personally:

- Identify one way you can improve and do so.
- Then do it again.
- Accept responsibility.
- Apologize when you offend or make mistakes.
- Don't make excuses.
- Stay positive, even in difficult times.[5]

Vignettes

An interesting coverage dilemma faced editors at the *Sarasota Herald-Tribune* in Florida, where the executive editor and managing editor not only disagreed over a decision but published competing columns explaining their differences.

At stake was whether the news organization should run the names and addresses of sexual offenders released into the community.

Managing editor Rosemary Armao favored publication. "If a convicted sex offender moves in next door to me, I want to know about it," she wrote. "Face it, news is often about people's private lives."

But executive editor Janet Weaver argued (and eventually decided) against publication. She raised concerns about accuracy and about the "public shaming" of "people who have served their prescribed sentences." Publishing the names, Weaver concluded, "starts to move us across a line, from being an independent press to serving as an extension of government."[6]

10 Making decisions about presentation

When the *Montgomery Advertiser* looked back at that Alabama city's momentous civil rights bus boycott of 50 years earlier, it naturally offered a major package in the printed newspaper. But the *Advertiser* also developed a dramatic web presentation: a video introduction featuring civil rights pioneers, voices from the boycott, a varied package on the life and legacy of Rosa Parks, biographies of other key figures, a gallery of historic front pages, and free searching through an archive of 575 articles from 1955 to 1957. The web extravaganza won an Online Journalism Award, and readers gained multiple ways to consume an important historical retrospective.

The massive effort underlined another way times have changed for editors. Just a generation or two ago, newsrooms divided fairly neatly into "word people" and "picture people," who got along about as well as the Montagues and the Capulets in *Romeo and Juliet*. Word people issued assignments, reported, made news judgments, and determined play. Picture people took photos and laid out pages, generally under the direction of word people. Occasionally, when more exotic illustration was called for, picture people provided locator maps to accompany news of foreign coups or supplied drawings of enlarged fruits for the Thursday food pages.

All this took place back in the Neanderthal age of print journalism, when editors assumed unshakeable audience loyalty, hardly ever fretted about declining readership, sniffed at television, and had never heard the word *Internet*.

Then panic erupted. Editors (and, more menacingly, publishers) noticed that (a) mainstream readership and penetration were drooping, (b) splashy new specialty publications were cutting into circulation and advertising, (c) television and its visual images had succeeded in displacing typography as the central form of audience experience, and (d) looming on the horizon were even more advanced electronic media.

So, like adolescents suddenly discovering romance, newspapers and magazines scurried to spruce up appearances, catch up with fashion, and woo the newly fickle audience. *Design* arrived. A process once left mainly to printers (and known as *makeup*) and later handled by harried editors scribbling furious diagrams on dummy sheets (a process known as *layout*) was transformed into a rejuvenated art form. *Design* came to denote the conception, coordination, and execution of an overall artistic and journalistic plan. Advancing technology (particularly innovations in color photo usage, better presses, and the advent of computers) further spurred the rush toward brighter, sharper, more orderly, more attractive print publications. Like a locomotive, the design revolution surged forward at full throttle.

Then the Internet emerged, bringing even more competition for the audience and even more options for presentation. Designers rushed to use its powers to craft visually elegant home pages. It seemed certain that attractive contemporary design would reach new crests and drive the development of websites into an exciting age blending words and images. But two problems soon became evident:

- Because of slow download speeds, especially in the early years of the web, designers found that relying on large dominant images, as they were increasingly doing with printed pages, was not practical. Viewers did not have the time or patience to wait as a lovely photo slowly unscrolled on the screen. So designers had to settle for small or thumbnail shots, not display art, and to re-think how the printed page should be modified in its transfer to the screen.
- Online audiences turned out to value function far more than attractiveness in design. They demanded well-organized home pages with maximum choices that took them, with no more than one or two clicks, to desired destinations. Where print pages were headed in the direction of orderly, modular design featuring fewer elements than in the past, web pages evolved in the opposite way. Consumers preferred more and more choices and links on the first screen they saw, often dozens per page, rather than an elaborately planned and unified page showing off modern design aesthetics.

For editors dealing with presentation, all these changes brought new demands as well as new opportunities. As newsroom decision makers, editors now faced a broader role in serving as master coordinators of various means of presentation: the traditional newspaper page, special sections and spin-off publications, and the suddenly all-important web pages. Many also had associations with radio and television stations or cable channels. No longer was the editor's work cycle a step-by-step progression toward the production of a single printed newspaper. Instead, it was a near round-the-clock multimedia, multiplatform production pageant.

Clearly, new technical skills were required. As production became increasingly computerized, editors confronted complex advances in software and hardware. Editors using computer coding and formatting in essence replaced compositors and printers. Desktop publishing and pagination supplanted hand-drawn dummy sheets. Web coding required a mastery of new software, and subsequent computer generations (which came quicker and quicker) brought fancier and flashier programs for producing and displaying text, art, graphics, animations, audio, and video.

These rapid developments revolutionized the daily routines of editors, but, interestingly, they didn't really change the role. The editor remained the newsroom decision maker charged with making presentation selections that best served the intended audience. As we pointed out in the first chapter, success called for the same three skills editors have always needed: strong strategic and conceptual thinking to envision the best journalism, technical capabilities to turn the vision into reality, and management dexterity to coordinate all the people involved.

Now that the multimedia world is firmly in place, the new editor must refine and employ these skills in multiple ways. The new editor must work toward integrating words, sounds, and visual elements, understanding the fundamental role of presentation in both the form and the substance of journalism. Design is not just a pleasant cosmetic for enhancing appearance, although that role is important, but it is also a central vehicle for conveying substantive information and impressions. The many tools available today let journalists deliver their messages more effectively and powerfully than traditional typography alone. Presentation is a powerful engine in improving the effectiveness of communication and in helping deliver more informative, interesting, understandable, and competitive news packages.

So the new editor, like a movie director or orchestra conductor, oversees and coordinates an increasingly elaborate assemblage. It begins, as it always has, with ideas and assignments. It ends, these days, with the use of computer technology to blend text, headlines, artwork, audio, and video into coherent packages over different media. If the traditional newspaper editor was the equivalent of a department store manager, today's editor oversees the entire media mega-mall, from boutique to superstore.

In managing these duties, editors should, as always, start early, plan carefully, and coordinate fully. Before we examine requisite skills and techniques, here are some broad concepts to guide editors' thinking:

- *Embrace the big picture from the outset.* Every outlet, whether print, broadcast, online, or otherwise, has its own special demands, schedules, and protocols. Not every editorial project will appear on every platform. Your job in the beginning is to fasten on the main purposes of the project at hand, envision all the presentation options, and adapt your material to whatever modes, channels, or formats will most effectively achieve the given purposes for the designated audiences. As always, editors must remain flexible as circumstances change, but they should begin with at least an overview of the most desirable master plan.

- *Exercise leadership*. In the mainstream media, in particular, audiences pay good money for editorial discretion and guidance. Decisions made by editors directly affect credibility and value. News media serve as both profit-making enterprises and public-service trusts. They are partly satisfying audience desires and partly providing essential social services. Like others such as pharmacists or teachers, editors should both respect their audiences and offer independent professional judgments that sometimes run counter to short-term popularity. As Shakespeare might have said but didn't, neither a tyrant nor a ninny be. Be a leader, open-minded but committed to quality.

- *Plan, plan, plan*. Maybe you remember reading this before, but the advice fits here too. As journalism becomes increasingly complex, then it becomes even more vital to think ahead, plan carefully, and recognize and solve problems early rather than late. You cannot provide audio feeds to your website if no one has thought to record them. You can't post the full text of the mayor's speech if no one bothered to collect it. You can't create a timeline to go with the story on your community's 150th anniversary if you start it a half-hour before deadline. Multimedia, multiplatform journalism requires multi-faceted planning from the start.

- *Communicate inward*. Unless you are blogging from your home computer, the chances are you will do very little alone in today's journalism. These days, projects are far more likely to involve more people than those of the past. Some will be generalists (an assigning editor overseeing a project), and others will be specialists (a web producer creating a slide show). You may deal with writers, photographers, artists, videographers, print designers, web producers, copyeditors, assigning editors, bloggers, podcasters, and all their counterparts from the cable and broadcast side, not to mention supervising editors and various bosses and executives. Whether you are the editor in charge or simply a mid-level team member, your goal should be full, ongoing communication and coordination across the board. Keeping everyone informed, *both orally and in writing*, is more important than ever before.

- *Communicate outward*. Then there is the matter of audience participation. Today's readers and viewers seldom will settle for sitting passively at the receiving end of your brilliant work. They want to participate. The interactivity associated with online journalism has empowered the audience in irreversible ways. Through the many available interconnections, audience members can be included in generating ideas, developing reporting strategies, and choosing presentation options. They can make their own contributions of words, sounds, and images, both on their own and through the news media.

Then they can respond instantly to what is published, engage in live discussions and forums, offer their own comments and feedback, and feel like active participants in the evolution of the news. Making it easy and inviting for the audience, establishing and enforcing standards where appropriate, and capitalizing on the two-way nature of today's journalism are all requirements for the new editor.

- *Direct with skill.* Planning means little without execution, of course. So the editor also must mix leadership traits with a sound knowledge of the journalistic basics. It is important to repeat that not every editor will have every skill. Often you will rely on specialists who have expertise you do not. But the successful editor will be sufficiently skilled to recognize good journalism, do good journalism, and help others do good journalism. As the process moves closer and closer to publication, appreciating and applying specific skills and techniques occupy more of the editor's energy.

The power of visuals must never be underestimated. Consider these research findings, reported by Monica Moses of the Poynter Institute in an issue of the *American Editor* devoted to design:

- We know that 90 percent of readers enter pages through large photos, artwork, or display type (headlines, promos, etc.).
- We know that running a visual element with text makes it three times more likely that at least some of the text will be read.
- We know that headlines are more likely to be read when a photo is nearby.
- And we know that the bigger the picture, the more likely readers are to be intrigued and read the cutline. . . .
- Graphics, photographs, and headlines get far more attention from readers than text does. The reader takes in 80 percent of the artwork and 75 percent of the photographs. . . . She sees 56 percent of the headlines. But she's aware of only 25 percent of the text, and she reads a fraction of that. . . . All top editors should be visually savvy.[1]

Although a detailed technical discussion of presentation methods is beyond our scope here, every editor, as part of being "visually savvy," should be exposed to at least some key issues and techniques. In the sections that follow, we examine several elements related to design and presentation: headlines for print and web; photos, illustrations, and other visuals; and design for print and web.

Headlines for print and web

Recall your own reading style. You probably do not read everything in a newspaper, a magazine, or a website. Few of us do. Instead, you select from the dozens, sometimes hundreds, of choices. Typically, you flip through the printed pages or scan those online, glancing at headlines or key words, stopping when they capture your attention, breezing on hurriedly when they fail to arouse you. Notice the very words we use for web readership, *surfing* and *browsing*, suggest someone skimming along, moving quickly from item to item, not paying careful attention. It is the headline, more than anything else except the topic itself, that must bring this busy consumer to a stop.

Headlines serve both content and design functions. They summarize stories, set a tone, help distinguish news and features, and provide a dollop of information for readers just looking for a quick summary. In their design role, headlines provide visual variety, dress up pages, and act as a kind of carnival barker calling attention to special attractions waiting in the small type. Headlines also help determine which items are returned when consumers use search engines.

Given this massive influence over readership, headlines receive far too little attention. This has long been true in the printed media, and it continues to be true under the even faster-paced editing style of online media. Consider the following scene, common in every newsroom: Deadline nears. A frantic reporter paces the floor, struggling with the lead on a major project. The story has been in the works for days. Leads have been written, discarded, revised, rewritten. Fellow reporters have been consulted. Various editors have weighed in with suggestions. The lead is *almost* there, and the writer is whirling in the final fevered stages of creativity.

Now ask yourself this question: How often have you seen a similar scene featuring the headline writer?

For most journalists, the answer would be seldom, if ever. Sweating for hours, even days, over a lead is common, even routine in some newsrooms. Unfortunately, headline writing more typically takes place at the last minute, under excruciating time and space constraints. The copyeditor may spend 15 or 20 minutes pondering a head for a project that has taken weeks. The slot person may help, and occasionally on extremely big projects senior editors may get involved in head writing. But those instances are exceptions. In online newsrooms, producers often key in headlines on the fly. Although it is true that online heads are often revised and improved as time passes, the original heads regularly draw minimal attention.

Yet, is the headline any less important than the lead? Of course not.

Too often editors see headlines as mostly a design convenience, not as the all-important gateway leading the reader into, or away from, the entire package. The result can be stark one-column, three-line heads with such flat, obvious messages as "President/to speak/Wednesday" or "Big storm/causes havoc/on highways."

Other times, whether because of time pressure or other reasons, headline writers simply fail to focus on an interesting point. Bland, boring, inaccurate, and sometimes unintentionally hilarious headlines regularly circulate around the web and are reprinted by trade publications *American Journalism Review* and *Columbia Journalism Review*. My own files include such beauties as "Grammer hotline available," "Man found dead in cemetery," "If strike isn't settled it may last a while," "Barbecue benefits animals," and "Cold wave linked to temperatures." On vacation one summer, I clipped such headlines as "Panel seeks probe of allegations" and "Governors OK waste figure examination." Would you stop to read those stories?

Good headlines sell their stories and enhance their pages without any compromise in accuracy and without resort to sensationalism. They stress what is most interesting, important, and special. They give readers a reason to slow down and enjoy an unusual article or posting. Some effective headlines: on a *Newsweek* column about dating, "Will you go out with me?"; on a *Washington Post* essay on parenting, "Read this article—or your kids will be stupid"; on an *American Health* piece on exercise, "How to eat more and weigh less."

Try this exercise: Go to an online aggregate site, such as news.google-.com, and compare the headlines on multiple versions of a current story. For instance, the following headlines all appeared over the same story in various newspapers and websites:

Biological brain changes make teenagers moody
Hormone paradox may explain teen moodiness
Hormone may boost teen mood swings
Moody teens: the excuse is chemistry
Hormone turns cute kids into horror teens
Why your teenager is so vile!

From somber to sensational, the range is great, and so is the impact. Granted, writing headlines can be arduous. Labeling a daily health story about teenagers is hard enough, but strong editors go pale at the idea of reducing a 2,000-word, six-month investigative project to six or seven words—which, of course, must be scrupulously accurate, incomparably clever, and sculpted to fit a given space. It may be fair to say that writing great headlines is the hardest single act in journalism.

Why do poor headlines get published? Typically, several reasons apply. First, headlines are often written at the last minute, at the very end of the cycle of publication. Second, editors often must produce so many headlines that they begin taking the process for granted. I often ask copyeditors how many headlines they write during a typical shift, and the answer usually ranges from a dozen to 20 or more. It is difficult if not impossible to be creative 20 times a day. Finally, not enough collaboration and quality control go into writing heads. They are often written, checked over, and published or posted by only one or maybe two people.

Here are some techniques that can help improve headlines both on paper and online:

- *Collaborate*. Copyeditors and web producers should work together more often in producing headlines. Write several options; pass them around; brainstorm toward improvement. Too many headlines are written and seen by only one or two people.
- *Start earlier*. You don't have to wait until a story is finished and a design or posting is final to begin mulling a headline. On major stories and postings, start toying with potential headlines or themes as early as possible. Work from leads, budget lines, general knowledge of what the story will likely say. You can't complete the head until the final specs are set, of course, but often you can get a valuable head start on phrasings and angles by beginning early and spreading your headline writing over a longer period.
- *Read headlines aloud*. It turns out to be a little like singing. You will hear the difference between the tuneful and the flat.
- *Ascend the ladder of excellence*. If you examine headlines in most news media, almost all are *accurate*. Somewhat fewer are *clear*. Even fewer are *clever*. And only a handful are *irresistible*. Work to move every headline as high as possible up the ladder, from accurate up to accurate and clear, then to accurate, clear, and clever, and ideally all the way to accurate, clear, clever, and irresistible.
- *Revise*. Don't settle for publishing the first headline you think of that fits. Keep trying. When writing web heads, go back and revisit the head a few minutes after posting. If you can think of something better, make the change.

Although some editors take to this task with an apparently congenital genius, most learn through practice, practice, practice. It also helps to internalize the qualities of successful headline writers. Best practices include the following:

- Use a subject and verb in most headlines, especially on news articles; try special effects, such as questions, phrases, or fragments, on features or packages that would benefit from an impressionistic rather than informational approach.
- Try not to split verbs, phrases, or nouns and modifiers between lines. Avoid splits such as "District Judge Rules Boy/Scouts Can Play Around/City-Owned Parkland."

- Use action verbs, active voice. A headline, like a lead, should express action, change, or movement.
- Avoid the verb "to be" and its forms.
- Build on key words and thoughts from the story but do not mimic the exact language of the lead or give away a good punch line.
- Be specific. Say "Man robs downtown bank/to get money for Christmas" instead of "Downtown bank robbed/of undetermined amount."
- Be precise.
- Don't exaggerate.
- Avoid headlines that state a continuing condition ("Meetings planned," "Mayor to speak") or fail to single out what is unusual about a particular story ("Defense spending criticized").
- Avoid double meanings and double entendres, as chronicled regularly by *American Journalism Review* and *Columbia Journalism Review* in such examples as "Rape classes planned," "Police can't stop gambling," and "Tornado victims begin picking up pieces."
- Take care with words that can be used as both nouns and verbs (loves, races, moves, plays). In a headline such as "U.S. hopes/dashed in Olympics," readers may be confused by whether "hopes" is meant as a noun or verb.
- Avoid contrivances or words used in ways you would not normally use or accept ("Solons flay prez").
- Use words that have high visual or descriptive power (grandmother, tax increases, flash fire) and avoid words that do not summon any image at all (process, system, activity).
- Surprise the reader.
- Do not waste words. Make every word in a headline add to the reader's visual image.
- Use secondary headlines—decks, subheads, blurbs, and the like— to add information and intrigue. Don't simply repeat the main point in different words or add something routine. Instead, stress the meaning or find one detail that would make a reader want to know more.

These qualities generally apply to headlines for both print and the web. In addition, online heads offer some extra challenges:

- Headlines may be even more important on websites than in print, since readers have far more options and eye distractions.
- Editors may be asked to write several heads, tags, or teasers for web packages: for example, for the home page, the story page, and one or more mobile alert systems. Web editors and producers often work from a content management system that provides a template for keying in these heads.

- Online heads should be both free-standing story summaries (for those who won't read any further) and tantalizing morsels that encourage as many people as possible to continue. Few home pages offer more than a few sentences, at most, of any one story. Whether people click to the full story depends hugely on whether the five- or six-word headline captivates them.
- Web heads also need to feature specifics and key words that can be detected by search engines, which can lure more viewers to the site. Designers sometimes talk about "SEO," or search engine optimization, as a contemporary goal of online headlines.

The new editor cannot reform overnight a system that tends to save headlines to the last minute or deprive them of creative energy. But it is a reasonable goal to move toward a system that decides on headlines earlier in the processing of stories, that allows more time for copyeditors to ponder, write, and rewrite them, and that recognizes the vital role headlines play in achieving any news organization's number one goal: to attract and communicate with a busy audience.

Photos, galleries, and slide shows

Photos have many uses. They often tell a story better, more dramatically, more profoundly than words. Such classic images as the World Trade Center towers in flames in 2001 or President John F. Kennedy's young son saluting his father's passing coffin linger in our minds years, even decades, after we first see them.

Photos also add color, capture moods, make pages more inviting, and intensify reader interest. Like many elements we discuss, photos have a role in both the form and the substance of journalism. Just as editors must consider the structure and the content of news articles, they so must judge photos.

Where does photo editing begin? It does not begin with viewing images or processing film or handling prints. Photo editing begins with the *assignment*. Photo assignments should be clear and complete, reflecting the vision and coordination of an editor thinking ahead and working together with the photographer.

Traditionally, given the relatively small photo and art staffs of most news operations, editors had to direct their forces carefully or risk wasting resources on projects that fell through or photos that would never see print. Today, editors face a broader challenge. They continue to depend on a finite band of professional photographers. But the spread of digital cameras, photo-taking phones, video captures, and other simple-to-use technology makes it easier than ever for nonprofessionals to capture and transmit important, interesting photos. Today's editors receive far more photos than ever before, not only from staff photographers, but from writers armed with small cameras and, increasingly and importantly, from members of the public.

Luckily, as the supply of good art has vastly increased, so has the opportunity to present it. Where a generation ago an editor could publish a relatively few photos per day in the printed newspaper, today's websites can display almost as many photos as an editor can supply. Most news websites regularly provide daily galleries and slide shows, often of several dozen images each, featuring photos generated by wire services, staff members, and public contributors. These developments underscore the role of the editor as coordinator and planner. With photos as with other aspects of editing, good work begins early and involves decisions of both content and structure.

- As an editor, you should make clear assignments. Make your intentions fully known. Do you want a stand-alone shot for a print news or feature story, a photo to illustrate a special tone or theme, a full story in photos that can be presented as a gallery or slide show?
- Alert readers early if you are actively soliciting photos—for example, shots of a big snow storm or traffic tie-up.
- Give the photographer as much information as possible about story-line, tone, any preliminary plans for packaging.
- Ensure that writers, photographers, artists, and editors consult and coordinate.
- And follow up to see that plans get carried out and that all parties get alerted if conditions change.

As with so much else in journalism, the editor's initial investment often proves crucial to the outcome. When the work arrives, you have little remedy if a fundamental early miscommunication has sent the reporter and photographer out with divergent views on the nature of their assignments.

Once photos have been shot, editors face a new round of decisions: choosing which shots to post or publish, then *cropping, sizing*, and *shaping* them, and preparing any special effects.

Cropping involves deciding which area of an image to publish. Typically, photos can be cropped from the top (eliminating, for instance, vast expanses of sky), the bottom or the sides to focus attention on the key point of the shot. *Sizing* means determining how wide and deep to display a photo. Generally, bigger photos are more dramatic and effective than smaller ones, but well-chosen small shots can be vital for a web home page. *Shaping* means considering whether a vertical, horizontal, or square photo works best. In most cases, squares are avoided as less pleasing.

Using photo processing software, editors also can improve sharpness, contrast, brightness, and other technical aspects. When preparing feature projects or web packages, they can also produce any number of special effects, from zooms to rotations to allowing readers to interactively select and control the images.

As do words, photos raise content issues that must be considered, starting with the amount of digital manipulation that is regarded as appropriate. In so many ways, the digitizing of photos was a remarkable advance. It allowed photos to be shipped quickly over very long distances by transmitting the precise codes from one computer to another. But this system also raised and still raises serious ethical issues. Once a photograph or graphic is encoded in computer memory, then an editor (or anyone with access) can change the code, and therefore alter the photo, merely by pressing some keys, in much the same way as editors can make insertions and deletions in written copy.

This may make it easy, and tempting, for editors to rearrange photos electronically, for example to delete unwanted background scenes or to move two people closer together for a tighter shot or even, at extremes, to add elements that were not in the original picture. To take an obvious example, a photo could be doctored to show, say, a political candidate in the same frame as a prostitute.

Most newsrooms now have written or at least widely understood codes for handling digital images. Photos presented as news or as candid, for example, should appear as close as possible to their original state. Appropriate cropping and minor technical fixes are generally acceptable, but nothing should be added, deleted, enhanced, subdued, or otherwise manipulated to make the photo misleading or dishonest. It is widely considered a firing offense for a photographer, editor, or producer to modify the content of a photo presented in a news setting.

In cases where staging, enhancements, and other special effects are permitted, for example, on magazine covers or advertisements, readers should never be misled about whether an image is real or manipulated. Editors often use the term *photo-illustration* to acknowledge that an image has been modified.

In addition, because of their inherent power, photos often trigger deeper, more emotional reactions from readers than articles that describe the same events in words. Shots of bodies, gore, and nudity cause some readers to recoil and to protest. Scenes that seem to embarrass or disregard the dignity or privacy of their subjects call for judicious handling. The editor must anticipate such problems and make considered, defensible decisions about how to proceed.

Cutlines or *captions*, the brief explanatory material accompanying a published photo, must also receive the same attention as any other copy. Cutlines should be double-checked for accuracy (and, in particular, cross-checked for consistency with the text), fairness, and tone. Some guidelines for captions:

- Identify anyone who can be clearly seen in the photo.

- Avoid the obvious ("Players celebrate after win") and make sure the caption adds something interesting ("Star player waves to her 90-year-old grandmother after win").
- Consider telling the story behind the photo if it is unusual; or explain something confusing; or write about an unusual detail in the shot.
- Be clever, but not cutesy. A common piece of advice: If you have heard the bit of wordplay before, don't use it.

Graphics, illustrations, and other artwork

Early newspapers used "dingbats," or small typographic devices, to break up columns of type, providing contrast and increasing readability. Magazines, with their higher-quality paper and longer lead time, led the way toward more elaborate and sophisticated artwork. A generation or so ago, the bold graphic style of *USA Today* and the introduction of computer graphics technology fueled the trend toward increasing use of non-photographic art on newspaper pages and later websites. Now, editors use all these tools, plus advanced software for animations, 3D effects, and multimedia packaging, to craft a rich blend of both simple and elegant images and illustrations.

Like photos, these graphics, or infographics as they are often known, go far beyond the cosmetic. They can highlight or amplify information contained within a text article, stand alone as powerful storytellers and information conveyers, or join with audio or video elements into full-scale, interactive, multimedia presentations. The editor's job has expanded into making decisions about which single element or set of elements—text, photo, drawing, map, chart, graph, animation, or combination—works most appropriately with each topic and medium.

Infographics can range from simple locator maps to doubletruck illustrations of heart transplant techniques to multimedia Internet animations combining text, illustrations, animations, audio, video, and interactive components.

In the months following the devastating Hurricane Katrina in 2005, the *New Orleans Times-Picayune* published hundreds of infographics, both in print and online (see www.nola.com/katrina/graphics). Some were simple charts or graphs ("Demographics of the dead"), but others were complex, multimedia photo-illustrations conveying massive data in easy-to-absorb visual form ("Why the levees broke," "Battle against the sea," "Where the levees failed, and where the water settled"). Other examples can easily be found by typing "infographics" into a search engine.

Few editors will be full specialists in all the software, programs, and plug-ins used to produce such displays, but, as always, the editor's job is to help. As with photos, the editing of graphics begins at the conceptual stage and requires coordination throughout the process. Veteran designer and teacher Alberto Cairo lists four stages in developing an infographic:

- *Information gathering*, by reporters and artists
- *Planning*, involving consultation among all parties and artists' sketches and storyboards
- *Design* of main and secondary art, for both print and web
- *Final editing*, including review, revisions, corrections, layout, and production.[2]

Through these stages, editors, along with reporters, artists, designers, and others, must plan carefully and communicate regularly. For a complex package to have unity and maximum effect, it needs an editor's attention at every stage.

Again, just as stories and photos can produce both structural and content problems, so can graphics. Structurally, graphics must be correct and in clear, appropriate, easily grasped form. Their content, often necessarily simplified or abstracted, must not distort or exaggerate. Because graphics often deal with statistics and other mathematics, editors must show extra care in examining them for careless or logical errors.

A typical case might involve a graphic used to illustrate an unusual fall of the stock market. One way to illustrate the drop would be with a "fever line" charting the course of the stock price average over several weeks, up until the day of the fall. But does one draw the chart with a base point of, say, 0, or of, say, 10,000? Using a base of 10,000 will show a steady increase followed by a dramatic plunge almost to the bottom of the chart. Using a base of 0 will show a far less dramatic falling line. The choice may be between providing context or drama.

Print design

"These are happy times for newspaper design and designers," the design guru and theorist Mario Garcia has said. "We have technology that allows us to do it almost all. We as designers enjoy a greater acceptance among editors. Cooperation between those who deal with words and those who work with visuals is at its best."[3]

It is probably true that printed pages have never looked nicer. For evidence, visit on any day the large selection of front pages compiled on the Freedom Forum's Newseum website (www.newseum.org).

For our purposes, we will define *design* as the overall planning and coordination of a publication's look and *layout* as the arrangement of elements on an individual page. Some editors specialize in layout, others lay out pages occasionally, and still others never touch the keys of a pagination program. But, as part of their overall understanding of design, all of today's editors should become familiar with the essential principles and techniques. The new editor should (a) understand and appreciate design and layout, (b) feel comfortable working with design and designers, and (c) know how to develop attractive pages.

Design can be both highly subjective and highly technical. It is subjective because, like other aesthetic judgments, design choices can be rooted in personal, debatable ideas about style and beauty. And it is technical because designers use a host of methods and devices, both large and small, to create subtle, cumulative impressions. Ultimately, a reader sees a page in its entirety and may seldom notice individual techniques such as the size of rules, the space between headlines, or the careful matching of colors. The designer, however, begins with a collection of parts and must blend them one by one into a coherent, orderly, and attractive whole.

A successful page is not one that induces a reader to exclaim, "What a beautiful layout!" Instead, it is a page that the individual is attracted to, reads, and enjoys. Likewise a poor page does not cause readers to comment on its ugliness. It simply causes them to turn away.

Some principles of layout

- The goal of layout is to attract and assist readers. Layout editors try to package material in a neat, considered way that invites attention, makes it easy to understand and read the material, and encourages reading as much of a page as possible.
- A successful page layout should be orderly, easy to follow, visually exciting, and consistent with the general tone of a publication.
- Page layouts tend to employ similar aesthetic values to those used in other areas, such as fashion, decorating or art: grace, neatness, imagination, symmetry, order, cleanliness, elegance.
- Three key principles to keep in mind are *balance, variety,* and *proportion*:

    Balance refers to the arrangement of elements (photos, graphics, body type, headline type, and white space) on the page. A page should be somewhat top-heavy, with the most important items above the fold. But the bottom should not be ignored, and the page should not seem right-heavy or left-heavy, or very heavy in one area and very light in another. Each quadrant should have some appealing visual item.

    Variety, or contrast, means mixing elements to avoid monotony. Variety can be achieved in size (for example, using headlines of different sizes), shape (mixing horizontals and verticals), and weight (incorporating blacks, whites, grays, and colors). Notice that most pages use two or three widths of body type, both one-line and multiline headlines, and several different rectangular-shaped packages (known as *modules*).

    Proportion rests on the assumption, supported by research, that strongly rectangular shapes are more pleasing than squares and that several different shapes on a page are preferred to several similar ones.

With these principles in mind, an editor can turn to the detailed process of creating pages.

Some techniques of layout

Almost all contemporary layout is done on computer, using what first was called *desktop publishing* and later became better known as *pagination*. Designers often start with pencil-on-paper sketches, and some still use the traditional "dummy sheets," or blank paper forms on the scale of a news page. Pagination programs begin with the online equivalent of a dummy sheet: a blank form in proportion to the actual page size. Editors can import type, photos, art, and other elements onto the page, arrange and rearrange them at will, make all necessary edits, and produce a final design for printing.

Here is a step-by-step work flow for laying out a page. We will assume it is a news page, although the process is similar for feature pages and others.

1   List available articles, photos, illustrations, and other elements. Develop a general idea of what should go at top of page (generally the most important material) and what at bottom (lesser material, but at least one unusual or eye-catching element). Do not try to cram too much onto a page. For a news page, using four to six elements is typical. For a feature page, use two to four elements, giving more emphatic play to at least one.

2   Begin with your most important art and most important story. Decide where you want them, and how much space they should get. Usually, these two items should be clearly dominant, and they should go near the top of the page.

3   Make it unmistakable as to where you want the reader to begin. Arrange the dominant elements so a reader's eye naturally focuses first on them. This usually means placing the most important visual element at the *optical center* of the page. The optical center is the place where the human eye most naturally falls first, just above and to the left of the geographic center. (Think, for example, of where the first page of a book chapter typically appears—about a third of the way down the page and a little to the left of center.)

4   Place an item of interest at the bottom of the page: a package that can be attractively boxed, a story that can be "stripped" across all columns, a feature with a nice piece of art, a horizontal index, or teasers promoting material elsewhere in the publication.

5   Note what elements you have remaining. Think of your page as

having three sections: top, middle, bottom. Working toward the middle, find places for each remaining element.

6   Work with *modules* (blocks of material that form rectangles). Make each package, whether text only or text with art, "square off" at the bottom to form a rectangle. This gives distinct status to each module, prevents items from interfering with one another, and makes pages seem clean and uncluttered.

7   *Wrap* as little copy as possible, except for strongly horizontal modules. A wrap is copy that is continued from one column to the next. Do not require more than 4 or 5 inches of vertical jump for the reader's eye from the bottom of one leg of type to the top of the next.

8   Use photos large and strongly horizontal or vertical. Give special stress to one piece of art per page.

9   Use a variety of shapes, most horizontal, some vertical. Do not stack similar shapes and do not divide pages in half either horizontally or vertically.

10   Avoid massive areas of gray type (a massive area is defined as one where you can put down a hand on the page and touch only body type). Use white space to add contrast and to let a page "breathe."

11   Use summaries, boxes, checklists, enlarged quotes, tables, charts, and similar devices both to convey information and to provide page variety. Use tools such as rules, screens, colors, small typographical devices, and white space to call attention to special stories and to add variety.

12   Be careful about bumping headlines. It can have the same confusing effect as reacting to two people shouting for your attention at exactly the same time. Some designers detest bumping heads, but others believe it isn't as irritating as once thought. A good compromise: Don't overdo it.

13   Vary headline sizes and shapes: bold/italics, one-line and multiline, one column and wider. Use subheads, secondary decks, kickers, labels, and other special headline devices where appropriate.

14   Do not run a story out from under its headline. The headline should be an "umbrella" that covers the entire package, making the boundaries clear to the reader.

15   Use biggest headlines at top of page and one fairly large headline at the bottom. Use smallest headline sizes in the middle. For one-column headlines, use three or four lines. For two-column headlines, use two lines. For wider headlines, use one line. Make sure to provide adequate room for an informative, compelling headline.

Feature pages follow many of the basic principles, but they often may be designed more like magazine pages, striving to be bold, innovative, and eye-catching. They use fewer elements than news pages, and often one huge element will consume half the page or more. Art may be stylized or staged for effect (using models, posed scenes, collages, and other combinations, as long as they are not presented as reality). Drawings, cartoons, diagrams, and other non-photographic illustrations appear more often than on news pages.

Impressionistic elements give feature pages a distinctive tone. More variety is expected in type style and the sizes and shapes of art. Designers often use numerous special effects, including unconventional headlines, enlarged initial letters, unusual boxes, screens, splashes of color, ragged copy margins, and silhouetting.

Sports pages double as both news and feature pages. Typically, they resemble the former in presenting information in an orderly way based on its news value and the latter in the use of large art and striking packaging. In fact, sports designers enjoy one key advantage over their colleagues from other sections: the almost daily presence of strong, dramatic, action photographs. Use them and use them big.

Overall, specialty pages such as features and sports begin with the fundamental precepts of design, including balance, variety, proportion, and the use of modules, and then adapt them to suit particular audiences and tastes. As always, the goal is to create clear, interesting, creative, dramatic pages that will lure and serve readers.

Web design

One word sums up the essential philosophy behind web design: *usefulness*.

Web readers move fast. They prefer well-organized, easy-to-navigate sites offering maximum choice and efficiency without seeming cluttered, confusing, or junky. Bright, attractive design helps, but, if the choice is between beauty and utility, web users want utility. They look for a full menu of choices that will direct them to their desired destination in one or two or certainly no more than three clicks of the mouse.

News web pages differ in significant ways from their print counterparts. They have unlimited space. They support multimedia presentation. They are interactive. They are nonlinear. They offer immediacy. They can be changed at will. So the designer's challenge becomes to respect the needs of the hurrying consumer, employ the vast powers of the web, and deliver pages that are journalistically sound, aesthetically pleasing, winningly imaginative, and rewardingly usable.

Look at a news organization's home page on a typical day, and here is what you may see:

- The screen divided into a grid of from two to five vertical columns, each providing a relatively short, easy-to-read line width
- One dominant photo (proportionately smaller than the lead photo on a printed page), generally around the optical center, plus one or more smaller photos

- Six to eight, sometimes more, news items featured in the interior columns, with a headline, perhaps a secondary head, a sentence or two summary, and often a time stamp to show their freshness
- At least one column, often the left-most, devoted to a list of menu choices (world news, local news, sports, and so forth), sometimes using windows that open with dozens more choices
- Overall, a huge number of links: often 50 or 60 or more within the first screen
- Audio clips
- Video clips
- Slide shows or galleries
- Ads integrated onto the page, often toward the right or the bottom of the screen
- Search boxes
- Interactive features (quizzes, comment boxes, polls, searchable maps and charts)
- Blogs
- Customization options (for instance, to localize the weather report or stock tables or to arrange for feeds to your cell phone or other mobile device).

Whereas a print newspaper will design its front page fresh each day, starting with a blank screen or dummy, its online site typically uses a standardized design tool that offers several templates from which to select. Web producers choose a template, create a page, and then revise and update it seamlessly by plugging in new items as time progresses. If necessary, for example when a huge story breaks, they can easily switch to another template already designed for such a situation.

As they develop and deliver their templates and designs, online editors keep in mind several other considerations not found in print:

- People end up at a website in many ways. While they may type in the site's address and travel directly, they often come through links they have seen elsewhere. So they surface in the middle of the site. Pages need clear brand identity so readers recognize where they are, and interior pages and features need strong links that encourage newcomers to visit the home page and stay awhile.
- Similarly, readers tend to jump rapidly from site to site, so web designers should work hard to encourage additional clicks within their own sites. Captivating headlines, logical forward and backward linking, and tantalizing teasers at the end of each block or item can help keep viewers within the site.
- Nearly everyone appreciates the web's immediacy, but a lesser-appreciated attribute is its permanence. Special projects, award-winning presentations, and popular reader-service features can be

displayed indefinitely. But designers need to periodically check that they still are displaying properly and perhaps refresh or update them.

- Readers coming to a web page should find something exciting and unavailable elsewhere. For example, the web presents unprecedented opportunities for integrated, nonlinear storytelling, blending text, images, graphics, audio, video, and audience reaction and participation.

For all its modernistic differences from plain old print, web design ultimately has exactly the same goal: to grab and hold a time-starved audience by offering worthwhile content and services in the most useful possible way.

Conclusion

Design links news organizations to their audiences. Like translators, designers stand in the middle. They are connectors. As journalists, designers must appreciate the subtleties and sensitivities of content, whether news or features, whether on paper or online. As friends of the audience, they must recognize the needs and tastes of potential readers and viewers and the never-ending competition for time and attention. Then they must shape the content into formats that hurried readers find engaging and meaningful, without letting format misshape or overwhelm substance.

Without doubt, presentation decisions are editing decisions, fully intertwined with and equally important to judgments about coverage, coaching, content, and structure. They bring editors to the end of the production cycle, and they demand creativity and vigilance to the very last moment. It is with these final touches that success of the whole enterprise rides. Poor presentation undermines everything that has gone before it, but good presentation enables journalists to achieve their foremost goals of maximizing readership and communication.

Sidebar 10: A visit to an online newsroom

The *USA Today* web staff is gathering for its 8:15 a.m. "cabinet meeting," so called because the nine editors huddle around a row of metal filing cabinets.

Usatoday.com staffs its home page around the clock, although less gets posted once the newspaper's contents are uploaded by midnight. The home page editor this day, Brett Molina, 30, has been on duty since 6 a.m., updating stories about a mine fire and a terrorism tape.

The news meeting, one of several daily, resembles the typical print get-together, except more attention goes to multimedia and special effects. For example, Chet Czarniak, 55, the online managing editor who presides, expresses concern about live coverage of the mining disaster. "If raw video comes in," he warns, "be careful what we use."

Another exchange highlights the costs and benefits of immediacy. An editor has spotted what he calls a classic dumb headline, "Flawed coin was a mistake." Unlike in a print edition where it would live forever, the head has been quickly rewritten.

USA Today was an early mover toward print–online staff integration, with editor Ken Paulson pushing for "a single 24-hour news organization." The printed paper and its website face an unusual mission, since they don't produce local news. Their national audience spills over several time zones. Viewers come for assorted news, sports, and the special packages and surprises associated with the *USA Today* brand. Usatoday.com puts less stress on breaking-news updates from its reporters than on special stories, imaginative packaging, and web-only features.

"What we're trying to do online," says one producer, "is celebrate a new way of storytelling that leverages our expertise in visuals, graphics, and multimedia."

The action seems nonstop, with the home page changing almost constantly.

"The pace is just incredible," says managing editor Czarniak. "Saturday at 11 p.m. is just as important as Monday at 11 a.m. Speed to market is vital. It's not even a deadline a minute. There are constant deadlines. Our train is always leaving the station."

News editor Randy Lilleston, 46, sees "print people" learning "broadcast sensibilities." "Stories are not permanent," he says. "They evolve. The story you read now is not the same as the one you'll read in two hours."

Lilleston worries about balancing accuracy and speed.

"Do you get the vetting you get in a newspaper? No, you do not," he says. But he adds crisply, "I reject the idea that online is an excuse for sloppiness. One of my goals is to knock down the idea that it is okay to be temporarily wrong. It is not okay."

Lilleston sees progress toward online safeguards. For example, most items posted directly are short, so typos and errors may be relatively easy to spot. Without a copydesk, editors are expected to turn to the person sitting next to them for a "second set of eyes." They constantly read behind each other, before and after postings. "I'd rather wait a minute or two and make sure it's right," says home page editor Molina.

News director Patty Michalski, 33, who oversees the home page, supports the point. "Get it right the first time," she says. "If it means taking two seconds longer, so be it."

Michalski also stresses those small but all-important headlines, subheads (known as "chatter") and blurbs. Those few words often determine readership. She pushes posters to seek suggestions from others and to consider "anything to make it a teensy bit more specific."

Even here, where the printed newspaper helped revolutionize design, the look of the home page remains relatively constant. Except for mammoth stories, the home page sticks to two or three standard looks, with templates for easy posting.

Consolidating print and web journalists was a culture shock, but Czarniak says merging makes sense for production, quality, and content. "The ultimate vision is that there are conversations about content among everyone," he says. "You're not concerned about the platform. You're concerned about how to tell the story."[4]

Vignettes

The *American Editor*, the fine publication of the American Society of Newspaper Editors, once compiled advice from designers and presentation experts around the country. Here are some of their wise words:[5]

- "Good design starts with critical thinking by designers, photographers, graphic artists, text and photo editors, copyeditors, and reporters."—Marcia Prouse, *Orange County Register*
- "You, the editor, need to care about the presentation of stories. Planning is key—daily, weekly, and monthly. Your planning meetings need to include a designer, a photo editor, and a graphic editor."—Nanette Bisher, *San Francisco Examiner*
- "There are, for me, two key elements for doing—or attempting to do—great design. One is knowing and loving content. . . . The second element is immersing yourself in others' work. Studying all design all the time lets you build a mental repertoire of tactics."—Geoffrey Giordano, *Journal News*, White Plains, N.Y.

11 Making decisions about legal issues

The early 21st century brought two major developments destined to revolutionize the relationship between journalists and the law: the surge in tightened access and secrecy following the September 11, 2001, terrorist attacks and the maturing of the Internet into a world-changing social, political, economic, and journalistic institution.

These milestones complicated editors' duties in protecting their ever-expanding news outlets from ever-growing challenges in an ever-litigious society. But despite all the changes, they did not alter the individual editor's role. Instead, they underlined it as an eternal principle of good journalism. The editor is not a *lawyer*, but a *noticer*. The editor's job is not to solve legal problems but to identify them, notify senior editors, and see that they receive proper attention from managers and actual lawyers.

The 9/11 attacks triggered vast concerns about security. In the aftermath came controversial new limits and pressures on free speech, open government, and access to records and documents. At least for a while, the government seemed to gain the upper hand in deciding what records and actions became public, and an increasingly conservative federal judiciary largely went along. "Post-Sept. 11 actions taken by the government regarding information policy have greatly damaged what citizens know about government operations," concluded Lucy Dalglish of the Reporters Committee for Freedom of the Press.

> Since Sept. 11, we've seen Justice Department directives restricting use of the Freedom of Information Act, an increase in the number of classified documents, frequent use by the government of the state secrets privilege, and zealous pursuit of government "leakers" who speak to the media.[1]

As the Internet exploded around the world, its ubiquity and scope challenged and sometimes overwhelmed earlier understandings of speech limits, intellectual property rights, and legal jurisdictions. Early court decisions seemed to promote openness and broadly interpreted speech rights, but many fundamental questions remained without definitive legal answers. On issues such as obscenity or defamation, what country's laws apply when web postings go around the world? Do host media (including journalistic websites) share liability for libelous postings or comments on reader blogs, message boards, and links? What rules should guide copyright and intellectual property concerns in an age where documents, images, music, news and entertainment programming, and audio and video clips of all kinds can be easily and universally accessed, exchanged, and even manipulated?

For all these reasons and others, few areas of editing have expanded as much in recent times as those dealing with legal concerns. Journalists have become masters of defensive editing, striving to anticipate problems and ward off legal challenges before they develop. Lawyers stand on call for reporters facing subpoenas, photographers worried about invasion of privacy, or web producers concerned about copyright infringement.

In part, this defensiveness stems from growing professionalism within journalism itself. As standards rise, editors naturally give content more scrutiny. After all, few if any journalists actually want to violate the law or provoke a lawsuit. But what is happening today also evidences more troubling conditions. One is journalists' widespread concern about public hostility toward the press. In our large and contentious society, the mass media may seem to many people to be big, impersonal, heartless money machines and, consequently, inviting targets for complaints and lawsuits. Fearing an aroused public, journalists tend to watch their step.

In addition, many journalists perceive that the judicial system, up through the U.S. Supreme Court, has become less friendly to the press, more willing to compel reporters' testimony, for example, or to restrain publication. If so, court action is even more to be avoided. The distinguished press lawyer Bruce Sanford put it starkly: "First Amendment law is stagnating in a nation grown as cynical about the value of free expression as it is enraptured with the dream of becoming a software millionaire."[2]

Then there were fears of being labeled as unpatriotic in the nervous climate of constant terror threats. Lisa Finnegan, a journalist turned psychologist, examined press behavior following the 9/11 attacks and concluded that "journalists were shaken ... they were focused on the fact that the United States was vulnerable, and deemed everything else unimportant." So they didn't aggressively resist government moves to suppress information or dissent.

The press hardly reacted, Finnegan wrote, when President George W. Bush's spokesman warned, "All Americans ... need to watch what they say," or when then Attorney General John Ashcroft complained, about those who questioned newly restrictive laws, "Your tactics only aid terrorists."

"We are giving the government the benefit of the doubt," CBS News

President Andrew Heyward said. "We'll do whatever is our patriotic duty," News Corporation head Rupert Murdoch added.[3]

Whatever the full range of causes, one result is probably more careful, responsible journalism. Another, however, may be excessive self-doubt and self-censorship, editing grown overly defensive. This is called the *chilling effect*.

For all these reasons, then, editors find themselves acting almost as paralegal trouble-shooters, sandwiched between gung-ho reporters and photographers on one side and cautious lawyers and publishers on the other:

- A reporter has discovered juicy information after overhearing jury members in conversation. The news organization's lawyer warns that, if published, it could lead to contempt proceedings.
- A reporter has sworn herself to secrecy to protect a source. The publisher fears huge fines and jail terms from an angry judge insisting on the source's name.
- A photographer has shots of a violent police–labor confrontation. Lawyers for both sides demand published and unpublished files.
- A website solicits comments on a music review. Many are profane and perhaps defamatory.

Although such examples are not unusual, they regularly are accompanied by lengthy deliberations involving lawyers, publishers, editors, and line journalists. What can sometimes be even more dangerous are the routine, everyday legal issues that may arise without fanfare and that may slip past less-than-alert reporters and editors. In fact, it is something of a truism among lawyers and editors that legal trouble may arise as much in the small items and tidbits as in the high-profile projects that get painstaking scrutiny.

In view of such an environment, what is the editor's role? How can editors balance the tension between their duties as law-respecting citizens and as unfettered journalists? Many years ago, editor Bill Schultz offered an answer that still stands: "Our challenge as editors is to respond to [these] concerns—to teach our reporters and editors how to be careful without becoming timid."[4]

Needless to say, editors should increase their understanding of potential legal problems. In addition, they should try to develop a philosophical framework for analyzing their obligations and expectations. Before getting to some specific trouble spots, then, we should try to delineate a strategic overview for editors confronting legal issues. It might begin with the following major tenets:

- *The editor's job is to edit:* to gather and publish material of value to the readers. It is not to solve crimes, protect government secrets, or prosecute cases. Those are worthy roles, and editors seldom oppose them, but fulfilling them is a task assigned to others.

- *The editor must respect courts but see them in context.* Unlike police and lawyers who swear to uphold the law, journalists do not do that. Certainly, they are not exempt, but extreme circumstances may lead them to challenge current readings of the law, as editors have done from John Peter Zenger to the publishers of the Pentagon Papers.
- *Editors should learn about the law, but never try to be lawyers.* Do not try to outguess lawyers. They do not think like other people. When you need legal advice, consult a good lawyer with a commitment to First Amendment values.
- *Editors should listen to lawyers but make their own decisions.* To a lawyer, the judicial process can be an end in itself. To an editor, the end is the best interests of truth and the audience. Sometimes this means taking a chance by publishing investigative material that could spark a lawsuit. Other times it means defying politically motivated efforts at censorship. And still other times it means leaving out risky copy that serves no overriding purpose. Lawyers should offer advice on the law and the risks of certain action. Journalists should decide what course to pursue and what risks to accept.

If editors cannot be expected to fully understand complexities of the law, how can they do their jobs with least risk? As is true with content and structural editing, a start is for each editor to develop a sense of the danger areas, a working understanding of where potential trouble most likely lurks.

Further, editors must not relent on the fundamentals. Carelessness and inattention can bring legal battles just as quickly as irresponsibility. The name you do not double-check may be the one that is misspelled or transposed so as to libel an innocent person. The columnist's work you approve each day with a glance may one day contain plagiarism. The human-interest photo you select at the last minute may depict a disabled child and produce a privacy claim. The assistant barely mentioned in paragraph 19 of an otherwise perfect investigation of a local official may have a case against you even if the official doesn't. Simply put, never take editing shortcuts with even the most innocuous-seeming items.

In the following sections, we briefly examine several areas relating to press law. Remember, this is not a law textbook providing legal advice. It is a sharing of experience, from journalist to journalist, about how to sense impending trouble.

Libel

This is the hardy perennial, the sleeping ogre all journalists tiptoe softly around. Libel has many complex legal definitions, but they boil down to the following: Libel is published, false material that defames someone. Libel laws apply to all media, from print to broadcast to the Internet. Beyond that, what editors need to know is that libel is what a judge and jury say it is. Because it involves issues like reputation and character, libel can be subjective and slippery. That means lots of work for lawyers and lots of confusion for journalists.

Common categories of libel include:

- Accusations of a crime
- Charges of immorality
- Insinuations of insanity or loathsome diseases
- Claims of incompetence in business

Defenses for libel begin with *truth*. You need not worry about libel if you can prove to a jury's satisfaction that what you published is true. Clearly, however, truth is a sticky term. How, for instance, does one prove the truth of concepts such as "immoral" or "loathsome" or "incompetent"? Although truth is an adequate defense, it can be a slippery one.

Two other defenses are important. First is *fair comment*, an individual's right to express an opinion about public affairs (such as politics) and public performances (such as movies or books). An opinion, even a harsh one, is not libelous if it is founded on facts and relevant to a public matter. However, opinions that rely on false assertions, such as calling someone a liar without any proof, are not protected and can draw suits.

Second is *qualified privilege*, the right to report on official proceedings (like city council meetings) and official documents (like most court papers), as long as the reporting is fair and accurate. A key point here is that the material in question must have been uttered or written in an official forum. If a member of Congress takes to the floor of the House of Representatives and calls a colleague a tax cheat, you can publish the charge without fear of libel. However, if the member makes the same charge in conversation while walking to the chamber, it is unofficial, and publishing it could constitute libel.

In the past, some judicial jurisdictions recognized what was called a doctrine of *neutral reporting*, which allowed journalists to report, without libel jeopardy, the informal statements of public officials even when they might be defamatory. In 2005, however, the U.S. Supreme Court let stand a Pennsylvania Supreme Court decision nullifying the neutral reporting protection. Because the top U.S. court simply let stand the state decision rather than conduct a full review on its own, the case did not definitively settle the issue. But the action certainly put the neutral reporting doctrine into such doubt that editors would be unwise to depend on it.

Since the landmark 1964 *Sullivan decision* of the U.S. Supreme Court, distinction has been made between *public figures* and *private figures*. In its 1964 decision and follow-ups, the court ruled that under the Constitution the press and public have great freedom to debate controversial public issues, without undue fear of libel suits. For public figures to collect libel damages, they must prove not merely libel but also *actual malice*.

Unfortunately, when the court chose the term *malice*, it did not use it in the ordinary meaning of "bad motives." In libel, actual malice has a much narrower meaning. It generally means either of two things: knowingly publishing untruths (lying) or "reckless disregard for the truth" (excessively unprofessional conduct such as deliberately publishing a defamation you know is almost certainly false). Motives are not really relevant, although courts do allow some questions about a journalist's "state of mind." What matters most is what journalists knew and did at the time of publication.

Generally, in libel cases involving public figures, the burden of proof lies with those suing the press. That is, they must prove the press acted with malice. But, pragmatically, it makes sense for editors to assume in their own minds that they carry the burden of proof. When confronting potentially libelous material as an editor, ask yourself this question: Can you convince a jury that you acted without malice and in the public interest? Is the evidence adequate for the assertions being made, and is all conflicting evidence being carefully considered? If not, reconsider.

The rise of the Internet has so far had relatively little effect on the basic premises of libel law. That is, it hasn't changed much about the definition or defenses. But it has raised some procedural questions of especial meaning to editors:

- *Jurisdiction.* Cyberspace is universal not local. Web postings cross all borders and can be accessed from almost anywhere. Does that mean a news organization in Idaho could be successfully sued for a posting that violates the libel laws of Pakistan? Kevin Goldberg, a lawyer for the American Society of Newspaper Editors, put the issue this way: "The ultimate question posed by defamation lawsuits for publishing on the Internet: Will jurisdictional issues erase borders or build impenetrable walls?"[5] Goldberg found several conflicting court decisions, leading him to conclude that the matter remains unsettled and should be carefully watched by editors.

- *Responsibility for blogs and posts from outsiders.* Interactivity is a hallmark of the web, and news websites teem with audience comments and two-way conversations, sometimes carefully monitored, sometimes spontaneous, live, and raw. Congress acted in the 1990s to shield website owners from liability for what outsiders post, but the posters themselves (whether outsiders or associated with the website) are subject to libel laws. A *USA Today* survey found that in just two years, 2005–2006, dozens of suits were filed based on comments on blogs and message boards. They included suits for libel, invasion of privacy, and negligence. Early decisions suggested judges would give "wide latitude" to web postings, *USA Today* reported, but the issue remained alive and subject to change.[6]

- *Live appearances by journalists.* Broadcasters long have known that libel laws apply to their work. But today, as more and more journalists operate across various media, reporters and editors trained in print also find themselves appearing increasingly on live radio, television, cable, and online programs. Where their journalism may be carefully vetted before publication, their off-the-cuff comments are not, and they can cause trouble. At least one libel case has arisen based on a reporter's amplification, on cable, of a story published in a newspaper. Press lawyer James Grossberg warned that reporters appearing live "need to be aware of potential legal problems when [they] speak outside of the pages of the newspaper or outside the confines of the broadcast booth." Further, he said, a journalist "should think about what he or she is saying in the same context as when he or she is composing a story."[7]

Finally, several possible misconceptions and pitfalls surrounding libel should be clarified:

- *Don't depend on the word "allegedly."* It is a hedge word that does not help in fending off libel. You should consider the sentence, "Smith allegedly robbed the bank" to be the same, legally speaking, as "Smith absolutely robbed the bank." Better to say "Smith is *charged with* robbing the bank" (assuming, of course, that charges have been filed). I recommend eliminating "allegedly" from your vocabulary.
- *Attributing libelous material to a source doesn't necessarily relieve journalists of responsibility for what they publish.* If you quote Jones as falsely saying, "Smith is a drug dealer," you may be as guilty of libel as Jones, and even more likely to be sued because news organizations are easy targets. In general, it is best to consider yourself responsible for the content of what you publish regardless of source or attribution, unless the material falls under a protected category such as qualified privilege.
- *Beware of headlines and cutlines.* They can libel too. In fact, big type can exacerbate libel problems. Do you know how often journalists spend months on investigative projects, only to have the headlines and cutlines slapped on minutes before deadline? That can be very dangerous.
- *Beware of big problems in small places.* Libel can occur, for instance, in the agate-type police roundup column or in a paragraph mentioning a bit player in an otherwise perfect story focused on someone else. Precision is important. One paper lost a classic judgment after using the term *testimony* when *affidavit* was correct.[8]

- *As in every legal matter, recognize that state and local laws aren't all alike.* Learn the peculiarities of your own state's laws. In some places, for instance, a publication can reduce or eliminate libel liability by publishing a correction or retraction as soon as an error comes to its attention. Some courts have indicated that quickly correcting an erroneous web posting can reduce the harm and therefore reduce potential liability.
- *As an editor, remember your quality-control function.* Insist that copy have satisfactory evidence, documentation, and sourcing for any potentially damaging charge. Do not fear challenging a reporter or source. Better to argue out tough points in the newsroom than in the courtroom. And do not shrink from getting legal advice when you need it.
- *Use common sense and common courtesy.* Surveys have shown that people tend to sue for libel *after* they have tried vainly to get satisfaction more informally. Some sue after being treated rudely or being patronized when they try to reach a news organization to complain. An easy but appallingly overlooked point: Train people who answer your newsroom telephones or screen email to be respectful to individuals (even angry ones) and to pass complaints along to someone with authority. When I was a supervising editor, I always told my staff to assume that every caller was the publisher's cousin.

The press also might benefit by helping educate the public in the difficulties of journalism. Reporting is a complex and imperfect craft, where the truth is elusive and often deliberately obscured. It would help if the public showed more patience with the inevitable errors and abuses that get into journalism and if it supported open records, public meetings, and the general forthrightness needed to bolster fair and accurate reporting.

Then, journalists should stop being such know-it-alls. They should remember how much there is, on nearly every story, that they do not know. They should distinguish between fact on the one hand, and opinions, inferences, or hunches on the other. They should acknowledge when evidence is conflicting. And, of course, they should give their critics ample opportunity to comment and to respond.

With such steps on both sides, the desire to resort to court battles might abate.

Invasion of privacy

Compared to libel, privacy is a newer, more confusing area of press law, but editors should keep in mind one bit of perspective. Whereas libel law has evolved in ways generally calculated to protect speech, privacy law contains much less built-in respect for the press.

Privacy actions divide into four categories:

- Intrusion, or the common-sense definition of invasion of privacy as an infringement on someone's solitude or property, either physically or electronically
- Disclosure of embarrassing private facts, such as medical or sexual records or old indiscretions no longer relevant
- Placing someone in a false light, making an individual appear (through a photo or a docudrama technique, for example) to be something different from what is true
- Misappropriation of likeness, using someone's name or image for commercial advantage without permission.

Defenses begin with *permission*. Individuals can waive their privacy claims by inviting you onto their property or signing consent forms for your use of certain material. Otherwise, privacy cases tend to turn on issues such as *newsworthiness* and *relevance*. For example, if an individual was convicted 20 years ago of assault, reporting on the case now, for no good reason, might constitute invasion of privacy. If the individual chooses to run for the local school board, however, the old conviction might gain renewed newsworthiness.

As with libel, the Internet age has brought new concerns over privacy, many of them affecting the news media at least indirectly. For instance, many blogs, personal web pages, and social networking sites include highly personal discussions of health and sexuality, intimate photos and video, and disclosures by and about under-aged minors. Web cams and microphones capture images and voices of people in private as well as public settings. Smaller cameras and recorders can be used with less chance of detection than in the past. As news sites increasingly accept contributions from citizens, venture into interactive partnerships, and link to other sites, they raise the risk of connecting to legally troublesome material.

Awareness and vigilance are the editor's best defenses. Try to avoid posting unedited or unmonitored material, to know the standards and practices of affiliated sites, and to alert all reporters, web producers, and other staff members about the potential for privacy concerns. Obtain written permission if possible when privacy questions may be raised, for example in articles or postings that deal with sensitive personal matters such as illness or abuse. As always, immediately seek appropriate legal advice anytime possible privacy issues arise.

In privacy as in libel and elsewhere, the editor is not expected to fully comprehend the legal intricacies. The editor's clear duty, however, is to know enough to spot potential problems and then get whatever expert help is needed to solve them.

Courts and contempt

In 2005, *New York Times* reporter Judith Miller spent 85 days in jail for refusing to reveal sources in a government leak investigation. Eventually, Lewis Libby, chief of staff to then Vice President Dick Cheney, was convicted of obstruction and perjury in the case. In what a *Times* news analysis called "a spectacle that would have been unthinkable only a few years ago," 10 of the 19 witnesses at Libby's trial were journalists.[9]

The case, which centered on leaks about CIA agent Valerie Plame, ended what investigative reporter and journalism professor Mark Feldstein called a "truce" that had held for a generation between the authorities and journalists. Although the U.S. Supreme Court ruled in 1972 that reporters have no special First Amendment privilege to shield sources, prosecutors and judges had shown reluctance to push the issue.

Journalists long had firmly opposed forcing their testimony, claiming that it makes them arms of law enforcement and discourages nervous sources from taking reporters into their confidence. Although most courts did not embrace this argument, many judges and the government did tend to set strict conditions on when journalists could be subpoenaed. Two typical conditions were that (a) the material being subpoenaed must be specific and central to a case and (b) every effort should be made to get it elsewhere so that subpoenaing a journalist became only a last resort. Even though some journalists did go to jail for what was regarded as an ethical imperative to refuse to reveal sources, the conditions tended to minimize such confrontations.

The Plame case changed nothing about the law, but it did spotlight a powerful new government tactic: asking (or, as some worried, pressuring) sources to sign waivers invalidating their confidentiality agreements with journalists. Once such waivers were signed, the government argued, journalists no longer should feel ethically compelled to stay mum. But reporters, including Miller, whose source (Libby himself) finally waived confidentiality and ended her jail stay, worried that the waivers might not be truly voluntary. The outcome was a high-visibility test case showing reporters for the nation's major news organizations submitting to government interrogation.

Surveying the issue for *American Journalism Review*, writer Rachel Smolkin concluded:

> Prominent First Amendment attorneys and activists say an alarming spate of high-profile court cases in which reporters have been ordered to disclose confidential sources and other materials could have sobering ramifications for newsgathering. They warn of a chilling effect on sources' willingness to share unflattering information about employers, stifling reporters' ability to unearth—and to tell the public— government secrets such as Watergate and the Abu Ghraib prison

abuse scandal. Disturbing new techniques ... such as asking government employees to sign waivers releasing reporters from confidentiality agreements, could spread into the corporate sphere and imperil reporting there.[10]

For editors, the operational question becomes how to instruct reporters to deal with sources in the first place. Clearly, it seems advisable to limit confidentiality agreements to minimal, exceptional circumstances where the source cannot be convinced to go on the record and there is no other way to get vital information. "The starting place should be let's put everything on the record and then work towards confidentiality," lawyer Mark Bailen said at a conference on the issue.[11]

What happens when reporters' notes or testimony is sought?

First, all staff members can be directed to volunteer nothing. If contacted by a prosecutor or lawyer, they should make no agreements and immediately refer the inquiry to their editors. I have known reporters who, in a naive willingness to be helpful, have volunteered on the spot to testify in court or cooperate in a case. Despite the good intentions, they should know that such actions have serious implications. For example, once reporters have been subpoenaed in a controversy, they may become a part of the story and therefore no longer free to cover it. Worse, once they testify even on something innocuous, they may lose any leverage to decline to reveal more important confidences. News organizations should develop policies for these occasions, and editors should explicitly stress them to reporters.

What should a reporter do if subpoenaed while in court? This occasionally happens when a reporter is covering a case she or he knows a great deal about. In such an event, reporters can be directed to ask for a brief recess in order to consult their employers and attorneys. Judges usually will honor such a request.

However, reporters often find themselves tongue-tied when forced, under such pressure, to interrupt a court proceeding. So it may help if editors provide, in advance, wallet or purse cards with an appropriate statement written out. As a city editor, I once devised such a statement with help from the newspaper's lawyer. It read as follows:

> Your honor, I am _____, a reporter for (a local media outlet). I request that the court allow a brief recess in order for me to consult with my editor and with the paper's legal counsel.
>
> I have been advised by my editor and the paper's legal counsel to seek a brief recess if ordered to testify on short notice because I may be asked to provide information that is privileged.

Once a request for notes or testimony has been referred to editors, how should they respond? That will vary, depending on the editor, the nature of the issue, and the policy of the news organization. Often, editors will try to explain the First Amendment concerns in a way that causes a lawyer to back off. Other times, editors will refer the inquiry to company lawyers.

How should the lawyers respond? Several things help. Often, when news organization lawyers explain the legitimate journalistic concerns involved, the inquiring lawyers will yield. Most lawyers have more important things to do than to bog down in time-consuming First Amendment battles. So delay and determination can be important allies for the journalist. If these tactics fail, challenging subpoenas in court may come next.

What if all this fails? While traditionally the majority of subpoena cases could be deflected, some cannot be. If such cases, editors should explore every option. In some cases, for instance, a court may settle for a sworn statement vouching for the accuracy of information in a story or negotiate limits on questioning. This can reduce the extent of the disclosure and sometimes prevent a reporter's appearance in court.

Usually, it is a line reporter threatened with jailing, not an editor. But editors (and publishers) can certainly stand with their reporters, to the point of demanding to be held accountable *instead* of their staff members. Matters tend to go far better if the entire news organization—including publisher, editor, and reporter—is perceived as standing side by side before the court.

It should be noted that many states have *shield laws*, which grant journalists protection from some court-ordered disclosures. However, these laws vary greatly and typically contain loopholes and exceptions. While all editors should become familiar with the pertinent laws in their states, they may not be able to fully depend on them for protection.

Access and court coverage. Another matter that sometimes engages journalists and legal authorities involves access to court proceedings. Several Supreme Court rulings have underlined the nation's commitment to open court hearings and trials, but some lawyers and judges still occasionally push for secrecy. In such cases, reporters should immediately contact their editors and lawyers. Some editors also instruct their reporters to protest to the judge on the spot. Again, the best course is to prepare the reporter, in advance, with whatever wording and procedures are appropriate when a judge threatens to close court.

Similar action is called for when officials attempt to close public meetings or forbid access to public documents. Editors should see that they and their reporters learn state and local laws regarding open meetings and records. In fact, many reporters carry copies of the laws with them and pull them out in protest when officials try to halt access. Often such challenges are sufficient to make bureaucrats and politicians reconsider.

Free press versus fair trial. This once-hot issue hinged on whether news stories and editorials, particularly in spectacular criminal cases, could prejudice the public so much that individuals could not get fair trials. This argument raged more furiously a few years ago than now.

Traditionally, it has been compromised in a way that generally favors freedom to attend trials and publish most material. "Gag orders," or other court-ordered restraints on the flow of information, should be last resorts. Before they are allowed, courts try alternatives such as interviewing large numbers of potential jurors in order to find enough unbiased jurors, delaying trials until public furor cools, moving trials to new locations, and sequestering jurors to prevent their access to press reports.

For its part, the press has tended to voluntarily accept a duty to avoid unduly inflammatory pretrial publicity. Journalists also have cited research showing that most jurors can and will decide cases on the evidence, not the advance coverage. More important may be the need to keep courts open so the public can see justice in action.

Behavior in and around courts. Courts and judges tend to vary somewhat in what rules apply to covering court cases. For instance, are cameras allowed in the courtroom? Are photographers allowed in the court building or restricted to some distance away? What kinds of technical equipment (recorders, cell phones, laptop computers, pagers) are allowed, and when and where? Usually judges set fairly clear rules on these matters in advance, but journalists should take pains to become aware of them. If the restrictions seem too rigid, editors should be consulted, and editors and lawyers should consider whether to approach the court with requests to negotiate.

Copyright

Very early in the digital age, a reporter I know discovered that a story she wrote had been copied and was circulating on the Internet. She was proud—until she read the online version. Her original story, published in a major metro newspaper, had been a balanced look at a controversial topic. But the online version contained only one side. Someone had systematically deleted all the balancing comments but had left the reporter's byline and media affiliation, making it appear that the unfair and incomplete story was her doing.

In journalistic terms, there was no way to answer the question of "who" had done it. But the "how" was easy. The electronic storage and transmission of information make it simple to find, retrieve, store, manipulate, share, and spread content of every kind, from text to rock music to movie clips. In most cases, the trail is so complicated that even expert technicians cannot retrace it to a source.

Information is everywhere. The web is infinite. And as more and more of the world's articles, books, songs, and movies become digitized, a huge power shift takes place. Where once content was almost entirely controlled by its *producers*, power now falls to *consumers*. The speed and ease with which information can be processed and exchanged online create an unprecedented challenge for our application of copyright and intellectual property laws.

The theory behind copyright is simple. The creator of an artistic product deserves a reasonable degree of control over how it is used in the marketplace, including copying, performing, distributing, and selling. *Copyright violation* is the unauthorized use of creative material owned by someone else.

Until recently, copyright rarely posed major problems for editors in a news setting. When they reprinted articles or photos from other sources, they gave credit and paid applicable fees, and that was about it. However, in a multimedia, interactive publishing environment, the situation becomes trickier. How do editors verify the originality of reader-submitted text and images? What restrictions apply in distributing blogs or compiling packages where text, audio, and video from online sources may be embedded? Conversely, what rights and concerns should journalists have when their original material turns up on other sites, especially the hugely popular portal and aggregator sites that collect words and clips from multiple sources?

Historically, it has been considered *fair use* to publish, *with attribution*, brief excerpts of copyrighted material, especially in journalistic or educational media. Again, however, the online revolution complicates the situation because web capacity is unlimited. A newspaper review of a book, for example, has space for no more than a few sentences from the work. Online, however, you could link to a whole chapter or the entire book. What should be considered "fair"?

In recent years, Congress has tightened federal laws regarding copyright infringement, notably in the Digital Millennium Copyright Act of 1998. It strengthened anti-piracy provisions and extended copyright terms, but it also generally relieved service providers of liability for simple transmission of problematic content.

Still, while exact copyright guidelines remain elusive and call for expert guidance, here are some generalities that can help guide editors' thinking:

- *Number of words.* There are no official quantitative rules governing how many words or what proportion of a work is allowed under fair use. A good rule of thumb is to avoid major damage to the work's commercial value. Publishing just a few excerpts of a short poem, for instance, may be considered unfair. Even with a book, posting a short passage that gives away the key point or most valuable information may undermine its value enough to cause problems.
- *Postings.* Email and web postings are copyrighted and are not in the public domain unless the poster expressly says so.
- *Linking.* Simple linking to a site does not usually violate copyright.

- *Permission*. Copyrighted material should virtually always be attributed, even under fair use. If you have any doubts about copyright, try to get permission before using or posting.

For now there are competing philosophies about the future of copyright. On one side are those who defend maximum protection for creative work and support tough enforcement against downloaders, file sharers, and those considered "pirates." On the other side are those who feel the web has rendered such strict enforcement unworkable and obsolete. This group tends to push for solutions such as central licensing arrangements. Under them, consumers pay fees for software or licenses and are permitted unlimited downloading, with the revenue distributed proportionately to copyright holders.

Editors, as always and above all, cannot be legal experts. Instead, they must know enough to notice potential problems and seek resolution, preferably before publication or posting but also by flagging questionable already-posted material as soon as possible.

Conclusion

Legal issues grow ever more specialized, but journalists must not leave the field to the politicians or the lawyers. They must respect the law and the public concerns underlying it. They must act with understanding and principle. They must protect the interests of their news organizations and the public.

At the same time, as a matter of substance and public duty, journalists should actively assert and defend the First Amendment and the values it represents. Otherwise, it might as well not exist. Editors share in this obligation.

When he was president of the American Society of Newspaper Editors, Rick Rodriguez of the *Sacramento Bee* expressed the point forcefully: "Now more than ever news organizations have to step forward to meet these regulatory and legal challenges. We can't wimp out, we can't be timid or cheap in these battles. Too much is at stake."[12]

As a matter of process, editors' top priority goes to identifying potential legal issues and raising them for discussion and decision. Every editor should feel duty-bound to sound such alarms. But individual editors should not feel obliged to settle legal quandaries alone. Top editors, as well as publishers and lawyers, must be supportive and closely involved. Debate should be extensive, and decisions should be reasoned.

In summary, given today's sometimes chilly and often complicated climate, editors should be sentinels on watch for potential legal problems. They should know how to get them resolved. And they should do so with both a commitment to the public's right to know and an understanding of legal limits.

Then, as we see in Chapter 12, they should be ready to move from the legal arena into ethics. Having determined, to their best ability, what "can" or "cannot" be done under the law, the next, perhaps even harder, step is to ponder what "should" be done by news professionals.

Sidebar 11: An editor's bibliography

There are fine books on reporting, copyediting, and design, on upper-level management, and on general matters of leadership and ethics. But shelves are relatively bare of materials aimed directly at those key newsroom figures, the midlevel assigning editors.

Fledgling and veteran writers can choose from dozens of useful textbooks and trade volumes in their area. Copyeditors and designers can select from at least a shelf-ful. But assigning editors still must piece together their libraries from a few books, a large but scattered field of articles, and the handouts and tip sheets collected at a relatively few websites.

Still, we must be heartened that some progress has occurred. The literature today, if not adequate, certainly surpasses what it was a few years ago. It falls into two broad categories: a few works expressly for midlevel editors and more general works that can help midlevel editors.

Here are some highlights. But bear in mind that the citations may change over time as books add editions or change publishers and as websites evolve. If the citations here do not work directly, try using a search engine.

Books about editing

Caught in the Middle: How to Improve the Lives and Performance of Newspaper Middle Managers, by Sharon L. Peters. Published in 1999 and downloadable from Northwestern's www.mediamanagementcenter.org. Peters surveyed more than 500 journalists and wrote about the problems of midlevel editors from their own view and also the views of their managers and their reporters. Great insights into the problems and some suggestions for help.

Coaching Writers: Editors and Reporters Working Together Across Media Platforms, 2nd edition, by Roy Peter Clark and Don Fry. Best book of its kind. Clark and Fry have been promoting collegial editing for two decades, and the book is full of wisdom, humor, and hands-on techniques.

The Editorial Eye, 2nd edition, by Jane T. Harrigan and Karen Brown Dunlap. Mostly for copyeditors, but includes friendly and helpful insights into "the big picture" of editing.

The Effective Editor: How to Lead Your Staff to Better Writing and Better Teamwork, by Foster Davis and Karen Dunlap. Slender volume filled with good humor and good sense, mainly about working with writers but with additional overall advice for the beginning assigning editor.

Newsroom Management, by Robert H. Giles. Hefty guide, pitched more toward top than midlevel managers, but full of guidance on motivating and supervising.

Books about editors

One can gain inspiration and insight by reading almost any editor's biography or autobiography. The three books below also contain material that is immediately and directly useful, including practical descriptions of editing style and methods, both good and horrid.

Genius in Disguise: Harold Ross of the New Yorker, by Thomas Kunkel. A look not just at *what* the master editor Ross did, but at *how*. Every editor can learn from this book.

Max Perkins: Editor of Genius, by A. Scott Berg. An in-depth look at the editor behind Fitzgerald, Hemingway and others. Not really journalistic, but inspiring anyway.

The Rose Man of Sing Sing, by James McGrath Morris. Charles Chapin was almost certainly the meanest city editor who ever lived (he died in prison after killing his wife). He was born to chase the news and had much success but at a very high cost. A good book about a bad example.

Books about managing and leadership

The books below are not directed primarily to journalists, but are among the most often recommended by top editors and trainers. The titles are pretty much self-explanatory.

First, Break All the Rules: What the World's Greatest Managers Do Differently, by Marcus Buckingham and Curt Coffman.

Getting to Yes: Negotiating Agreement Without Giving In, by Roger Fisher and William Ury.

Love and Profit: The Art of Caring Leadership, by James A. Autry.

Management of the Absurd: Paradoxes in Leadership, by Richard Farson.

Time Management for Dummies, by Jeffrey J. Mayer.

You Just Don't Understand: Women and Men in Conversation, by Deborah Tannen.

Sources of articles

All the journalism trade magazines deal with midlevel editors from time to time. One publication that has done so regularly is the *American Editor*, published by the American Society of Newspaper Editors. It frequently runs articles on pertinent topics such as writing, ethics and leadership.

Fortunately, content from the past several years is available online at www.asne.org. Unfortunately, the searching is rudimentary, so you have to know what you want or be willing to skim a lot of article titles.

Web resources

www.americanpressinstitute.org: Targeted at journalism broadly, but with some useful articles and links for midlevel editors. Example: "Critical Thinking Checklist."

www.copydesk.org: Site of the American Copy Editors Society. Good links, discussions, and other resources. For example, click on "site features," then "resources," and you read a long list of interesting articles, such as Jane Harrigan's "Why Editing Is Cool."

www.journalism.org: Affiliated with the Project for Excellence in Journalism. Both links and full texts of research reports and articles, including such practical ones as "Ten Tips on Time Management."

www.newsthinking.com: Run by writing coach and former *Los Angeles Times* editor Bob Baker. Outstanding material on how to find, write and help others write great stories. Try Susan Ager's "A Vocabulary List for Reporters and Editors" or Laurie Hertzel's "Yeah, I'm Defensive."

www.notrain-nogain.com: Gold mine. News trainers site, with links, exercises and tip sheets galore. Try Steve Buttry's "Helping Reporters Improve Stories" or Michael Roberts' "Six-Month Program for Line Editors."

www.poynter.org: A varied and constantly evolving site, geared more toward writers, but with numerous relevant essays and tip sheets on editing, coaching and leading.

www.readership.org: Comprehensive collection of research from Northwestern's Readership Institute. Lots of studies and reports, plus examples of how journalists are applying what is being learned.[13]

Vignettes

When the *American Journalism Review* convened a conference for top editors and bureau chiefs on dealing with "a hostile legal and political climate," several leading journalists and media lawyers offered advice. Here is a sampling:[14]

- "The first thing you need to do is contact your editor. There should be a protocol in every news organization about what to do. Don't go out and do something rash."—Lucy Dalglish, executive director of the Reporters Committee for Freedom of the Press, commenting on how a journalist should respond if subpoenaed
- "It's really important for us to redouble our efforts to independently corroborate the information through documentation and through on-the-record sources so there is no need to cite the anonymous sources or even hint that the original tip came from a secret source. This has the added benefit of giving the story credibility with the public."—Deborah Nelson, award-winning investigative editor and teacher
- "News organizations . . . should technologically equip their records so they don't show outgoing or incoming calls. That's a technological fix that will make it more difficult for prosecutors to get at phone records that way. It's really important to have discipline when you're sending and receiving emails. . . . use good judgment and common sense about the emails that you keep."—Lee Levine, media attorney.

12 Making decisions about ethics

Have you ever done anything bad? Did you know it was bad when you did it?

Chances are, the answer to both those questions is yes. Most of us do bad things, and most of us realize it at the time. While ethical dilemmas can become tangled and difficult, many if not most ethical lapses in journalism occur when someone knowingly does wrong. A columnist plagiarizes. A reporter fabricates. An editor manipulates an image. A web producer misappropriates video. A manager propositions an employee. A publisher promises favoritism to an advertiser.

When I initiate discussions about ethics, whether with students or professionals, I often ask whose values and interests deserve consideration. Answers usually come rapidly: those of the audience, of the people journalists write about, of the organization, of the news profession, even of the country itself. Often, though not always, I have to intervene with a reminder to each journalist present: Your values matter, too. Ethics should begin with one individual's personal and professional integrity.

Would you pester a public official to get an important story? Most people say yes.

Would you pretend to be a police officer? Few say they would.

In between persistence and impersonation comes a range of tricky issues, of course, but the starting point is simple enough. Journalists make countless ethical decisions every day, most of them guided more than anything else by personal standards of right and wrong. Before we let the ethics discussion get too deep, we should stress that point. Your ethics begin with you. Whether you are driven by idealism, or a fear of getting caught, or a (very valid) concern about throwing away your job and reputation, you can fairly resolve a huge proportion of ethical problems by doing what you know is proper. In journalism as in every other profession, it is important to stand for what is right and to act honorably.

Still, we all will fail at times, and we all will confront dilemmas where the best decision isn't obvious. That is one more reason we have editors.

Consider two notorious and widely publicized cases. In 2003, a 27-year-old *New York Times* reporter named Jayson Blair lost his job over what his own paper called "frequent acts of journalistic fraud" that included fabricating comments, concocting scenes, and plagiarizing material in at least 36 stories.[1] Early the next year, Jack Kelley, a foreign correspondent for *USA Today*, resigned under duress, and a subsequent inquiry by the newspaper found evidence he had "fabricated substantial portions of at least eight major stories, lifted nearly two dozen quotes or other material from competing publications, lied in speeches he gave for the newspaper, and conspired to mislead those investigating his work."[2]

What both cases had in common was at least twofold: (1) individual reporters making decisions they almost certainly knew were wrong and (2) editors failing to notice problems quickly enough.

For editors, the practical implications of these and other incidents are clear. Editors must be the conscience of the newsroom, and they must never let down their vigilance. Both Blair and Kelley were talented reporters; I personally knew them both. But the editor's job is not to closely monitor the supposedly *bad* reporters, whoever they may be, while never checking on the presumably *good* ones. The editor's job is to backstop *all the reporters*. From the newest greenhorn to the Pulitzer-carrying veteran, everyone makes errors, everyone's copy needs careful attention, and nobody can predict who will be the next to clash with the ethical rules. As with every other aspect of editing that we have discussed, editors must:

- Treat seriously all copy by all contributors
- Notice potential ethical trouble spots as early as possible
- Collaborate with their staffs to avoid or repair problems
- Encourage mutual discussion up and down the chain of command to see that dicey issues receive full deliberation before publication.

With these duties in mind, we can turn to areas where editors often encounter ethical quandaries, whether they be in news-gathering techniques and behavior, decisions about what to publish, or issues raised by new media and changing technology. Some, such as fabrication, are clear cut, but many others do involve complex collisions of values that don't always have an obvious correct answer. As always, the editor must be a primary noticer and conversation-starter.

Day-to-day news gathering

Actor Richard Dreyfuss was discussing his drug problems before about 850 people at the University of Maryland when he noticed reporters in the audience. Even though he was giving an open speech at a public university, the Oscar-winning film star declared the evening a "non-quotable experience." As the campus newspaper the *Diamondback* reported, Dreyfuss demanded that journalists abide by this "gentlemen's agreement."

Of two reporters present, one left the auditorium. The other stayed and took notes.

Which did the right thing?

Questions like this arise hundreds of times every day for journalists from campus weeklies to metropolitan dailies. They do not involve legal issues. In the Dreyfuss incident, leaving the auditorium or remaining to report both were perfectly permissible under the law. Instead, they involve ethics and values: what *should* be done in difficult situations. Should reporters defend the right to attend and cover public events, or accede to the privacy wishes of a celebrity talking to students about personal matters?

For many reasons, the matter of ethics has become a growth industry in journalism. As reporters and editors become increasingly professional, they naturally spend more time pondering standards for appropriate and inappropriate behavior. As society becomes more complex and contentious, journalists' decisions invite sharper public scrutiny. As the Internet opens more and more windows into media institutions, the public gains inside information and greater chances for comment and feedback.

The result has been rising concern both inside and outside newsrooms about what constitutes proper conduct, who decides what standards apply, and what, if anything, happens when journalists transgress the rules.

In the ongoing rhythms of the newsroom, it is of course the editors who must take the lead in resolving these issues.

Consider another example: You are a sports editor for your campus newspaper, investigating tips that star athletes are performing poorly in classes. As you and a reporter interview an athletic department official, she refers occasionally to a form apparently listing each athlete's grades. When you ask to see the report, she replies that it is private. Suddenly, she is called out of the room. She leaves the report in open sight on her desk. The reporter turns to you for guidance. Do you ignore the form? Sneak a quick peak? Read it carefully and take notes? Take it and leave the office?

To put the matter bluntly: Under what circumstances if any would you lie, cheat, or steal to get a story?

Although reporters commonly must make on-the-spot decisions about such issues as snooping around a source's desk, it is editors who set the tone for ethical behavior in a newsroom. The editor who looks the other way, reflexively defends reporters against all complaints, and demands "Get the story or else" projects a message of permissiveness that no reporter will miss. By contrast, the editor who constantly second-guesses reporters' conduct, kills stories over the tiniest lapses, and tries to promulgate legalistic guidelines for every contingency sends an opposite signal.

How do editors decide these things?

There is no one way, of course. Most editors try to avoid rigidity and inflexibility. The best articulate high overall standards and then encourage, expect, and reward adherence to them. Reporters who want to bend, or break, the rules bear a high "burden of proof" for persuading editors to acquiesce.

Thus, in most cases editors would argue that lying, cheating, and stealing are improper ways of acquiring stories. Deception taints the final product. It alienates sources, outrages readers, clouds both the reporter's and the news organization's credibility, and undermines future access to sources and information. And, simply but importantly, deception is wrong, and most of us know it.

Yet, as most of us also know, the line between deception and ingenuity can be hard to discern. For example, I once obtained an interview after a source, who had refused in advance to see reporters, mistook me for a cab driver as he left a hospital. For a minute or two, I did not correct him. In fact, I even walked with him in the general direction of a cab. Then, after some brief warming-up conversation, I introduced myself as a reporter, and the source courteously granted an interview.

Strictly speaking, I had not lied. Had I deceived? Is there a difference ethically between blatantly lying and simply neglecting to set straight a mistaken source?

In Chapter 9, I mentioned a reporter who staked out a grand jury that was considering allegations of misconduct against a public official. The reporter happened to be standing outside the room when the grand jurors took a break. As several jurors talked, he sidled up and listened quietly. Apparently assuming that he was a court official, they talked openly about the case they were hearing. Did the reporter have a responsibility to identify himself? Or is it sources' responsibility to determine to whom they are speaking?

Most editors, I suspect, clearly believe that it is unethical to break the law or breach ethics most of the time. But almost every editor can cite exceptions. I know of no editor who would condone shooting someone to get a story, but I also cannot imagine any editor complaining if a reporter jaywalked to reach a breaking news event.

Remember this essential point: *Suppressing or neglecting the truth is just as unethical as violating standards to get the truth.* The ethical imperative for journalists isn't to create a set of rules that limit what can be told to the public. Instead, the imperative is to carefully balance suitable behavior and aggressive reporting, so that the audience receives the information it needs but through a process that isn't contaminated by dishonest, hurtful, or otherwise inappropriate methods.

That means journalists must match *means* and *ends,* a tricky but inescapable reality in the news business. In so doing, they learn to examine situations systematically and to outline the issues at stake, the potential good and harm, all available options, and the likely response from every-one involved. Too often, however, reporters make such decisions by them-selves and under pressure. They may not trust their editors, may fear them, or simply may be conditioned to operating as lone-wolf individualists.

Almost as important as *what decision is made* is *how the decision gets made*. It is a basic duty for editors to create an environment in which reporters understand the importance of discussing ethical matters, in advance wherever possible, with their editors. Cultivating an air of trust and mutual dependence can prevent many ethical dilemmas from flaring into disaster.

One area where advance conversations help is in how journalists treat people during reporting. Editors should make their views clear on how they expect reporters to deal with the public. Some editors still adhere to the "story-at-any-price" philosophy. More often these days, editors can encourage reporters to be persistent and tough without belligerence. Simple courtesy and respect remain good standards.

Take an all-too-common situation: A child has been killed in a traffic accident, school shooting, or other tragedy. I see nothing wrong with approaching the grieving parents, identifying oneself as a journalist, and politely asking if they wish to talk about their child. Many parents do want to talk, and gentle encouragement seems appropriate. If they decline, then I think reporters should leave them alone.

Many editors firmly distinguish between private and public matters. To them, reporters are entitled to much more aggressively bulldog public fig-ures who refuse to return phone calls, hold press conferences, or other-wise discuss public issues. In those cases, the disrespect is not on the part of the media, but on the part of the officials dodging their responsibilities.

When faced with these everyday ethical conundrums, editors often can foster a cool, systematic, rational analysis, by suggesting such questions as:

- How important is the information being sought? Is it crucial to an important story, or of secondary importance? Is it public or private?
- Is there any other way to get it besides breaching ethics? For example, can documents be demanded under freedom-of-information laws rather than surreptitiously examined?
- Will the information be made public eventually anyway? Is there any real advantage to be gained by cheating to get it early?
- How do the consequences of an ethical violation compare with the consequences of not getting the story? An oft-cited hypothetical: Suppose a reporter, by stealing documents, could have gained access to plans for the September 11, 2001, terrorist attacks? Wouldn't the theft be outweighed by the lives that might have been saved? On the other hand, the benefits of a routine story that involved theft of documents might be more than offset by ensuing ethical and legal controversies.

- How would you explain your actions in print? How would you defend yourself if your methods were challenged?
- How would you feel is the story involved you or your family? Would you condone the questionable methods?
- How would a court or jury or a panel of subscribers react to border-line actions by a journalist? Would they understand and consider them reasonable under the circumstances?
- And, in a common way of formulating the question: How would your mother respond if she knew what you were doing?

On and off the record

President Lyndon B. Johnson, a crafty old gamesman, once upbraided a reporter for not publishing information Johnson himself had leaked. "But, Mr. President," the reporter protested, "you told me that was off the record." Replied Johnson, "I know that. But why didn't you use it?"[3]

That old anecdote still reveals much about the concept of "off the record"—a confusing and often dishonored technique that provides end-less opportunity and controversy for journalists. It exemplifies a category of ethical issues that line editors and reporters face routinely: the use and misuse of sources.

Most of journalists' information, by far, comes from sources. And most sources, including presidents, have their own reasons for using and abus-ing the journalistic process. At stake is the very nature of "the record" that sources are perpetually sliding onto and off of. "The record" is not, as some might assume, a faithful snapshot of reality. It is instead subject to revisions, deletions, and manipulations in a process governed by byz-antine codes that are applied inconsistently and self-servingly. Sources employ constant propaganda. Journalists face time and access limits. Most "news" is pieced together, second-hand, by journalists trying to catch up after the fact.

What we read and hear, then, is not reality, but a reconstituted reality. The struggle to control "the record" becomes a battle to shape what consumers are offered as "reality"—the common information base of our society. As journalists and sources jockey to produce "the record," they affect one another in many ways.

Journalists can "burn" their sources by misquoting them, taking remarks out of context, or violating agreements about confidentiality. Sources can undermine journalists by lying, exaggerating, distorting or omitting information, failing to divulge conflicts of interest, and refus-ing to stand behind the information they provide. Numerous surveys have shown public annoyance with the widespread practice of using anonymous sources, but journalists persist in doing so.

Over the years, a semiformal collection of rules has evolved to govern attribution of information to sources:

- *On the record* means information can be published and attributed to a source by name.
- *Background* means information can be reported but without identifying the source, such as by citing "a member of the mayor's staff."
- *Deep background* means information can be reported but without referring to any source at all, such as by writing, "It was learned that. . . ."
- *Off the record* means information is not being provided for publication at all. At one time, an off-the-record agreement generally prohibited the reporter from publishing the information even if it could be obtained from other, independent sources. Now, reporters commonly feel free to seek the information elsewhere as long as they don't compromise the identity of the original off-the-record source.

In my experience, several categories of sources routinely seek shelter behind some form of background or off-the-record agreements: *front people*, such as press secretaries or political aides whose job is to publicize their bosses not themselves; *celebrities and big shots*, who often are accustomed to giving orders and having everyone scurry to obey; *policy makers*, such as high officials who may want to advance information unofficially, to avoid the complications of formal announcements; *politicians*, who as a class are notorious gossips but do not like having a reputation for it; and *laypeople*, who often simply are shy or do not want to get involved in the publicness that attribution brings.

In most of the cases just mentioned, anonymity is neither necessary nor desirable. Anonymous information is as suspicious and lacking in credibility as a medication would be if its name were kept secret. Editors should insist that their reporters try extremely hard to persuade reluctant sources to talk on the record.

Several arguments or actions can help push information onto the record:

- Some sources, particularly public officials, can be shamed by a hard-headed reporter who insists on public accountability.
- Many sources will respond to reporters who say, "My editor won't allow me to take off-the-record information" or "I really need your help to get this right and do my job properly."
- Other sources will agree to attribution if they feel their story will not be fairly told in any other way. After all, most people who tell you something (such as the above-mentioned episode involving President Johnson) truly want the material made public.
- Sometimes editors can help, by contacting a wavering source and explaining the importance of on-the-record attribution.

Even so, some reporters all too easily accept spurious rationales for sources remaining unidentified. As an editor, you can save yourself many headaches by making clear to reporters, in advance, that you must approve any grant of anonymity and that you require a heavy burden of proof to do so. The more important or sensitive the information, the higher the need for attribution.

For one key group, confidentiality can be crucial. That group consists of sources with important information and with *specific* reason to fear for their jobs, lives, or families if they are associated with it. This includes employees exposing corruption, government whistle-blowers, and relative bystanders who learn sensitive information. But even if such sources remain confidential, their information should be checked and double-checked thoroughly. Most editors require at least two independent sources for any disputable assertion.

In short, editors should prod reporters to resist anonymity and to hold sources accountable. Under rules of the Associated Press, for instance, anonymity is permitted only when the information ("not opinion or speculation") is "vital," not available elsewhere, and from a source who "is reliable, and in a position to have accurate information."[4] Journalists at the *New York Times* are instructed to "resist granting anonymity except as a last resort to obtain information that we believe to be newsworthy and reliable" and "of compelling interest, and unobtainable by other means."[5]

Even when anonymity is deemed necessary, reporters should try to limit its scope. For legal as well as ethical reasons, a reporter might agree to withhold a crucial source's name from a story but reserve the right to divulge the name if the story results in court action. If a deal must be made, make the best deal possible. Blanket confidentiality is seldom necessary.

Once a deal is made, however, one point is crucial: *The terms of any reporter–source agreement should be absolutely clear to both parties.* Many sources, for example, do not understand the distinction between *off the record* and *background*. Reporters should make clear their precise interpretation of where confidentiality begins and ends. Then, they are duty bound, under the ethics of the profession, to honor any such deal, even to the point of going to jail if necessary. That, of course, is a big reason why granting confidentiality is risky and undesirable in the first place.

Good editors will develop newsroom policies and confer with reporters in advance about these issues, so reporters can operate with the clearest possible guidance about their organization's policies and expectations.

Deciding what to publish and what to withhold

A public official repeatedly calls a reporter late at night, slurring words and otherwise suggesting inebriation. A tipster provides evidence that an anti-abortion activist once received an abortion. The most-arrested person in town is a relative of the local prosecutor. A candidate for office was accused of domestic violence years earlier but never charged. A citizen blogger on your website wrote racist rants while in college. The married mayor may be having an affair. You, a local editor, are arrested for drunken driving.

Where do privacy, gossip, and sensationalism end, and news and legitimate public interest begin? For editors, sensitive questions of what to publish and what to leave out arise almost every day. Enforcing ethics requires a scrupulous balance between compassion and concealment.

A standard rationale for publishing personal information is that it sheds light on the character of people who are entrusted with public policy making or who seek the limelight. A leading argument against publishing is that individuals should retain their privacy unless their conduct can be shown to directly affect the public interest.

Gray areas abound, and editors frequently must referee such situations. In many cases, either decision—to publish or to suppress—will anger a large segment of your audience and newsroom. I often recall receiving a call from the mother of an individual being investigated by my newspaper. She argued that what we had unearthed was private and that publishing it might drive her son to suicide. Later the same day, I was called by the reporter on the story, who said his sources were questioning whether we planned to "cave in" and "cover up" the man's dubious activity. A decision either way was certain to antagonize a substantial constituency.

As life constantly reminds editors, the news media hold awesome power over people's lives and work. Bad reviews can close plays and restaurants. Investigative reporting can cost people their jobs and point them toward prison. Careless mistakes can ruin reputations. Sometimes, even innocuous material can bring unwanted and even dangerous public attention to individuals and families. The *Charlotte Observer* once published a simple feature photo of a young mother walking her daughter to school. The woman subsequently reported horrifying phone calls and mailings of sexual harassment to both herself and her child.[6]

Editors have long espoused *relevance* and *newsworthiness* as standards. But as we have seen, they can be hard to apply. It surprises many people that, despite the conflicts over what journalists do publish, news organizations routinely choose not to publish certain juicy material. Quite often, editors determine the information is not sufficiently germane to public issues.

It is not unusual for different editors to see the same case differently. In the Twin Cities of Minnesota, a high school athlete hanged himself in a school building. The *St. Paul Pioneer Press* withheld the boy's name. "This was a private act. I could not see any major public value to be served," said its editor. Next door, the *Minneapolis Star Tribune* named the youth, citing "the extremely public nature of what he had done and where he had done it."[7]

In 2004, Vice President Dick Cheney used what the *Washington Post* termed a "big-time obscenity" in an argument with a U.S. senator. *CNN* referred to it as "the F-word." The *New York Times* was satisfied with "an obscenity." But the *Washington Post* printed the four-letter word in full. Explained executive editor Leonard Downie Jr.:

> When the vice president of the United States says it to a senator in the way in which he said it on the Senate floor, readers need to judge for themselves what the word is because we don't play games at the *Washington Post* and use dashes.[8]

Nothing can anticipate every situation for editors who must raise, debate, and decide such issues, but it can help to develop policy guidelines in advance and to distribute them to staff members. As with so many other aspects of editing, an editor's insistence on care, thoughtfulness, and broad consultation can help produce wise, defensible decisions.

Ethics inside the newsroom

One of your general-assignment reporters is a 40-year-old parent of three school children. The reporter, who has lifelong ties to the community, wants to run for the city school board. How should the news organization respond? Approve the civic-spirited gesture? Forbid it as a conflict of interest for a journalist covering community events? Transfer the person out of reporting (for example, to a design job) or out of the newsroom entirely? Do nothing, on the grounds that personal time is beyond an employer's control?

Ethical conflicts arise within the newsroom as well as outside it, and editors must encode and then enforce the standards. Sometimes, the conflicts are purely internal (should a publication hire relatives of current staff members?). Occasionally, they pit the interests of different divisions of a news operation (should a website publish a marginal feature about a new business whose account the advertising department wants to win?). Increasingly, they involve the news organization and its corporate owner (can a television station owned by Disney fairly review a movie made by Disney?). Other times, they involve the media and the wider public (should the publisher chair the local united charities drive?).

Often the media evaluate such issues in terms of *conflict of interest* and *perceived conflict of interest*.

Actual conflict of interest occurs when a staff member stands to benefit personally from professional behavior. Accepting money or gifts from a source in exchange for favorable coverage is a direct conflict of interest and a firing offense. Buying stock on the basis of inside information gained while covering a corporation falls into a similar category, and is probably illegal as well. News organizations routinely forbid conflict of interest, and relatively few cases of it come to light. Simply put, it is wrong, and everyone should know it.

Editors, however, should never take for granted that everyone does know, or heed, it. They should spell out, particularly to new staffers, the importance the newsroom places on upright conduct. Consequences of unethical behavior, including demotion and dismissal, should be as explicit as possible.

Perceived conflict causes more problems. Newspeople must worry constantly about how people outside the profession will view their actions. Would the public feel coverage of city schools was neutral if a reporter sat on the school board, even if the reporter was honest and never involved in the coverage?

Sometimes such dilemmas extend into journalists' families. Suppose the reporter assigned to cover city hall decides to marry the mayor's press secretary. Would the public have reason to suspect conflict if the reporter remained on the beat? Almost certainly. Yet is it fair to penalize an employee because of a spouse's occupation?

Editors frequently must mediate between the newsroom's desire to appear above board and employees' rights as individuals. Written policies help. From the moment of employment, journalists need to know what their employers expect. Another useful vehicle is a newsroom committee established to monitor conflict of interest. If staff members understand that potential conflict issues should be raised and discussed in advance and in a fair setting, then touchy questions can be debated and resolved early.

The ethics of management

Your news site has a vacancy for a beginning reporter. Your newsroom contains fewer minority staff members than you want. Should you commit yourself to an affirmative hiring plan? What are the best methods to increase newsroom diversity? Are there steps you should avoid?

In an earlier chapter, we discussed hiring and recruiting in a management context. A word remains to be said about such practices in an ethical context. Fair hiring, training, and promotion contribute to an organization's overall ethical standing, as policed by its top editors.

As institutions that attempt to cover their total communities and that critically examine the personnel practices of other institutions, the news media should serve as models. Aggressive diversity plans are as important ethically as clean conflict-of-interest records. Diversity provides innumerable benefits for a news organization. It seems an obvious virtue in and of itself, like fairness. It contributes to broader, more representative, more innovative coverage. It extends staff experience and expertise. It brings additional points of view to discussions of content, ethics, and service. And it helps atone for our history of unfair hiring and promotion.

Veteran editor Gregory L. Moore offered several suggestions for editors seeking greater diversity:

- Recruit more aggressively, searching widely for diverse talent and building as big a pool of candidates as possible.
- Offer mentoring and better "care and feeding" to candidates and the newly hired.
- Take risks by giving minority journalists chances to show their talent.
- Listen to story ideas that "would not get done otherwise."
- Avoid labels, such as "development hires" or "projects," that single out minority journalists and affect how they are treated by others.[9]

At the operational level, journalists tend to devote their thinking about ethics to a narrow context, dwelling on individual incidents that force tough decisions on whether to lie, cheat, or steal for a single story. Such occasions provide provocative fodder for newsroom, classroom, and barroom conversation.

But editors should not neglect their duty to approach ethics more broadly, such as in their promotion of diversity. More profound than the individual episodes are the ethics lessons that flow from continuing policies and priorities. The effects of ethics are cumulative. Decisions about how to finance, organize, and operate newsrooms have an ethical dimension that publishers and editors should not overlook.

The following paragraphs give additional examples where patterns of behavior have ethics consequences.

The selection of stories to cover. Suppose your religion reporter proposes to investigate how a local television ministry collects and spends its money. The reporter has heard rumors of wrongdoing but has no evidence. She concedes that the investigation may take weeks and produce nothing. In the meantime, you will be short-staffed. But ignoring such tips and warnings means that inevitably some momentous stories will go unreported. Do you agree to her proposal?

Coverage is a function of staff, time, and money. As those resources tighten, it is tempting to push for higher percentage assignments, sure-shot stories done quickly. The premium may be lowered on chancy, time-consuming projects. Editors and reporters may grow wary of such proposals. Yet if the press takes its watchdog role seriously, then a commitment to some more expensive projects cannot be shoved aside by short-term calculations.

The messages editors send to reporters. Most editors regularly prod reporters to press hard for stories. These days, however, many editors also spring quickly to second-guess a reporter's methods, often on grounds of ethics. The newshound who stretches the limits to get at a source, a document, or a news scene may well face an editor's wrath. Much of today's scrutiny is well intentioned and proper, the natural outgrowth of higher standards and a desire to reduce arrogance and warm up to consumers.

But editors should realize that this increasing defensiveness may have unspoken, unexpected consequences. Reporters may react by becoming less aggressive, by not pushing hard enough, for fear of chastisement. Long-term service to readers could suffer. The answer is not necessarily to stop criticizing the ethics lapses, but to reaffirm, at the same time, that hard-nosed journalism has a place and will be rewarded when appropriate.

The resources spent on newsrooms and salaries. Good journalism is not cheap. For too long, news organizations have taken advantage of the idealistic nature of many recruits by offering low salaries and tolerating unreasonable working conditions. One result is a drain of talent to such places as law school and public relations. Another result is the high stress complained about in every newsroom. How the news industry treats its workers is an ethics issue equivalent to any that reporters face in their daily activities.

Ethical concerns in the multimedia age

As the Internet expanded in the early 21st century, news organizations welcomed the chance to incorporate increasing levels of user-generated content onto their websites. Comment boxes allowed readers to respond in volume to stories. Audience members joined journalists in discussion groups and live online chats. Blogs were assigned to community experts and gadflies alike. So-called hyperlocal news was solicited from neighborhood freelancers. An entire genre of "pro-am" content emerged, private citizen journalists teaming with full-time professionals to examine community issues.

With this new content came significant ethical questions:

- Should citizen contributors be vetted for criminal history, conflicts of interest, or patterns of misconduct or inaccuracy?
- Should citizen posts be edited for accuracy, taste, decency, fairness, or any other such standard? Whose standards? Who decides?
- Should posts, chats, and other features be truly live, or time-delayed for editing purposes?
- What about live images, audio, and video, and the constant potential for legal, ethical, taste, and privacy problems?
- Should anonymity be allowed always, never, or under special circumstances?

- Should audience contributions be monitored before being posted? Should editors and producers spot-check them after posting? Should readers be encouraged to complain about out-of-bounds postings?
- Should copyeditors or other professionals scrutinize citizen postings with the same intensity that staff copy receives?
- Should staff members participating in chats and blogs adopt the more informal tone of the web, express personal opinions, deviate from the more distanced manner of traditional media?
- And, of course, where will the added resources for effective oversight come from?

The rise of the web also intensified problems involving *plagiarism* and *copyright violation*. The web's vastness, coupled with its formidable search-and-retrieve capabilities, made it easier than ever for journalists to find, adapt, or copy information, whether willfully or accidentally, and for that compromised information to make its way to publication. Powerful search software also made it easier for editors to catch such offenses, but the tools were far from foolproof. To take just one of scores of examples, no less a figure than the CBS News anchor Katie Couric was embarrassed when an on-air commentary she read—written as it turned out by a producer—was found to be plagiarized. The producer was fired, but the damage was immense.[10]

In some ways, these challenges brought little change to the fundamental principles of editing. Editors needed to carefully inspect all copy, notice potential problems, seek the proper help in resolving them, and apply the best values and practices of their organizations.

What changed most was the circumstances under which editors worked. For example, the web's 24-hour news cycle made it obsolete to submit all copy, in a linear and graduated fashion, through one copydesk. Instead the concept of *on-the-fly editing* emerged, with individual editors and producers, scattered across a newsroom and website, on duty to read copy whenever necessary. Some sites encouraged *buddy editing*, where someone about to post to the web would turn to the nearest journalist, whether an editor or not, and ask for a second eye on the copy. However, the very phrase, "on-the-fly" editing, implied a haste that raised the prospects of error and embarrassment.

As time passed, news organizations continued to struggle with developing editing protocols that would both ensure accuracy and quality and serve the fast-paced needs of the multimedia age.

A framework for decision making

It is tempting to conclude that all ethics are relative and that every situation should be decided on its own by judicious and thoughtful journalists. However, such a conclusion would be facile. In truth, philosophers, ethicists, journalists, and many other professionals have articulated numerous widely accepted standards and principles that can help. To decide each case in a vacuum, ignoring history and precedent, would invite inconsistency and confusion. Instead, it is worth considering some of our society's core values.

The late James Carey, a leading thinker about journalism's role, wrote that while doing good journalism "is always a matter of judgment. . . . there are good choices and bad choices." Carey added that the key

> is the process those who produce the news go through in making their decisions. Once a journalist begins to develop a disciplined, thoughtful way of making choices, he or she will build on it and refer to it over and over again.[11]

In citing more formal and disciplined methods of analysis, for example, one popular ethics textbook recommends a grounding in the following virtues:

- The Golden Mean of Aristotle and Confucius: finding the appropriate location between extremes
- Kant's Categorical Imperative: acting in a way that you think should be universal law
- Mill's Principle of Utility: seeking the greatest happiness for the greatest number
- Rawls's Veil of Ignorance: making decisions behind a veil that suspends your personal interests and assumes you could be any party affected by the results
- The Judeo-Christian creed: loving your neighbor as yourself.[12]

More particularly, journalists can examine where their obligations lie. Reporters and editors have duties to themselves as individuals and professionals, to clients and subscribers paying for their services, to employers, to the overall profession, to sources and subjects of their copy, to the law, and to society. Ethical dilemmas often involve choosing between competing obligations.

The Code of Ethics of the Society of Professional Journalists (see Sidebar 12) begins by stressing "seeking truth and providing a fair and comprehensive account of events and issues." It would follow, then, that ethical conduct lies in the spirit of service to truth: in representing the truth, pursuing the truth, and publishing the truth whenever possible.

Lying, cheating, and stealing to obtain stories do not, in most cases, serve the truth. It is only when the value of a story is so urgent, its good ends so overwhelming, the harm from not publishing so clear, that the truth of the ultimate story may redeem questionable methods employed to get it. Direct involvement in making such judgments constitutes a prime duty of editors as they operate daily in the newsroom.

Conclusion

Advance discussion and reasonable guidelines greatly assist editors in making decisions about ethics. The decision-making process should encourage honesty, openness, fairness, and broad deliberation, both within the newsroom and with the audience. The direction should be toward truth.

For editors, managing ethics means more than advising reporters on how to resolve the tough calls. Journalists make important ethics statements every day but vastly more important ones over time. Good editors monitor their long-range performance as well as referee the daily dogfights. More than their response to isolated ethical predicaments, how they deal with the broad issues has a cumulative effect on how staffs perform and readers are served.

In part, journalists do assert their ethics by applying codes to individual situations. But even if they are blemish-free by those standards, there remains an overriding judgment, based on the collective amount and depth of coverage and the overall behavior of newspeople and news media. By those standards, editors, and all journalists, are more than the sum of their situational ethics.

Sidebar 12: Resources in ethics

Probably more than ever before, today's editors can find considerable help in making decisions about ethics. Numerous journalism societies, educational bodies, news organizations, and even individuals offer advice, codes, case studies, and discussion forums, most of them easily accessible on the web.

Three especially notable sites are run by the Society of Professional Journalists, the American Society of Newspaper Editors, and the Poynter Institute.

The Society of Professional Journalists

This umbrella organization, known as SPJ, has long focused on ethics as a main topic. Its home page, www.spj.org, includes a direct link to a large and helpful ethics section. There editors will find the SPJ Code of Ethics; case studies of actual examples and how they were handled; an archive of relevant articles from the society's *Quill* magazine and elsewhere; an ethics hotline; an active discussion board;

information about the SPJ Ethics Committee; and many other resources. Professionals, teachers, and students, as well as members of the public, can find invaluable assistance there.

The SPJ Code of Ethics

The code opens with a preamble committing journalists to "seeking truth" and serving the public with "thoroughness and honesty." The code itself has four major sections:

- "*Seek truth and report it*. Journalists should be honest, fair and courageous in gathering, reporting and interpreting information."
- "*Minimize harm*. Ethical journalists treat sources, subjects and colleagues as human beings deserving of respect."
- "*Act independently*. Journalists should be free of obligation to any interest other than the public's right to know."
- "*Be accountable*. Journalists are accountable to their readers, listeners, viewers and each other."

Each section contains more specific advice, such as "distinguish between advocacy and news reporting," "avoid pandering to lurid curiosity," and "refuse gifts, favors, fees, free travel and special treatment."

The American Society of Newspaper Editors

This group, known as ASNE, is the professional organization of top editors of newspapers and related websites. Its site, www.asne.org, highlights issues regarding diversity, credibility, and the First Amendment, with articles from the *American Editor* and helpful links. An especially valuable link goes to ethics codes and resources from dozens of national and regional news organizations.

The ASNE Statement of Principles

Also available from www.asne.org, this document's preamble declares that journalists have a "particular responsibility" to pursue "a standard of integrity proportionate to the journalist's singular obligation."

The statement includes sections on responsibility, freedom of the press, independence, truth and accuracy, impartiality, and fair play. It exhorts journalists to defend a free press "against encroachment or assault from any quarter, public or private" and to "observe the common standards of decency and stand accountable to the public for the fairness and accuracy of . . . news reports."

The Poynter Institute

This nonprofit educational body based in St. Petersburg, Fla., maintains a varied website, www.poynter.org, with a direct link from the home page to ethics resources. They include almost daily topical articles, blogs, and commentaries on current ethics issues; a hotline and email address for ethics questions; and numerous case studies and tip sheets from Poynter's staff ethicists and others.

For example, Bob Steele, a former reporter who became Poynter's "scholar for journalism values," offers a simple checklist called "Ask These 10 Questions to Make Good Ethical Decisions."[13] The questions include:

- "What is my journalistic purpose?"
- "How can I include other people, with different perspectives and diverse ideas, in the decision-making process?"
- "What are my alternatives to maximize my truthtelling responsibility and minimize harm?"

Vignettes

On its 100th anniversary, *Editor & Publisher* magazine published a vast and fascinating collection of articles, tidbits, and excerpts from its past century covering journalism. Especially interesting were early examples of efforts to articulate the values and ethics of the practice.

From "Cardinal Rules," a creed by James McClatchy, founder of the *Sacramento Bee* and namesake of today's chain, developed during the late 19th century and published in *Editor & Publisher* in 1908:[14]

- *The Bee* demands from all its writers accuracy before anything else. Better lose an item than make a splurge one day and correct it next.
- Sneers at race, or religion, or physical deformity, will not be tolerated. . . . This rule of regard for the feelings of others must be observed in every avenue of news, under any and all conditions.
- Consider *The Bee* always as a tribunal that desires to do justice to all; that fears far more to do injustice to the poorest beggar than to clash swords with wealthy injustice.

From "The Canons of Journalism," ethical rules adopted by the American Society of Newspaper Editors in 1923, reprinted in *Editor & Publisher* in 1931:

- The primary function of newspapers is to communicate to the human race what its members do, feel and think.

- Good faith with the reader is the foundation of all journalism worthy of the name.
- Lacking authority to enforce its canons, the journalism here represented can but express the hope that deliberate pandering to vicious instincts will encounter effective public disapproval or yield to the influence of a preponderant professional condemnation.

13 Toward excellence in editing

The excruciating photo ran in the local news section of the *Bangor Daily News* in Maine. It showed the aftermath of a fatal crash between a 14-year-old bicycle rider and a dump truck. In the background is the truck. Beside it, rescue workers hover over the body, which cannot be seen. In the foreground are harsh skid marks, the mangled bicycle, and two tennis shoes.

To many readers, the decision to publish the photo was tasteless and even heartless. "You seem to have forgotten that there was a living, breathing human being with a family and loved ones who lost his life," one objected.

Mark Woodward, the paper's executive editor, took the anger seriously. He wrote a heartfelt column both defending the decision to publish and explaining the anguish it brought journalists:

> Every editor here was moved by the photograph. They are parents with kids, who have bikes. It is a photo that wallops you, where it really hurts. Put it up on the refrigerator, said one editor. Let your children see it. Death is real. It's out there, even on hot summer days. . . .
>
> Readers can't see the photographs we don't run. Pictures of piles of slaughtered Albanians . . . the murdered Columbine High School student dressed for graduation and lying in his coffin. . . . None of these photos ran in our paper. . . .
>
> Why run the photo last Saturday? It graphically reminded us of life's sharp edges. . . . Criticize us. . . . But our concerns and compassion are constants. We have children and families. Those empty sneakers will never leave our thoughts.[1]

Editors are human beings who make decisions. Their work is powerful, meaningful, sometimes distressing, and often consuming. "Is editing a job," a young editor asked me once, "or a lifestyle?"

It is a good question.

Like priests or police officers, good editors never really go off duty.

One reason, as the young editor had surmised, is that editing is not simply a mechanical regimen that one turns on and off at will. It is a way of thinking and an ability to analyze. It is an ever-sharp eye and a tuned-in ear. It is a capacity for leadership and direction. It is, in some sense at least, a way of life.

And it is a rare one. As every top journalist knows, trustworthy editors are far scarcer than good reporters and writers. They are harder to find and harder to keep.

Yet, as we have seen, they matter so much. What most often separates weak publications from strong ones is the quality of the editing. Through good editing, the good ideas get better, finishing touches get applied, and the raw edges get smoothed. Tough decisions get made with both compassion and a dedication to providing the truth even when it hurts. Without good editing, superior journalism seldom happens.

While reporters and writers can take journalism much of the way to excellence, it is the editors' work that accounts for the remaining distance—the difference between good and excellent, or between good and mediocre. The deciding factors, often, are the attitude, ability, and professionalism of the editors, along with the environment in which they work and the support they receive from their own superiors.

Preceding chapters have shown that becoming a good editor today requires diligence and drive. Although editing has never been easy, we have discussed several reasons why the job is becoming more and more complex as journalism undergoes important transitions. We can summarize as follows:

- Editing is hard work, calling for special capabilities distinct from those of reporting and writing. Too often incoming editors are selected on the basis of outstanding performance as reporters, without regard for whether they have the qualities editors really need. These editors seldom receive sufficient training for their new roles, and they face trouble from the start.
- The editing environment grows increasingly complex and stressful. News organizations operate as part of big business, aiming to sustain profits in the face of unprecedented competition for advertising and audiences. In such a climate, editors' journalistic ideals can collide with marketing imperatives.
- Editing increasingly means managing, a job made tougher by the modern workforce's unwillingness (understandable as it may be) to submit to the endless hours, low pay, and semi-dictatorial regimes of some traditional newsrooms. The ever-expanding administrative demands of helping run a sophisticated business and lead a volatile staff can overrun the unprepared editor.
- Innovations sparked by new technology compel editors to know more than ever about integrating all aspects of journalism into a

multimedia context. The idea of the editor as a "word person" is quaintly outmoded. Editors need to know more and more every day.

The result is a demand for what we have called the *new editor*, a better prepared and trained specialist in newsroom quality control. Not just "word people," new editors must be comfortable with all phases of editing in all manner of media.

New editors, like their predecessors, take pride in their profession, enjoy working with reporters and copy, and are thoughtful and serious. They know how to use their minds creatively and in different gears. Unlike many of their predecessors, perhaps, new editors see editing as more than a conventional "step up the ladder" after reporting. They see it as a specialized career opportunity, quite distinct from reporting, requiring preparation for a variety of duties, from assigning articles to overseeing web pages, from fine-tuning daily copy to directing long-range projects, from hand-holding anguished writers to planning corporate strategy. New editors understand that haphazard, up-by-the-boot-straps, on-the-job training rarely produces, by itself, enough confident, competent editors.

Demand for new editors is high, and supply is not. Throughout this book, therefore, we have been exploring ways of thinking and of working that can foster the age of the new editor. As we look toward the future, we conclude by itemizing some proposals for more effective recruitment, training, and nurturing of editing talent.

In some cases, students can make immediate use of the suggestions. In others, the material may seem more appropriate for those who are teachers and managers or who hope to assume those positions one day. Because a goal of this book has been to prepare young journalists for editing careers, not simply an introductory editing job, I hope they will carry along (and build on) these ideas as they make real the ideal of the new editor.

Developing new editors

For many students and young journalists, editing is an alien art. Although most students practice writing in grade school, few receive exposure to editing. For many, their first editing experience comes in college copyediting classes, which journalism departments often use as ground-level, "weeding-out" boot camps and which consequently loom before students as onerous obstacles. Such courses may concentrate so heavily on drill and structure that students never leave the stylebook long enough to appreciate the larger, fascinating context in which most editors work.

Like exercising new muscles, learning to edit can prove painful, especially for the novice. Many students become discouraged at this stage and depart with the permanent impression of editing as something sour-tasting and medicinal. More fortunate are those students who study under instructors—and there are many of them—gifted enough to inspire and ignite the editing potential inside many journalists-to-be. When early courses energize rather than squash this dormant talent, young people often awaken to new, exciting career possibilities and turn on to a future of editing.

There, at the moment students first encounter editing, lies the biggest opportunity to identify and develop new editors. To turn them on, and not off, challenges every teacher and journalism school. Of course, not all journalists attend journalism school or gravitate easily to editing. Many reach the profession without a full understanding of editing or a recognition of their own potential as desk people. Many veteran reporters wonder whether editing is for them, unsure even after years in the business of exactly what editing means and requires. So the newsroom, too, plays a central role in the talent search for editors.

Both in the classroom and in the newsroom, changes can take place to spur the development of new editors.

In the classroom

Teachers and students can help refocus journalism education so that potential editors get more attention. For too long, journalism training centered nearly exclusively on reporting and writing. Eventually graphics, design, and visual literacy worked their way into more prominence in the curriculum. Then came online journalistic skills. Now educators must recognize that students need even firmer grounding in editing and managing if they are to be ready for the changing newsroom.

Journalism schools, like newsrooms, can respond to the demand for new and better editors by examining their programs and ensuring that graduates are well prepared for life beyond reporting. Students interested in editing can push to make these changes happen faster. The following paragraphs round up some specific suggestions for how students, through their education, can prepare themselves to be new editors:

Study editing. Knowledge about editing is too important to be restricted to editors. All journalism students, including those who are positive that they want to be lifelong reporters, should study editing. It will make them better at their own jobs, it will help them appreciate good editing, it will prepare them to raise the standards of their editors, and it will equip them for the day when, inevitably, many find themselves bound, to their surprise, for desk work.

As for students who already aspire to editing, study can help reduce the shock of being submerged pell-mell into the job. Some editing skills are instinctive and inbred, but most can be developed and refined through study and practice.

Students, then, should learn writing and reporting but not neglect courses in editing. Basic editing courses can pay off not only for potential editors, but also for reporters and others who need, in their jobs, to better understand and appreciate editors' roles. Advanced courses can target those students with special interest or aptitude for editing.

Seek courses that teach editing broadly. Too many editing courses stop with language skills. That is where they should *begin*, not where they should *end*. Without neglecting traditional copyediting instruction, today's courses must aim for more. A good editing curriculum should have at least the following qualities:

- It should underline the basics of language. It should make students aware of their strengths and weaknesses in grammar, punctuation, spelling, and usage, and see that they address the weak spots. It should make them care passionately about precision and correctness.
- It should cover the spectrum of editing: structural editing (grammar, style, language), content and conceptual editing (clarity, completeness, organization, tone, and above all accuracy), news and policy judgments, design, headlines, graphics, photography, management, and ethics, in print, broadcast, online, and nontraditional settings.
- It should treat editing in all its breathtaking breadth. Editors must have the vision to comprehend both traditional and futuristic media; to meet the audience through the most conventional legacy publications and the newest mobile marvels; and to imagine and execute sound plans for multimedia, multiplatform, multipurpose journalism. They must also be provided opportunities—both in class and outside—to refine the technical and software skills to operate across these many frontiers.
- It should stress the human and intangible dimensions of editing. Editing involves instincts, analytical skills, respect and sympathy for writers, and a flair for recognizing and solving a variety of puzzles.
- It should convey that editing requires alertness and resourcefulness. It should foster good reading and news-monitoring habits, and encourage observation, curiosity, and questioning. Editing demands thinking—and caring.

In summary, students should strive, in their editing courses, to not simply push toward an entry job on a conventional copydesk but to soak up training for the full range of duties and challenges facing the professional editor at all levels, in all media, and in the yet-unimagined media of the future.

Emphasize management and human relations. Much good journalism can be learned outside the journalism school. Students can benefit from courses in areas such as psychology, personnel development, and business management, to supplement training in journalism classes.

Stress critical thinking. Editors need to be good analyzers and strategic thinkers, advanced concepts that are not easily teachable. In addition to editing courses, classes in math, philosophy, research methods, and problem solving can help immensely and should be sought after by students with editing potential.

Obtain editing internships and experience. This should not come at the expense of reporting and writing, which editors-to-be need also. But collegiate editing experience can prove invaluable. College newspapers and websites are an obvious and valuable opportunity for young people to edit on the job. Many community publications and sites also welcome students as part-time (and occasionally full-time) editors, editing interns, summer fill-ins, or just periodic observers. National programs, including one long sponsored by Dow Jones, also offer editing internships.

In the newsroom

Given the well-documented difficulty of finding and keeping good editors, newsroom managers cannot leave those projects to journalism schools. The profession has its own special interest in taking steps to locate and prepare new editor talent.

In the same way that journalism schools have tended to stress writing over editing, newsroom recruiting and training programs have followed. In recent years, the industry has come a long way in recognizing its problem in attracting and holding editors, but there are many more steps that publishers and editors can take to combat the problem.

Recruit early. Look for potential editors in journalism schools, at rival news operations, and within their own newsrooms. Identify potential editors early and track them.

Broaden the pool. Remember the laws of supply and demand. If the supply of good editors has fallen low, then news organizations must move aggressively to expand it. One of the best editors I ever worked with was a former laundry-truck driver whose quick mind and natural genius with words brought him to the attention of a top editor.

Ask reporters for names of potential editors, because few people can spot good and bad editing more quickly than writers can. Woo reluctant candidates by taking editing seriously and treating editors well. Build a reputation as a well-edited product, and watch the magnetic effect it has in attracting both editors and writers.

Provide editing internships. Be certain that internship programs make room for editors as well as reporters and photographers. If possible, offer broad internships on various desks and web operations, giving potential editors wide exposure to editorial duties.

Define what is wanted in an editor. Develop an understanding of what qualities good editors have and how they differ from the qualities of good reporters. Many, such as leadership ability, diplomacy, resourcefulness, or teamwork skills, may not show up on resumes or in clips or in tests typically given applicants. Reference checks often uncover them.

Interview reporting candidates with editing in mind. Most editors begin as reporters. They should; they need reporting experience. But managers should recognize that a percentage of the reporters they hire will go on to become editors. Try to hire accordingly, placing a premium on hiring some candidates who seem to have long-range editing potential.

Immerse new editors gently. When managers identify reporters as having editing talent, move them along slowly and cautiously. Give them an editing mentor. Assign them to the desk one or two days a week. Watch their performances closely, treat them as apprentices, and give constructive feedback.

Recognize that editing and reporting differ. Managers should never toss good reporters onto the desk in the assumption that they automatically are ready for the job if they have (a) succeeded as reporters and (b) seen editors in action. This is no more effective than giving a piano to a novice whose only experience is listening to virtuosos play.

Isolate the real problems. If a manager's complaints center on poor reporting and lackluster writing, that does not necessarily mean the newsroom has a reporting and writing problem. It probably has an *editing* problem whose symptoms are poor writing and reporting. The best journalists in the world will look like drudges if their work must pass through lousy editors on the way to the doorstep or screen. Because editors affect so many stories, it is true that hiring, promoting, and inspiring one editor has a multiplier effect far more powerful in many cases than adding a star reporter.

Nurturing editors

Complaints about supervisory editors often center on their inability to work with people, encourage subordinates, and offer helpful feedback. Such complaints can be summarized in the concept of *nurturing*. Editors need to be nurtured themselves, and they need to nurture others. Considering the built-in strains and difficulties of journalism, the work can become overpoweringly frustrating unless superiors share their support, energy, and information.

For newsroom managers, then, the objective cannot be merely to recruit talented editors, as hard as that is in itself. Equally important is keeping good editors, by maintaining the kind of newsroom where good editors are valued, teamwork is rewarded, stresses stay within reasonable check, and the special gratifications of editing are not overwhelmed by exhaustion and exasperation.

Here are some steps that managers can take to help bring about such a newsroom climate:

Pay attention. Much editing is nonglamorous, often invisible. Many editors feel overlooked and alone. So managers and senior editors should carefully monitor subordinates' work, praise and critique it regularly, and make editors feel that good work is noticed and prized. Small touches can mean a great deal, such as thank-you notes from the managing editor to a copyeditor who has written an unusually good headline or to an assignment editor who has helped a marginal reporter produce unexpectedly sizzling copy or a web producer who has packaged a breaking story with energy and imagination. It usually is not hard to determine which editors produce quality work under fire and which need help, and good managers know and respond to both situations.

Teach editing. Make editing an exciting topic in the newsroom, through newsletters and online discussions, critique sessions, markups, and in-house training. Get the newsroom talking about editing the same way it talks about writing. Many news organizations have internal writing coaches. How many have editing coaches?

Take advantage of external resources. Often it is easier to learn about editing after one has been in the news business for a while. Set against a professional's frame of reference, the subtleties of editing have more impact. Managers can take advantage of this by sending an editor to a college class or a professional seminar at the Poynter Institute, American Press Institute, or somewhere similar. Do not overlook training in management, teamwork, and other so-called nonjournalistic areas that might help editors. Periodic outside refreshment is good for the soul—and the employer

Encourage collegial relationships instead of rigid hierarchies. Sharing the responsibilities helps disperse the pressures. Robert Haiman, former executive editor of the *St. Petersburg Times*, told author Robert Giles of taking his first editing job at age 25 and "learning a lesson that probably every young lieutenant has to discover":

> There are a number of senior staff members who are your single best resource in running the group. Not only is there no shame in asking them for advice as to how the outfit runs, but it is almost essential to do that if you want to avoid giving everybody heart failure, including yourself.[2]

Reduce or offset stress wherever possible. Editors are often victims of their own idealism and high expectations. They are perfectionists working under time and resource constraints that make perfection impossible. Recognizing those characteristics, managers should act to reduce the tension that inevitably mounts. Have enough editors so that each editor's workload is manageable. Periodically rotate editors out of draining overnight or weekend shifts. Delegate enough authority to give editors reasonable control and latitude. Give candid feedback, but do not second-guess so much that editors despair.

Anticipate burnout and exhaustion. Editors handling big stories tend to put in long, hard hours and then go home burdened by the knowledge that the stories (and the long, hard hours) may go on for days, to be followed by other big stories requiring long, hard hours. For most editors, this scenario produces a combination of exhilaration (big stories are fun!) and exhaustion (big stories are tiring!). Managers should make sure that editors have some relief from this energy-emptying, unending spiral. Insist that they actually take earned vacation time and days off, instead of sending subtle (and not-so-subtle) messages that promotion and success depend on toiling round the clock. Left on their own, editors will overwork themselves to the point of burnout. So, do not leave them on their own.

Reward editors fairly. Providing pay commensurate with responsibility and generous vacation time is obviously important but too often neglected. Managers should look for other rewards as well. Some news operations offer paid sabbaticals ranging from a few weeks to several months. Travel to conferences and seminars can be used as rewards. Occasional one-day special projects (attending a workshop, taking a recruiting trip with the managing editor, running a task force on a current problem) can be timely escape valves. Simple breaks in the routine can go a long way toward heading off potential exhaustion.

Provide feedback and encourage dialogue with editors. It is a management truism, as we have already shown, that employees never feel they know enough about what the boss is thinking. Managers should share their thoughts. Level with editors about expectations and performance. Provide periodic formal evaluations but recognize that ongoing communication is even more important. Do not hold grudges or let sore points fester.

At the same time, feedback should flow two ways. Managers should listen to editors. Editors need regular opportunities to make suggestions, offer advice, issue complaints, define problems, and ask for help. Having an open-door policy is not enough. Take the next step to invite editors through the door on a regular basis.

Celebrate diversity. A former editor of mine, John Walter, talked about how each job is just one part of the whole. No individual can do it all, he said, and no editor can operate alone. One sign of a great editor is the knack to gather people of many talents and backgrounds, encourage them at what they do best, and coordinate their work into overall success.

Help editors enjoy their work. For all its problems, few jobs beat editing for fun, excitement, and stimulation. Every day brings interesting, unexpected challenges and opportunities. Good newsrooms reflect this spirit. Maintaining a sense of humor and a good-hearted perspective can make the difference between a newsroom ground down by the pressures or one uplifted by the daily wonders of it all.

Some specific starting points

Here, finally, are several specific recommendations that can help reporters, editors, and their newsrooms move immediately and painlessly toward better writing and editing. They cost very little but return championship interest:

- *Create a newsroom writers' and editors' group* to meet monthly and discuss topics such as writing leads that sparkle, coordinating multimedia coverage, improving relationships between editors and writers, or using web images and headlines to best advantage.
- *Distribute a newsletter or web posting* praising, critiquing, discussing, and generally celebrating writing and editing. Invite everyone in the newsroom to contribute ideas, examples, and observations. Such newsletters are often produced monthly by someone such as the city editor, news editor, or copy chief.
- *Hold occasional critique sessions* in which you invite people with various points of view to discuss writing and editing. Some possibilities: a reporter, a copyeditor, a web producer, the publisher, the circulation director, a local writer or teacher, a high school journalism student, a reader who's always emailing you with gripes.
- *Form a newsroom "book club,"* in which you read other newspapers and magazines, both online and in print, and discuss their writing and editing.
- *Publicly praise* good writing, editing, headlines, art, design, and web packaging, using a newsroom bulletin board.
- *Demonstrate from the top down that good editing and writing have priority*. Top editors should read their sites and publications carefully, recognize good writing and editing, and encourage and praise it. If they don't notice, the newsroom will stop caring.
- *Coach one another*. Foster a newsroom climate where writers gather around to discuss their leads, where editors spend time talking with reporters about writing, and where junior and senior editors compare notes about issues and problems.
- *Reach out*. The journalism of today and tomorrow will not be dominated by news professionals alone. Citizens will increasingly use their new powers to make their own media, participate in and influence the mainstream media, and share gatekeeping power over what information, ideas, and images emerge and endure. Newsrooms should connect with their audiences and make the most of their ideas and energy.

Overall, nothing will contribute more toward better journalism than better editing. In the classroom and in the newsroom, we should welcome every opportunity to identify, spotlight, and build upon the qualities of leadership, sensitivity, and aptitude that will be the hallmarks of the best new editors.

Conclusion: To the future

Editing will never get easier.

New demands of our ever-changing world will continue to magnify the editor's role as coordinator, quality controller, and decision maker. More than ever, newsrooms will require savvy leaders able to promote good journalism and sensitive management in increasingly competitive corporate environments.

The age of the new editor will be an era of unprecedented opportunity and challenge. Well-rounded new editors will need the full arsenal of traditional skills in writing, editing, and design across a variety of channels. They will need a flair for analytical thinking and problem solving. They will need adaptability and shrewdness to cope with the nonstop changes in society and in journalism. And they will need the intangible, personal qualities enabling them to juggle so many disparate duties and constituencies with grace and efficiency.

Perhaps most of all, the new editors will need to maintain their trust in themselves, their colleagues, and their readers, and in the words, ideas, ideals, and images that constitute good journalism.

If there is one lesson to absorb above all, it is that trouble hounds editors who see their jobs as working mainly with *things*, with the sentences, punctuation marks, headline calls, web tools, and computer projects that fill their days.

At the heart of good editing are *people* and *ideas*, powerful, living forces worthy of respect and recognition. In the hands of good editors, content comes alive, journalists flourish, and journalism shines. Few satisfactions, in any field, can top those.

Notes

1 The dynamic world of editing

1 J. Greenman, (2006, spring). Listening to editors' difficulties helps find solutions. *Nieman Reports*, 72.
2 *Line Editors Speak Out* (1997). Associated Press Managing Editors, 13.
3 C. Bernstein, & B. Woodward (1974). *All the president's men*. New York: Simon & Schuster, 51.
4 K. Schenck (2005, April). How to find—and keep—copyeditors. *American Editor*, 28.
5 H. Glamann (2000). How papers can find and retain copyeditors. Retrieved August 14, 2006, from www.copydesk.org/words/ASNEFebruary.htm.
6 J. Krim (1987, August 24). Personal communication.
7 L. Ansley (2006). *Retaining minority journalists*. Retrieved August 16, 2006, from www.notrain-nogain.org/recruit/minor.asp.
8 S. L. Peters (1999). *Caught in the middle*, 3, 6. Retrieved August 17, 2006, from www.mediamanagementcenter.org/publications/caught.asp.
9 J. Geisler (2005, Feb. 24). Out of balance. Retrieved Jan. 11, 2007, from poynter.org/content/content_view.asp?id=78725.
10 Inland Press Association (2006). *Newspaper industry compensation survey*.
11 Project for Excellence in Journalism (2006). *Median TV news salary comparisons over time*. Retrieved August 17, 2006, from www.stateofthenewsmedia.org/2006/narrative_localtv_newsinvestment.asp.
12 Information Please (2006). *Median weekly earnings of selected occupations, 2005*. Retrieved August 17, 2006, from www.infoplease.com/ipa/A0873324.html.
13 A. S. Berg (1978). *Max Perkins: Editor of genius*. New York: Simon & Schuster, 170.
14 *Line Editors Speak Out*, 25, 5.
15 American Society of Newspaper Editors Diversity Committee (2004). *The passionate editor*, 2.
16 Peters, *Caught in the middle*, 14, 47.
17 G. Overholser (1998, December). Editor Inc. *American Journalism Review*, 55.
18 Associated Press (2005, September 22). JetBlue flight lands safely. Retrieved September 27, 2005, from www.foxnews.com/printer_friendly_story/0,3566,170076,00.html.
19 This section condensed from C. S. Stepp (2006, April/May). Center stage. *American Journalism Review*, 46–53.

2 What makes a good editor?

1 J. Charlton (Ed.) (1985). *The writer's quotation book*. Stamford, CT: Ray Freiman, 98.
2 J. Franklin (1994). *Writing for story*. New York: Plume, 162.
3 M. Dawidziak (1996). *Mark my words*. New York: St. Martin's, 69.
4 W. Zinsser (1994). *On writing well*. New York: HarperPerennial, 278.
5 D. Murray (2000). *Writing to deadline*. Portsmouth, NH: Heinemann, 174–175.
6 R. P. Clark, & D. Fry (2003). *Coaching writers*. Boston, MA: Bedford/ St. Martin's, 1.
7 S. Biagi (1987). *NewsTalk 1*. Belmont, CA: Wadsworth, 100.
8 J. Schutze (1981, March). A view from the trenches: The editor as enemy? *ASNE Bulletin*, 20.
9 J. Hart (2000, March). What makes a great editor? *Second Takes*, an internal publication of the *Oregonian*, 1.
10 B. Baker (2002). *Newsthinking*. Boston, MA: Allyn & Bacon, 171.
11 G. Foreman (2000, March). What reporters want from mid-level editors. *American Editor*. Retrieved September 11, 2006, from www.asne.org/kiosk/editor/00.march/foreman1.htm.
12 Zinsser, *On writing well*, 278–279.
13 L. Ross (1981). *Reporting*. New York: Dodd, Mead, 5.
14 T. Kunkel (1995). *Genius in disguise*. New York: Random House, 242–243.
15 D. Halberstam (1978, January). Time Inc.'s internal war over Vietnam. *Esquire*, 100.
16 J. Ward, & K. A. Hansen (1987). *Search strategies in mass communications*. New York: Longman, 220.
17 A. S. Berg (1978). *Max Perkins: Editor of genius*. New York: Pocket Books, 33.
18 Used by permission.

3 The rise of the new editor

1 D. Brian (2001). *Pulitzer: A life*. New York: John Wiley & Sons, 6.
2 A. Kapr (1996). *Johann Gutenberg: The man and his invention*. Brookfield, VT: Scolar Press/Ashgate, 173–180.
3 J. Updike (1988, February 22). Many Bens. *New Yorker*, 105.
4 B. Franklin (1955). *Autobiography*. New York: Washington Square Press, 119.
5 D. Halberstam (1979). *The powers that be*. New York: Knopf, 212–213.
6 T. Porter (2004). Training for managers: Forget the beast. Retrieved August 15, 2006, from www.tomorrowswork.org/newsletter_training.htm.
7 M. Nemko (2006). Career changers. Retrieved October 17, 2006, from change.monster.com/articles/website_editor.
8 G. Overholser (1998). Editor Inc. In G. Roberts (Ed.) (2001). *Leaving readers behind: The age of corporate newspapering*. Fayetteville, AK: University of Arkansas Press, 157–158.
9 D. E. Graham (1984, March). New times, old values. *Press-Enterprise* lecture series, University of California, Riverside, CA.
10 News release (2006, September 6). Knight Center in Editing Excellence creates new leadership role. John S. and James L. Knight Foundation, Miami.
11 C. S. Stepp (1987, December). As writers see editors. *Washington Journalism Review* (now *American Journalism Review*), 32.
12 R. H. Giles (1987). *Newsroom management*. Indianapolis, IN: R. J. Berg, xi.

13　C. S. Stepp (2002, April). If I went back. *American Journalism Review*, 43.

14　Stepp, If I went back, 44.

15　D. Barry (1985, March/April). Defining the typical editor: How come so many of them tend to be geeks? *ASNE Bulletin*, 3–4. Used by permission.

16　Adapted from Stepp, If I went back, 40–45. Used by permission.

4　The editor as decision maker in a multimedia age

1　J. McPhee (1993, January 4). Remembering Mr. Shawn. *New Yorker*, 137.

2　J. Madden (1985). *Hey, wait a minute*. New York: Villard Books, 224.

3　Adapted from C. S. Stepp (1993, December). How to save America's editors. *American Journalism Review*, 29–30. Used by permission.

4　Adapted from C. S. Stepp (2000, July/August). Reader friendly. *American Journalism Review*, 22–35. Used by permission.

5　Making decisions about people

1　K. Kelleghan (2001). *Supervisory skills for editors, news directors, and producers*. Ames, Iowa: Iowa State University Press, vii.

2　R. H. Giles (1987). *Newsroom management*. Indianapolis, IN: R. J. Berg, x.

3　Readership Institute (2006). The state of people management practices at newspapers. Retrieved December 18, 2006, from www.readership.org/culture_management/people_mgt/stateofpeople.asp.

4　Readership Institute (2006). Inside newspaper culture. Retrieved December 18, 2006, from www.readership.org/culture_management/culture/insideculture.asp.

5　K. Graham (1997). *Personal history*. New York: Alfred A. Knopf, 388.

6　Giles, *Newsroom management*, 9.

7　Musings from editor-managers on their management styles (1981, March). *ASNE Bulletin*, 6.

8　A. B. Sohn, C. L. Ogan, and J. Polich (1986). *Newspaper leadership*. Englewood Cliffs, NJ: Prentice-Hall, 37.

9　A. N. Morgan (2004, May–June–July). From the helm of a small boat. *American Editor*, 27.

10　Kelleghan, *Supervisory skills for editors, news directors, and producers*, 59.

11　B. Baker (2002). *Newsthinking*. Boston, MA: Allyn & Bacon, 85.

12　E. D. Miller (2005). Reflections on leadership: Managing conflict. Retrieved January 11, 2007, from www.newsroomleaderhip.com/Reflections/e-050530-managingconflict.

13　S. Libin (2004, December 28). New Year's resolutions for newsroom leaders. Retrieved January 11, 2007, from poynter.org/content/content_print.asp?id=76271.

14　S. Coffey (2002). *Best practices: The art of leadership in news organizations*. Arlington, VA: Freedom Forum, 109–113.

15　T. Kunkel (1995). *Genius in disguise: Harold Ross of the New Yorker*. New York: Random House, 243–245.

16　A. J. Liebling (1961). *The press*. New York: Ballantine, 31.

17　S. Peters (1999). *Managing newsroom employees*. Evanston, IL: Northwestern Media Management Center, 9–13.

18　J. Geisler (2005). Out of balance: Poynter survey reveals journalists' pressure points. Retrieved January 11, 2007, from poynter.org/content/content_view.asp?id=78725.

19　C. Scanlan (Ed.) (1986). *How I wrote the story* (2nd ed.). Providence, RI: Providence Journal Co., 15–18.

20 R. P. Clark, and D. Fry (2003). *Coaching writers: Editors and reporters working together across media platforms.* Boston, MA: Bedford/St. Martin's, 1.

21 Clark and Fry, *Coaching writers*, 3.

22 H. Broun (1975, October 24). The copy reader ... sharpened 7 pencils. *Guild Reporter*, 7.

23 Scanlan, *How I wrote the story*, 34.

24 Clark and Fry, *Coaching writers*, 187.

25 Adapted from C. S. Stepp (1999, July). Important lessons from a first editor. *American Editor*, 24. Used by permission.

26 Remembering Mr. Shawn (1993, January 4). *New Yorker*, 134–145.

6 Making decisions about copy: Editing for content

1 Recipe for disaster (2006, June 21). Retrieved February 12, 2007, from www.regrettheerror.com/2006/06/recipe_for_disa.html.

2 Take 2 (August/September 2004). *American Journalism Review*, 21.

3 E. Liburt (2000, March 6). Cyberspace is forever. *Editor and Publisher*, 9.

4 Newspaper apologizes for offensive caption (2005, November 11). Retrieved November 14, 2005, from www.norwalkadvocate.com/news/local/state/hc-11171423.apds.

5 J. Gerick (1986, August 24). 3 awarded prestigious prize for breakthroughs in math, *New York Times*, A13; and T. Lofgren (1986, August 24). Nobel's wife. *New York Times*, 20E.

6 And now, a few words we wish had never been written (2002, January 20). *New York Times*, section 4, 7.

7 Making decisions about copy: Editing for structure

1 R. H. Copperud (1986, November 8). Editorial workshop. *Editor & Publisher*, 4.

2 G. Cooper (Ed.) (1980). *Squad helps dog bite victim.* Garden City, NY: Dolphin Books.

3 R. C. Born (1993). *The suspended sentence.* Ames, IO: Iowa State University Press, 80–85.

4 M. Mencher (2006). *News reporting and writing* (10th ed.). New York: McGraw-Hill, 153.

5 W. Lutz (1996, October 17). Life under the chief doublespeak officer. *USA Today*, 15A.

6 NCTE Doublespeak Award. Retrieved February 19, 2007, from www.ncte.org/about/awards/council/jrnl/106868.htm.

7 J. Charlton (Ed.) (1985). *The writer's quotation book.* Stamford, CT: Ray Freiman, 43.

8 B. Walsh (2000). *Lapsing into a comma.* Chicago, IL: Contemporary Books, 91, 16, 17.

9 J. Alter (2006). *The defining moment.* New York: Simon & Schuster, 267.

8 Coaching writers

1 Adapted from C. S. Stepp (1994, December). A dying breed. *American Journalism Review*, 35–41. Used by permission.

2 J. Hart (2006). *A writer's coach.* New York: Pantheon Books, 72, 91, 218.

9 Making decisions about coverage

1   M. Stephens (2007). *A history of news* (3rd ed.). New York: Oxford University Press, 4.
2   M. Mencher (2006). *News reporting and writing* (10th ed.). Boston, MA: McGraw-Hill, 58.
3   H. J. Gans (1979). *Deciding what's news.* New York: Vintage Books, 39–52.
4   G. Tuchman (1978). *Making news: A study in the construction of reality.* New York: Free Press, 104.
5   Steve Buttry is a veteran editor and newsroom coach, associated with various newspapers and the American Press Institute. This article is adapted from a posting on http://www.notrain-nogain.org, a website for newsroom trainers. It is used by permission.
6   C. S. Stepp (2000, July/August). Reader friendly. *American Journalism Review*, 29–30.

10 Making decisions about presentation

1   M. Moses (2000, April). Consumer mentality. *American Editor*, 6–7.
2   A. Cairo, The terror of the south. Retrieved March 14, 2007, from www.albertocairo.com/imagenes/articledinosaur.pdf.
3   M. Garcia (2000, April). We've come a long way. *American Editor*, 5.
4   Adapted from C. S. Stepp (2006, April–May). Center stage. *American Journalism Review*, 46–53. Used by permission.
5   The editors' guide to newspaper design (2000, April). *American Editor*, 10, 18, 19.

11 Making decisions about legal issues

1   L. Dalglish (2005, fall). Four years of uncontrolled secrecy affected Katrina coverage. *News Media and the Law*, 1.
2   B. Sanford (1999). *Don't shoot the messenger.* New York: Free Press, 8.
3   L. Finnegan (2007). *No questions asked: News coverage since 9/11.* New York: Praeger, 4, 45, 37. See also C. S. Stepp (2007, April/May). Books. *American Journalism Review*, 65.
4   B. Schultz (1985, September). We're consulting with him more often on stories. *ASNE Bulletin*, 11.
5   K. Goldberg (2006, November/December). The world wide web of legal ramifications. *American Editor*, 12.
6   L. Parker (2006, October 3). Courts are asked to crack down on bloggers, websites. *USA Today*, 1A.
7   G. Penrod (2005, spring). Safely shining in the spotlight. *News Media and the Law*, 25.
8   M. Massing (1985, May/June). The libel chill: How cold is it out there? *Columbia Journalism Review*, 35.
9   A. Liptak (2007, March 8). After Libby trial, new era for government and press. *New York Times*, A14.
10 R. Smolkin (2005, February/March). Under fire. *American Journalism Review*, 19.
11 J. Meyers (2006, April 4). The confidentiality crisis. *American Journalism Review*. Retrieved March 6, 2007, from www.ajr.org/article.asp?id=4105.
12 R. Rodriguez (2006, January/February). Don't be timid. *American Editor*, 2.
13 Adapted from C. S. Stepp (2006, spring). Resources for midlevel editors. *Nieman Reports*, 77–78. Reprinted by permission.

14 J. Meyers (2006, June/July). Fighting like tigers. *American Journalism Review*, 58–61.

12 Making decisions about ethics

1 D. Barry (2003, May 11). Times reporter who resigned leaves long trail of deception. *New York Times*, 1.
2 B. Morrison (2004, March 19). Ex-USA Today reporter faked major stories. *USA Today*, 1.
3 J. Deakin (1984). *Straight stuff*. New York: William Morrow, 72.
4 AP statement on anonymous sources. Retrieved April 5, 2007, from www.apme.com/committees/credibility/052705anonymous.shtml.
5 B. Keller (2005, June 23). Assuring our credibility. Retrieved April 5, 2007, from nytco.com/pdf/assuring-our-credibility.pdf.
6 G. Ring (1986, February). Are exact addresses always part of the news? *ASNE Bulletin*, 20–22.
7 C. S. Stepp (1986, December). When a public figure's private life is news. *Washington Journalism Review*, 40.
8 H. Kurtz (2004, June 26). Post editor explains decision to publish expletive. *Washington Post*, C4. See also H. Dewar, and D. Milbank (2004, June 25). Cheney dismisses critic with obscenity. *Washington Post*, A4.
9 G. Moore (2003, March). Keeping the faith. *American Editor*, 5–10.
10 B. Carter (2007, April 12). After Couric incident, CBS News to scrutinize its web content. *New York Times*. Retrieved April 16, 2007, from www.nytimes.com/2007/04/12/arts/television/12cbs.html.
11 T. Rosenstiel, and A. Mitchell (2003). *Thinking clearly: Cases in journalistic decision-making*. New York: Columbia University Press, 3.
12 G. C. Christians, K. B. Rotzoll, M. B. Fackler, K. B. McKee, and R. H. Woods (2005). *Media ethics* (7th ed.). Boston, MA: Pearson, 12–22.
13 B. Steele (2000). Ask these 10 questions to make good ethical decisions. Retrieved April 16, 2007, from www.poynter.org/column.asp?id=36&aid=4346.
14 *Editor & Publisher* (March 31, 1984), 130, 188.

13 Toward excellence in editing

1 M. Woodward (1999, July 22). The capacity to care about news, and pain. *Bangor Daily News*, B1. See also C. S. Stepp (2000, July/August). Reader friendly. *American Journalism Review*, 33–34.
2 R. Giles (1987). *Newsroom management*. Indianapolis, IN: R. J. Berg, 130.

Index